MIS MEMORIAS

Aunque la verdad duela...

ENCARNA FÚNEZ CRUZ

*Este libro se lo quiero dedicar
a mis padres, por todo lo vivido,
por todo lo sufrido y porque
gracias a mi madre,
pudimos salir adelante.*

©2021 Encarna Fúnez Cruz

©Fotografías: Encarna Fúnez Cruz

Escrito y maquetado: Mercedes R. Cervantes

Diseño portada y contraportada: Mercedes R. Cervantes

Todos los derechos reservados. No se permite la reproducción total o parcial de este libro, ni su almacenamiento en un sistema informático, ni su transmisión por cualquier procedimiento o medio. Ya sea electrónico, mecánico, por fotocopia, por registro o por otros medios sin permiso previo y por escrito del titular del copyright.

Cualquier forma de reproducción, distribución, comunicación pública o transformación de esta obra solo puede ser realizada con la autorización del autor de los derechos del libro.

Encarna Fúnez Cruz

Era primavera, los árboles y las flores rebosaban en colores. Ese día tan soleado, brillante y luminoso, el 25 de marzo de 1926 nací yo, Encarna Fúnez Cruz. Gran parte de mi vida ha transcurrido en Las Casas (Ciudad Real), el pueblo que me vio nacer y sufrir en cada etapa de mi vida. En ese momento en el que tan solo tenía unas horas de vida, nadie podía presagiar las duras situaciones que me iba a tocar vivir. No solo a mí, sino a toda mi familia.

Mi madre se llamaba **Prado Cruz Notario**, nació el 23 de febrero de 1901 en la caseta del peón caminero que hay en la carretera entre Ciudad Real y las Casas. La guardo mucho cariño y me acuerdo de ella cada día. Cuando veo sus fotos, me vienen a la mente recuerdos del pasado. Un pasado duro, triste y sombrío. Aunque siempre salimos adelante con grandes esfuerzos.

En 1898 nació mi padre Ángel Fúnez González. A él lo recuerdo con tristeza, (más adelante sabréis por qué) pero también con mucho cariño. Conoció a mi madre en el pueblo. Eran muy jóvenes, pero eso no impidió que se hicieran amigos. Aunque esa amistad, en poco tiempo se convirtió en algo más. Tanto, que les llevó a estar 10 años de novios. Tras ese largo noviazgo, decidieron casarse.

Se casaron en la iglesia de la Merced de la calle Toledo en Ciudad Real. Se encontraban solos ante

Mi abuelo Pedro Cruz y su hija Prado (mi madre).

el cura, los testigos tuvieron que buscarlos entre la gente que pasaba por la calle y dos personas fueron a acompañarles. Lo hicieron así porque los padres de mi madre murieron antes de la boda. Su madre, o sea, mi abuela se llamaba Eustaquia Notario y falleció cuando mi madre tenía tan solo 3 meses de vida, y su padre, mi abuelo, se llamaba Pedro Cruz, pero no recuerdo bien si vivía o no.

Los padres de mi padre Ángel, mis abuelos por parte paterna, se llamaban Alejandro Fúnez y Aurea González, creo recordar, porque hace ya tantos años de eso…

Mi madre Prado tuvo 10 hijos, yo fui la primera, Encarnación pero solo vivieron siete. Después de mí nacieron mis hermanas Eustaquia, Prado, Pilar, Angelita y mis dos hermanos Ángel y Alejandro. Además, tuvo dos abortos y un hijo que falleció con 14 meses.

Recuerdo una mañana, era el 5 de Julio de 1938 yo tenía doce años, me encontraba en casa y estaba en la cocina con mi madre. En ese preciso momento se puso de parto. Iba a dar a luz a mi hermano pequeño Alejandro. Yo salí asustada y preocupada a la calle para avisar que mi madre estaba dando a luz. Solo estábamos ella y yo y necesitaba que la asistieran. Afortunadamente dos mujeres que nos conocían llegaron a casa, y rápidamente les ayudé a preparar lo que necesitaban.

Mi padre estaba trabajando en el campo segando. Inmediatamente fueron a avisarle de que su mujer iba a dar a luz. Dejó de trabajar y se dirigió a casa nervioso. Cuando llegó, le dieron la grata noticia de que su hijo ya había nacido y que los dos se encontraban bien. Mi padre Ángel estaba feliz, se acercó a mi madre, la besó en la frente y después tomó a su hijo Alejandro en brazos.

Tengo una anécdota muy graciosa sobre mi hermano Alejandro. Había una vecina en Las Casas que criaba gorrinos. La cerda que tenía había dado a luz a diez cerditos y le dio a mi madre Prado uno. Mi madre para cebarlo le compró un bote de leche condensada y lo guardó para dárselo más tarde. Le advirtió a mi hermano pequeño, que eso no lo podía tocar, que era peligroso y le podía sentar mal.

Más tarde, cuando mi madre fue a por el bote de leche condensada para dárselo al cerdito, lo encontró vacío. Mi hermano Alejandro que por aquél entonces tendría uno o dos años, no hizo caso, se lo tomó todo y no dejó ni una gota.

Mi madre tenía muchas varices y en cada embarazo a causa de eso le costaba andar y tenía que ir con muletas. Pese a acabar de dar a luz a mi hermano Alejandro y encontrarse con el problema de varices en las piernas que le impedia andar con normalidad, tenía que ir a limpiar a la iglesia de Las Casas. Con el paso de los meses se iba recuperando y se le pasaba.

En aquella época eran pocos los niños que podían ir al colegio, yo no tuve esa oportunidad. Aunque pude aprender a leer y a escribir poniendo todo mi empeño en aprender. Cada vez que cogía un papel preguntaba a la gente qué letras eran, y así poco a poco fui aprendiendo. Mis hermanos tampoco pudieron ir al colegio. Yo, como era la mayor, tenía que trabajar para llevar dinero a casa. Pero aprendí lo suficiente, además me servía cuando algún familiar necesitaba escribir una carta o recibían correspondencia, era yo la que les escribía las cartas, y cuando les contestaban se las leía. A mi suegra le escribí y leí muchas cartas que enviaba a sus hijos cuando estaban haciendo la mili.

Éramos una familia pobre pero muy honrada. Pasamos mucha hambre, se trabajaba de sol a sol y se ganaba muy poco. Ni siquiera podíamos salir adelante con lo poco que nos pagaban. Solo vivíamos para trabajar y trabajar, pero comer, muy poco y en ocasiones nada.

Cuando nacieron mis hermanas, me tuve que quedar en casa cuidándolas para que mi madre pudiera ir a trabajar.

Mi padre era muy trabajador, siempre se preocupaba porque tuviéramos algo para comer. Trabajaba de jornalero en Las Casas, en la hacienda de un señor de buena posición. Por aquel entonces no había otra cosa que trabajar en el campo.

En casa teníamos una borrica, mis hermanas y yo, acompañábamos a mi padre al campo a recoger hierbas, espárragos, cardillos y collejas. A pesar de todo, de vez en cuando, lo pasábamos bien.

Me gustaba estar en familia aunque fuera a trabajar, me sentía segura junto a mi padre. Mi madre se quedaba en casa cuidando de los más pequeños y además, nos hacía albarcas de esparto para que no fuéramos descalzas. Si apenas teníamos para comer, ¿cómo iban mis padres a comprarnos sandalias para todos? Era imposible...

Lo cargamos todo en la borrica y cuando lo atamos bien, nos fuimos con mi madre a venderlo a Ciudad Real. Salimos de Las Casas y comenzamos a andar por la senda. Había unos siete kilómetros de distancia, nos cansábamos, pero ya estábamos acostumbradas. También llevábamos troncos de leña a la panadería para que nos dieran pan. Teníamos que trabajar y andar mucho para venderlo por unos pocos reales, pero era eso o nada. Aunque tuviéramos que trabajar para cobrar una miseria, teníamos que hacerlo. Como dice el refrán:

"Buenas son tortas"

Regresamos a casa cansadas pero contentas, lo habíamos vendido todo. A la borrica le dimos de comer grama (hierba) que cogíamos en el campo. Se portaba muy bien, en ninguna ocasión nos dio una sola coz.

Pasaron los meses y seguíamos trabajando sin apenas descanso, pero entonces, llegó el fatídico día. Yo tenía trece años y mi hermano pequeño

Alejandro, solo tenía cuatro meses cuando la Guardia Civil fue a buscar a mi padre. Él se encontraba trabajando en el campo podando cepas cuando se lo llevaron esposado. Fue muy duro vivir ese momento en el que lo vimos así, indefenso. Mis hermanas y yo nos mirábamos extrañadas porque no entendíamos nada. Pero antes de que lo metieran en el coche, mi padre se dirigió a la Guardia Civil y les dijo:

—Hagan el favor de dejarme que enganche los aparejos a la burra para que puedan ir mis hijas a casa.

La Guardia Civil accedió y mi padre nos subió encima de la burra, ató la cabra que teníamos a los aparejos de la borrica y desoladas, nos fuimos a casa. Cuando llegamos, le contamos todo a mi madre. Se puso muy nerviosa e inmediatamente se marchó para averiguar qué había pasado, porque él no había hecho nada malo.

A mi padre se lo llevaron al juzgado de Ciudad Real para interrogarlo. Mi madre tuvo que andar siete kilómetros hasta llegar allí. Cuando llegó, estuvo unas cuantas horas en ese lugar, sola y sin saber muy bien qué hacer. Tan solo deseaba que saliera libre y pudiera volver a casa con ella.

La espera se hacía interminable para mi madre, solo quería que le dieran noticias de su marido.

Varios agentes de la Guardia Civil lo interrogaron. Horas después lo llevaron ante el juez y este decidió que lo metieran en la cárcel. Cuando se acercaron los agentes a mi madre apenas le dijeron nada, únicamente que lo trasladaban a la cárcel.

Mi madre agachó la cabeza ante la noticia que le dieron los agentes y no tuvo más remedio que volver a casa sola, sin su marido. Tuvo que recorrer otros siete kilómetros de vuelta. Llegó a casa abatida y apenas sin ganas de hablar. Solo nos dijo que lo habían encerrado en la cárcel. Nos echamos las manos en la cabeza, no entendíamos nada…

Tuvimos que sacar fuerzas para ir a verlo a la cárcel. Íbamos todas las semanas, mi madre, mis hermanas y yo. Los martes era el único día que podíamos ir. Mi madre le recogía la ropa sucia y se la lavaba. Pero siempre tenía manchas de sangre en las camisetas. Un día de los que fuimos a ver a mi padre, mi madre no pudo más y le preguntó por esas manchas:

—¿Por qué tienes la ropa manchada de sangre?

—Por las palizas que me dan aquí... —respondió apenado—. El médico me ha dicho que tengo las costillas rotas.

Mi madre agachó la cabeza y se entristeció. Por esas fechas era invierno y nevaba. Fue entonces cuando le comentó a mi padre que no nos llevaría la próxima vez con ella porque hacía mucho frío. Pero él insistió en que nos llevara por si era la última vez que nos veía.

Para nosotros fue muy duro dejarlo allí, a sabiendas de las palizas que le daban. Mi madre lo pasaba mal, pero no podíamos hacer nada.

A mi padre le acusaron de ser contrario al régimen. Querían ejecutarlo tan solo porque era del PSOE. Y así fue como lo lograron, a las siete de la mañana del 17 de noviembre de 1939 lo fusilaron en las paredes del cementerio de Ciudad Real. Junto a él había nueve hombres y una mujer. A todos ellos los fusilaron esa misma mañana.

Después, hicieron un barranco y los echaron a todos juntos, unos encima de otros y la mujer fue la última. La dejaron caer encima de todos los hombres. Ni siquiera pudimos despedirnos de él. Fue muy doloroso el trago por el que tuvimos que pasar. Sé quiénes fueron los que los fusilaron y también sé, quién lo mandó fusilar allí en Las Casas. Unos ya han muerto y otros aún viven, pero yo no quiero venganza, no quiero igualarme con ellos, con los desalmados que hicieron fusilar a mi padre. No puedo olvidar lo ocurrido, y perdonar, es muy difícil para mí.

Esa misma mañana, a las doce del mediodía nos obligaban a cantar el "Cara al sol" y a rezar en el comedor social de Las Casas. Si no lo hacíamos, no nos daban de comer.

Tampoco nos permitían llorar porque nos atemorizaban con no darnos los alimentos. Así fue mi juventud, rota de dolor por la muerte de mi padre y de llanto a escondidas.

Desde esa fatídica tragedia, mi madre se convirtió en una luchadora nata para sacar a sus siete hijos adelante. Aún con el sufrimiento por la pérdida de su marido, sacó fuerzas de flaqueza para poder recomponer ese corazón herido que le arrebataron sin motivo. Aunque la salud de mi madre se resintió. Pasamos muchas penas, fatigas y calamidades, no teníamos nada que comer, solo teníamos el sol de día y la luna de noche. Pero aun así mi madre no se rindió nunca, trabajaba en lo que buenamente podía para sacarnos adelante, pero eso sí, muy honradamente y puedo decirlo con la cabeza bien alta porque estoy muy orgullosa de ella. Recuerdo esta frase que siempre decía...

"Tiene que haber una providencia divina muy grande cuando puedo sacar a mis hijos adelante tan honradamente."

Nunca olvidaré esa frase, siempre la tengo en mi memoria y en mi corazón.

En 1982 el Sr. D. Máximo redactó un informe diciendo que mi padre Ángel fue inocente para que mi madre Prado pudiera cobrar una pensión.

Yo tenía trece años cuando iba con mi madre a segar. Como ella no se encontraba bien de salud porque andaba con muletas, yo hacía mi surco y los dos de ella, mientras ella nos hacía la comida. A mi madre le daban el jornal entero y a mí por ser joven me daban medio jornal. También íbamos a recoger pitos, en fin, de todo lo que salía para trabajar en el campo.

Mis tres hermanas mayores Eustaquia, Pradito y Pilar, también trabajaban en el campo, pero cuando se acababa la temporada teníamos que buscar otra cosa. Encontramos un trabajo para hacer carreteras. Teníamos que extender la piedra y después con el capazo echábamos la arena. Por cada metro que hacíamos, nos daban tres reales (0,75 céntimos/peseta), una miseria para el trabajo que hacíamos.

Los domingos descansábamos pero nos obligaban ir a misa, si no íbamos, los falangistas nos decían que no nos darían comida.

Pasaron los años con mucho sacrificio, pero a veces, las cosas que nos sucedían, no nos ayudaban a avanzar. Recuerdo perfectamente el día, era el 2 de febrero (Candelaria) del año 1940 cuando nuestra humilde casa se derrumbó sobre nosotros. En ese momento nos encontrábamos durmiendo mis seis hermanos, mi madre y yo. Todos estábamos en la misma habitación y el tremendo golpe nos despertó.

La luz eléctrica se quedó a un palmo del suelo y la bombilla sorprendentemente, no se rompió. Mi madre estaba asustada y se temía lo peor. Aun así, mantuvo la calma para tranquilizarnos, no quería que nos alteráramos. Únicamente nos dijo que teníamos que salir de allí como fuera.

Vimos ese pequeño hueco que había y fuimos uno por uno arrastrándonos como si fuéramos gatos para poder salir por ese pequeño hueco. Estábamos muy asustados porque el mínimo roce podía hacerlo caer sobre nosotros y aplastarnos. Afortunadamente, todos pudimos salir del fatídico derrumbe. Aún recuerdo las palabras que mi madre dijo al vernos a todos fuera de la casa.

"¡Qué providencia divina tiene que haber...!"

En ese instante, yo también lo creí. A pesar del derrumbe, tuvimos que dar gracias porque salimos todos ilesos, algo que hasta ahora me cuesta creer.

Nos quedamos de pie frente a la casa observando el mal estado en el que quedó. No sabíamos dónde ir ni lo que hacer. Pero aún se complicó más si cabe. Ese día se puso a llover, no teníamos donde refugiarnos y tuvimos que pasar el día a la intemperie. Estábamos empapados, mi madre estaba acongojada aunque no nos decía nada, sabíamos que lo estaba pasando mal y que estaba preocupada por nosotros. Las pocas cosas que teníamos se encontraban dentro de la casa y no podíamos entrar a coger nada.

Mi madre recordó que mi padre Ángel tenía tres hermanos, mi tía Natividad, mi tío Florentino que era muy conocido por todos en el pueblo y mi tío Encarna (curiosamente se llamaba así, pero era un hombre). Mi tío Florentino tenía una casa y fuimos a verle. Cuando le contó lo ocurrido, se negó a dejarnos la casa para que pudiéramos refugiarnos y poder tener un sitio donde vivir. Él tenía en una habitación la cebada que tenía guardada y no quería sacarla para que pudiéramos tener un sitio donde dormir. Y eso, que la casa realmente era de mis abuelos.

Al ver la negativa de mi tío, mi madre decidió ir a La Falange a explicar lo que nos había pasado. Cuando llegó, le explicó al jefe de la Falange lo que nos había sucedido. Le dijo que se encontraba en la calle con sus hijos porque la casa se derrumbó, estaba lloviendo y no teníamos dónde ir. Le comentó que mi tío no quería desalojar la cebada para que viviéramos allí.

Después de meditarlo unos segundos, le pidió a mi madre que lo llevara a la casa de mi tío. Cuando llegaron, este señor se dirigió a mi tío y le dijo:

—Oye, si no le quieres dejar la casa a tus sobrinos para que se resguarden y tengan una casa donde vivir, donde ha ido tu hermano irás tú. Así que piénsatelo bien...

Así de seco, directo y firme fue en su afirmación. A mi tío no le quedó otra que sacar la cebada de la casa para que pudiéramos entrar a vivir.

Estábamos empapados por la lluvia pero contentos de tener un sitio donde poder vivir. Era una casa bastante grande, tenía tres habitaciones, el portal y una cocina. También había un patio en la parte de atrás muy amplio. Nos acomodamos con lo que teníamos puesto, encendimos el fuego para calentarnos y así pasamos la noche.

Al día siguiente nos levantamos para ir a trabajar. Todo transcurrió como siempre, trabajando de sol a sol. El cansancio se notaba cuando llegábamos de vuelta a casa. Pero al menos, podíamos descansar en el nuevo hogar. Aunque lo peor fue cuando se terminaba la temporada en el campo y nos quedábamos sin trabajo.

Aunque fue muy duro lo vivido hasta ahora, también tuve algunos momentos bonitos en mi vida. Yo tenía dieciocho años, era sábado y esa tarde salí con mi novio. Se llamaba Enrique, él tenía veinte años, y como os dije antes, éramos vecinos. Sus padres se llamaban Luis Oliver y Mª Jesús Pérez. Tuvieron diez hijos contándole a él. Sus nueve hermanos se llamaban, Lolín, Pepa, Jesús, Luis, Victorio, Juanita, Juan, Natividad y Mª Jesús. Cuando nos conocimos él trabajaba ayudando a un electricista llevándole las herramientas que necesitaba. Aunque no le pagaba con dinero, llegaron a un acuerdo para que a cambio de su trabajo le compensara con comida. Ese día, le comenté que me había quedado sin trabajo. A él no le gustaba que fuera a trabajar, pero se tenía que ir a la mili. La hizo en Madrid en Cuatro Caminos y allí estuvo tres años. Su hermano Jesús también la realizó en el mismo lugar pero apenas coincidieron. Enrique le comentó a su hermana mayor Lolín, que me había quedado sin trabajo. Ella trabajaba de criada en una casa de Ciudad Real con un matrimonio mayor. Este matrimonio tenía una amiga que necesitaba una niñera y ella me recomendó.

Mi novio Enrique

Así fue como empecé a trabajar cuidando a los hijos de los señores.

Mi madre no quería separarse de mí ni de mis hermanas, pero con todo el dolor de su corazón, nos llevó a Ciudad Real a mis tres hermanas mayores y a mí. Todas trabajamos de niñeras, a mí me pagaban veinticinco pesetas al mes, y yo era la que más cobraba. Esto lo hacíamos todos los inviernos, porque en el verano mi madre venía a recogernos para trabajar en el campo.

Así fue mi vida hasta que cumplí los veinticinco años, porque tomé una decisión muy importante.

A esa edad mi novio Enrique Oliver Pérez me pidió matrimonio y por supuesto, me casé con él.

Guardo un bonito recuerdo de ese día tan especial para mí.

La foto de nuestra boda.

Nos casamos el 1 de abril de 1951 aunque a mí me hubiese gustado casarme el día de mi cumpleaños y de mi santo el 25 de marzo, pero no pudo ser. La boda se celebró en la iglesia de Las Casas. Yo llevaba un vestido que me hicieron, era azul marino aunque parecía casi negro. Los hermanos de Enrique, Lolín y Luis, fueron los padrinos de la boda. En la iglesia se encontraban nuestras respectivas familias. Fue muy emocionante para mí entrar por el pasillo hasta llegar al altar. En ese momento, recordé a mi padre, lo echaba mucho de menos, pero la vida sigue a pesar de todo.

Cuando salimos de la iglesia después de todas las felicitaciones de cariño que nos dieron, nos reunimos en casa de mis suegros, ya tenían preparada la comida. Mi familia se marchó a reunirse a casa de mi madre.

Ya éramos marido y mujer, los once años de novios hizo que nos conociéramos muy bien, Él sabía perfectamente cómo era yo, y yo sabía cómo era él. Aun así, nunca sabes qué puede pasar, al final, todo es un misterio.

Nos pusimos a vivir en una de las habitaciones de la casa donde vivía mi madre con mis hermanos. Era la casa que nos dejó mi tío Florentino. Tenía varias habitaciones, era muy grande, había un patio que tenía un pozo y una higuera. Las habitaciones en las que estábamos eran la cocina y la cuadra. Las tuvimos que acomodar para poder vivir ahí.

Como curiosidad, os puedo contar que los gañanes eran las personas que se encargaban de cuidar los animales que se encontraban en la cuadra.

Mi madre y mis hermanos vivían en una habitación y mi marido y yo en otra. Bueno, en otra… es por llamarlo de alguna manera, porque en realidad donde dormimos esa noche y las venideras, fue en la cuadra, hicimos una especie de habitación. Tuvimos que echar tierra en el suelo y ahí nos acomodamos a pasar la noche de bodas.

En el mes de mayo empezamos a trabajar en el campo. Íbamos a segar como siempre, de sol a sol, y así nos pasamos todo el verano.

Tuve a mi primer hijo Luis, en el año 1951 era el día 20 del mes de octubre. En aquella época no íbamos al hospital a dar a luz, lo teníamos en casa. Normalmente siempre iba algún conocido o familiar a ayudar en ese momento. Pero mi madre Prado le pidió a mi marido que fuera a avisar a la comadrona. Así que Enrique no se lo pensó dos veces, cogió la bicicleta y se marchó a Ciudad Real.

Cuando llegó, dio el aviso para que la llamaran. Después dejó la bicicleta en casa de una tía suya y regresó en coche con la comadrona. Así que ella, mi madre y mi marido, me asistieron en el parto. Afortunadamente no se complicó y todo salió bien.

Mi madre estaba orgullosa de poder tener a su primer nieto entre sus brazos. Lo que más le llamó la atención fueron las manos tan bonitas que tenía. Se dirigió a Enrique para enseñárselas y a los dos se les caía la baba. Todos vivimos un momento muy bonito y muy especial. En ese instante, ya éramos padres y teníamos otra responsabilidad, sacar adelante a nuestro hijo.

Pasaban los días, las semanas y cómo crecía. Ya tenía nueve meses de vida cuando contrataron a mi marido Enrique por recomendación de su hermano Jesús. Este había trabajado anteriormente para ellos construyendo el secadero de tabaco junto a Máximo, el marido de su hermana Lolín. Así que nos fuimos a Picón a trabajar en la masía.

El señor era médico pero ya no ejercía. Vivía junto a su mujer en la masía. A nosotros nos gustaba la idea de ir a trabajar allí. Vivir en el campo le vendría bien a nuestro hijo.

La masía tenía un patio muy grande donde estaba la casa de los señores y tres habitaciones separadas para los sirvientes. Allí podían vivir tres familias y cada una de ellas tenía una cocina. Enrique y yo ocupamos una de las habitaciones junto con nuestro hijo Luis.

Yo aún le daba el pecho, por eso cuando le tocaba, dejaba de trabajar para darle de mamar. Cuando terminaba, esperaba un poco y lo acostaba en la cuna. Después regresaba a trabajar al campo. También iba de vez en cuando a echarle un vistazo a ver cómo estaba, afortunadamente dormía mucho y no daba problemas.

En la masía, trabajábamos sembrando y cosechando tabaco. También servíamos en la casa, y además Enrique, se ocupaba de cuidar a la yegua. Trabajábamos mucho pero no nos importaba, al menos teníamos un techo mejor donde vivir.

Al año y medio de tener a mi hijo Luis, me quedé otra vez embarazada. En ese momento me encontraba trabajando en la masía. Me querían mucho... allá donde iba a trabajar siempre me querían porque era muy limpia, trataba bien a los niños, era cariñosa con ellos y por eso estaban contentos con el trabajo que hacía.

Pasaron dos años cuando tuve a mi segundo hijo, era una niña. En esta ocasión di a luz en el hospital, aunque después de lo que sucedió, hubiera deseado que fuera en casa como en el anterior.

Cuando me puse de parto en la masía llamaron al médico de Picón y este me llevó en su furgoneta al hospital de Ciudad Real.

Estando en el hospital, me visitó la señorita Pura, su hermano era amigo de un cura. Ella vivía en Ciudad Real. La conocí cuando mi hermana Prado que trabajaba sirviendo para ella, se puso enferma y fui durante unos días a sustituirla. La señorita Pura quería estar presente cuando yo diera a luz con las monjas, insistió mucho en eso, cosa que a mí me extrañó un poco.

Ella iba a coser al costurero del hospital para ganarse un dinero porque quería meterse a monja. Cuando me puse de parto empecé a sangrar. A los pocos días di a luz a una niña que apenas pude ver, pero la escuchaba llorar. Una monja se la llevó enseguida. Cuando me llevaron a la habitación me trajeron supuestamente, a mi hija. Yo no podía cogerla, solo la tocaba con la mano y era como si fuera un témpano de hielo. Le decía a mi compañera de habitación...

—Llama a la monja porque mi niña está muy fría.

Pero después pensé...

—Esta no es mi hija...

Al insistir en que llamara a las monjas, mi compañera de habitación las avisó y vino una de ellas. Me miró, se la metió debajo del brazo y se marchó sin decirme nada. Al rato volvió y me dijo que había fallecido. Me comentó que le habían echado agua bendita para bautizarla pero que no sabían si ya había fallecido y ellas mismas le pusieron de nombre Inmaculada. En ese momento estaba confundida, no me lo podía creer. Se fue sin enseñármela para que la viera y se marchó con ella, o lo que fuera aquello porque mi hija no era.

Estoy cien por cien segura porque en aquella época, era cuando daban a nuestros hijos/as a otras personas y a las madres nos decían que habían fallecido. Algunas han podido encontrarlas tras muchos años de búsqueda y denuncias que pusieron. En mi caso, sé seguro que fue así porque mi hija no consta en ningún registro ni documento, no notificaron su nacimiento ni el fallecimiento, es como si no la hubiese tenido. Para una madre, vivir eso es muy fuerte, y más sabiendo que está viva, pero no sabes dónde ni con quién estará. Me engañaron y me mintieron para dársela a otra familia. Yo creo que fue la señorita Puri la que tuvo algo que ver, pero eso a ciencia cierta no lo sé. Lo que sí sé es que me robaron a mi hija y me trajeron un bebé congelado. Tenían bebés congelados para intentar justificar que había muerto, pero a mí no me engañaron, lo supe desde el primer momento en que la toqué. Así que, no consta en ningún sitio que tuve a mi hija.

Mi madre Prado y mi hermana Eustaquia vinieron a verme y se quedaron asombradas cuando se lo conté.

Lo que me consuela un poco es que todo esto se destapó y fueron a juicio. Estuvieron hablando sobre ello bastante tiempo en la televisión. Salió en todos los medios informativos. Aunque yo no lo denuncié, porque para eso se necesitaba tener dinero y no teníamos lo suficiente como para eso.

Pasaron los días deseando salir del hospital. No quería estar allí ni un segundo más, pero tenía que recuperarme. El domingo fue mi marido

Enrique a verme. Me iban a dar el alta el lunes pero pregunté si me podía marchar del hospital ese mismo día. Me desaconsejaron que me fuera con él en la bicicleta y que esperara hasta mañana para irme, pero después de lo que había sucedido no quise estar allí ni un día más. Recogí mis cosas, me vestí y regresé con mi marido a Las Casas. Esa noche la pasamos en casa de mi suegra, nos quedamos durmiendo cerca de la chimenea.

Al día siguiente nos fuimos hasta Picón en autobús. Mi marido tenía que trabajar en la masía. Yo aún tuve unos días de descanso para recuperarme y poder ponerme a trabajar.

Pasaron esos duros días, me recuperé del parto y el disgusto fue a menos cada día, pero hasta hoy, sigo recordándolo. Volví al trabajo, eso me servía para distraerme y no pensar tanto en ello. Así pasaban los días, los meses y los años, trabajando y criando a mi hijo Luis. Aunque tenía la pena de mi segunda hija que no pude ver, pero al menos sé que vive.

El médico que tenía la masía de Picón tenía otra finca en Toledo. La masía de Picón la empezó a gestionar un cuñado suyo y él se fue a la otra de Toledo. Así que Enrique y yo, nos fuimos con nuestro hijo Luis que ya tenía tres años, a seguir plantando tabaco como hacíamos en la de Picón.

Pasado un tiempo, volví a quedarme en estado, tanto mi marido como yo estábamos muy contentos. Aunque en ese momento recordé lo que me ocurrió en el hospital y aún tenía el susto en el cuerpo por si pasaba lo mismo que con la niña. En esta ocasión me las ingenié para que esta vez no me llevaran al hospital. Unos días antes de la fecha prevista para el parto, me fui con mi hijo Luis a Las Casas. Nos llevaron en el coche unos amigos del señorito que tenían que ir a Ciudad Real, y fueron tan amables que nos acercaron hasta la casa donde vivía mi madre.

Me puse de parto el 6 de noviembre del 1955. Esta vez me asistieron mi tía Natividad (hermana de mi padre Ángel) y mi madre. Todo salió muy bien. Era un niño y le pusimos Enrique como su padre. Ya estaba más tranquila y feliz de tener a mi hijo junto a mí en la cama.

Mi marido vino unos días después porque tenía que trabajar y aprovechamos para bautizarlo. Celebramos el bautizo en familia, me alegré de volver a verlos y estar de nuevo todos juntos.

Al día siguiente nos fuimos los cuatro a Toledo. Fue un largo viaje pero no me importó, tenía a lo que más quería junto a mí, mis dos hijos y mi marido. Cogimos un autobús que salía de Las Casas hacia Ciudad Real. Una vez allí, nos fuimos a la estación de tren que nos llevaba hasta Los Yébenes. Cuando llegamos, salimos de la estación y nos dirigimos a la masía andando. Llegamos algo cansados, sobre todo mi hijo Luis que no pensaba que el viaje sería tan largo. Nos fuimos directos a la habitación a descansar.

A la mañana siguiente, mi marido se levantó pronto para ir a trabajar. Yo me quedé cuidando a los niños, aunque pasados unos días, yo también me reincorporé al trabajo. Pronto volví a la rutina de trabajar y descansar para dar de mamar al bebé, cuidar del pequeño Luis, en fin, que fui una madre coraje, como tantas en aquella época. Mientras, mi madre estaba en Las Casas cuidando de mis hermanos que eran más pequeños. Los despertaba para que fueran a trabajar y ella iba a lo que buenamente podía hacer para ganar algo de dinero.

Un año después nos trasladamos a trabajar a otra finca, se llamaba "La Vinuesa". Esta se encontraba situada cerca de Las Casas. Así nos sentíamos más próximos a nuestras familias. En la masía,

Enrique trabajó de mayoral con las mulas y yo, en el campo segando y cuidando de mis hijos.

En el año 1957 me quedé de nuevo en estado y el día 22 de marzo de 1958 tuve a mi hija Encarna. Recuerdo con agrado que ese día nevó, me gustaba ver el rastro blanco que dejaba la nieve. En esta ocasión di a luz en la misma finca donde estábamos trabajando. Como mi madre no pudo desplazarse, vino mi suegra Mª Jesús a la masía para asistirme. Afortunadamente, todo salió bien. Di a luz a una niña, esta vez le pusimos mi nombre, Encarna.

Mi marido Enrique, nuestros 4 hijos y yo.

Pasaron los años y seguíamos trabajando con los señores. Tenían dos fincas en las afueras de Las Casas, la finca de "La Vinuesa", que era en la que estábamos trabajando y otra más. Un día nos dijeron que nos íbamos a ir a trabajar a la otra masía. La verdad es que para nosotros fue mucho mejor porque estaba todo mucho más nuevo.

Pasaron los meses y me volví a quedar en estado, en esta ocasión fue de mi hijo Ángel, que nació el 17 de junio de 1963 en la masía. Esta vez, sí que pudo venir mi madre para ayudarme a dar a luz.

En aquella época, parte de la familia y conocidos nuestros se desplazaron a Riba-Roja de Túria (Valencia) en busca de trabajo. El hermano de mi marido, Victorio, fue uno de los que se trasladó. Un día, regresó a Las Casas de visita junto con otros familiares. Nos contaron que les estaba yendo bien, así que nos animamos, y quisimos probar suerte a ver qué tal nos iba por allí. Por eso cuando se marcharon, Enrique se fue con ellos en el tren. Se alojó en la casa de su hermano Victorio hasta que encontró una casa para vivir. Los dueños vivían en la casa de al lado, y al ver que mi marido estaba interesado en ella, se la alquilaron.

En realidad, más que una casa, se trataba de una cueva, pero no nos importó. Se encontraba situada en la calle Velázquez. Por aquel entonces había muchas familias que vivían en cuevas rehabilitadas. Cuando Enrique acomodó la vivienda, yo viajé para allá con mis cuatro hijos. Íbamos en un camión que transportaba las pocas cosas que teníamos. Recuerdo que cuando salimos de Las Casas estaba nevando. Durante el viaje llovió mucho y tardamos bastantes horas en llegar a Riba-roja. En aquella época se tardaba entre 8 y 10 horas. Actualmente ese viaje se realiza en 3h y 30 minutos aproximadamente, porque las carreteras han mejorado mucho. Llegamos el

Aquí estoy trabajando en la naranja en Riba-roja de Túria.

19 de diciembre, nuestro hijo Ángel tenía tres meses. Todo parecía que estaba mejorando y que

ya quedaron atrás los sufrimientos y todo lo que padecimos. Ojalá hubiésemos tomado antes esta decisión, pero como dice el refrán...

"Nunca es tarde si la dicha es buena."

Mi marido y yo empezamos a trabajar en el campo, pero esta vez en la naranja. Era la primera vez que recogíamos este fruto y nos gustaba.

A los niños me los tenía que dejar solos en casa, aunque siempre he intentado compaginar el trabajo con el cuidado de ellos. No me gustaba nada dejarlos solos, pero no tenía otra opción. Luis era el mayor y se encargaba de cuidar a sus hermanos, pero él también era un niño. Aunque siempre hay alguien que te echa una mano cuando la necesitas. Los propietarios de la cueva donde vivíamos, Carmen y Agustín, en algunas ocasiones solían hacerse cargo de los niños cuando nosotros estábamos trabajando. Fueron muy amables con nosotros desde el primer día que llegamos, siempre les estaré agradecida, hicimos una bonita amistad.

Al poco tiempo de mudarnos al pueblo, empecé a notar que mi hijo Ángel, no se encontraba bien. Se quejaba mucho y no quería comer.

Un día noté que alrededor del ombligo tenía un bulto del tamaño de un botón. Lo llevé al médico que se encontraba en el ambulatorio del pueblo y después de examinarlo me dijo:

—Mañana tienen que llevar a su hijo al hospital Sanjurjo de Valencia.

Cuando se lo conté a mi marido, nos quedamos muy preocupados. Estaba deseando que amaneciera para llevarlo al hospital. Al día siguiente me fui en tren con mi hijo a Valencia.

Cuando llegamos al hospital empezaron a hacerle pruebas. Finalmente me dieron la mala noticia, le detectaron un cáncer en el riñón. Tuvieron que ingresarlo porque tenían que operarlo para quitarle el riñón dañado.

Con mi hijo Ángel, en el hospital.

Tras la operación, los médicos salieron a informarnos y nos dijeron que todo había salido bien. Todos nos quedamos más tranquilos. Pero con el tiempo se volvió a reproducir en el otro riñón y tras varios meses de hospitalización, falleció en casa a los dos años y medio rodeado de sus hermanos. Pasar por esa tragedia de enterrar a un hijo, es muy duro. Lo enterramos en el cementerio del pueblo. Otra vez tuve que pasar por una pérdida inesperada. Es muy duro ver a tu hijo enfermo y que no puedas hacer nada por él, pero es mucho peor enterrarlo…

A pesar de ese mal trago que tuvimos que pasar, nos alegró mucho venir a vivir a Riba-roja de Túria porque logramos tener una vida mucho más tranquila y más digna. Ojalá nos hubiésemos venido antes. Aunque también trabajábamos mucho, pero nos compensaba porque ganábamos bastante más. Nos cambió la vida como de la noche a la mañana.

En el campo íbamos a recoger naranja, patatas, cebollinos, cebollas y también cogíamos algarroba. Aunque yo tenía alergia y asma, seguía trabajando en el campo, pero en las épocas en las que había más polen, no podía ir a trabajar. Por eso buscaba casas para limpiar por horas, la cuestión era no estar parada y seguir trabajando.

Vivir en este pueblo cambió nuestras vidas a mejor, teníamos nuestra casa y algo más de libertad. Además, los dos niños más pequeños Enrique y Encarna pudieron ir al colegio público Miguel de Cervantes. El mayor, Luis, estudiaba en casa de un profesor por las noches junto con otros alumnos. Este profesor habitualmente daba clases en las escuelas parroquiales de Riba-roja de Túria. Teníamos que hacerlo así porque durante el día trabajaba para ayudar a la familia.

Con solo 12 años de edad, empezó como ayudante de pintor en Manises. Al principio, se encargó de limpiar los cubos de pintura y de ayudar en todo aquello que les hiciera falta. Como no tenía edad para trabajar, cuando realizaban una inspección de trabajo lo escondían en alguna habitación o en un cuarto de baño para que no le viesen.

La comunión de nuestro hijo Enrique.

Por fin llegaron días maravillosos por vivir, la comunión de mis hijos Enrique en 1966 y la de mi hija Encarnita, en 1967 justo un año después. Pudimos disfrutar de ese momento todos juntos y en familia.

El trabajo y el esfuerzo que hacíamos valieron la pena, lo dábamos todo por nuestros hijos. Hasta pudimos comprar una casa en la plaza del ayuntamiento, y tras acomodarla nos pusimos vivir.

Enrique, había trabajado de albañil y realizó algunos arreglillos en la casa para dejarla más habitable. Cuando terminó, nos mudamos con mucha alegría. En esa casa he pasado gran parte de mi vida. Guardo muy buenos recuerdos.

También os quiero contar un poco de historia. En el año 1982 fue cuando Felipe González ganó las elecciones. Desde ese momento, yo empecé a ser militante del PSOE. Eso es algo que siempre me ha enorgullecido mucho, porque lo hice en recuerdo a mi padre. Pero antes de todo eso, pasaron muchas otras cosas, como la muerte de Franco, que fue el 20 de Noviembre de 1975. Recuerdo muy bien ese día, en cada balcón ondeaban banderas de España con crespones negros. Algunos se alegraron mucho de su muerte, pero estaban preocupados por lo que pudiera venir.

El fin la dictadura, dio paso a la monarquía. El rey Juan Carlos I comenzó su reinado con una jovencísima y guapa reina, Sofía, su esposa. En ese momento, nosotros ya vivíamos en la casa de la plaza del ayuntamiento.

Entre los años 1975 y 1977 tuvo lugar la transición española. Las primeras elecciones fueron el 14 de Junio de 1977 que ganó el partido más votado, y fue la Unión de Centro Democrático (UCD) liderado por Adolfo Suárez.

El 6 de Diciembre del 1978 se aprobó la **CONSTITUCIÓN ESPAÑOLA** gracias a eso, en España se dio un gran paso hacia adelante, entramos en una democracia. Gracias a los partidos políticos que se crearon en aquella época, y que consiguieron llegar a un gran acuerdo como es el de la constitución, podemos hoy disfrutar de nuestros derechos y libertades.

Aunque esa tranquilidad no estuvo exenta de sobresaltos, como el que tuvo lugar el 23 de Febrero de 1981 que fue cuando se inició el golpe de estado en el **Congreso de los Diputados**. Aún se pueden ver los tiros en el techo. En ese momento nosotros no sabíamos nada. Mi hija Encarnita y yo entrábamos en casa cuando sonó el teléfono. Era Josefa, la mujer de mi hijo Luis, también natural de Las Casas. Llamó asustada para saber si habíamos visto las noticias. Nos comentó que los tanques habían salido por las calles de Valencia. Afortunadamente el golpe de estado fracasó y todo quedó en un gran susto.

Al poco tiempo, mi madre también se trasladó a este pueblo porque la única hija que vivía con ella en Las Casas, también quería venir. Por eso se vino con mi hermana, para no quedarse sola. Todos mis hermanos vinieron a este lindo pueblo que tan bien nos acogió. La verdad es que nos cambió mucho la vida. Mi madre también se acopló muy bien, se instaló en nuestra recién estrenada casa. En la buhardilla tenía su habitación.

Pasado un tiempo, mi madre se fue a vivir a un piso que además, tenía a dos de sus hijas viviendo en la misma finca, Pilar, que vivía enfrente de ella y Angelita, en la segunda planta. Ahí estuvo hasta sus últimos días, murió con 83 años en el año 1985. Se encontraba rodeada de sus hijos y la enterramos en el cementerio de Riba-roja de Túria.

Después de trabajar durante tantos años, casi toda mi vida, llegó la hora de jubilarme. Por entonces, ya tenía mucha artrosis y no podía trabajar. Aun así, tuve una vida muy activa. A mí nunca me ha gustado estar parada y participaba en todas las actividades que podía. Esta parte de mi vida la viví intensamente. Lo que no pude disfrutar de joven, lo disfruté de mayor.

Me animaron a ir a la escuela de adultos para mejorar mi lectura y escritura. No me lo pensé dos veces, siempre he sido muy decidida y echá palante, así que no me dio vergüenza ir al colegio para aprender más de lo que ya sabía, porque lo que no pude hacer de niña, lo hice en ese momento. La vida me estaba dando una segunda oportunidad y la aproveché. Hasta me saqué el certificado de escolaridad.

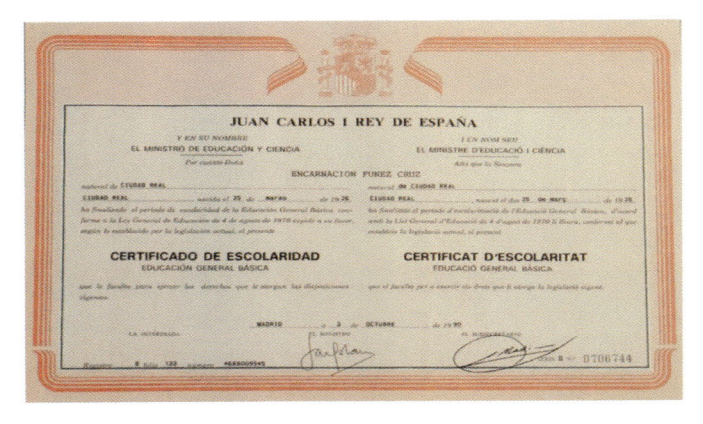

Incluso me apunté a gimnasia para la tercera edad que hacían en el pueblo. Hasta íbamos de excursiones a otros pueblos para realizar exhibiciones de gimnasia.

También me gustaba mucho la natación y me apunté a unos cursillos para aprender a nadar. Algo que durante mi juventud, me resultó imposible realizar. El agua me encantaba, disfrutaba mucho tanto en la piscina como en la playa. Además, también me venía bien para la artrosis.

Otra cosa que siempre me ha gustado mucho y que me ha caracterizado, ha sido que me encantaba recitar poemas. Durante mi juventud aprendí muchos. Algunos los escuchaba en la radio y otros los leía publicados en alguna revista o periódico de la época. A día de hoy, y con más de noventa años cumplidos, todavía recuerdo muchos de ellos, incluso soy capaz de recitarlos sin problema y dándoles su entonación, a viva voz.

Y ¡qué contaros del baile! Me encantaba ir con mi marido a los bailes de los jubilados los fines de semana. Nos encantaba bailar los pasodobles. Además, también formé parte de la ejecutiva de la Asociación de Jubilados de Riba-Roja de Turia.

Aquí estábamos disfrutando una tarde entrañable juntos, en el Hogar de los Jubilados.

A mi marido le gustaba mucho pasear e ir a la estación con los amigos y escuchar los clásicos de su época que eran, Manolo Escobar, Joselito, Peret, Machín... Aunque lamentablemente todo no fueron alegrías. Enfermó casi de repente, fue en marzo del año 2005 tenía 80 años.

Un día, cuando volvió a casa le notamos un poco extraño, llegó con temblores y con problemas para caminar. También observamos que no podía vocalizar bien, tenía dificultad para hablar. Nos

Paseando por el río Turia con mi marido, mi hija Encarnita y mi yerno Lorenzo.

asustamos porque no era nada normal en él lo que le estaba pasando. Rápidamente lo llevamos al ambulatorio. Esperamos impacientes al resultado del médico que lo estuvo reconociendo. Nos recomendó que sería conveniente hacerle un TAC para poder averiguar lo que le estaba sucediendo.

Se realizó la prueba radiológica y al poco tiempo, llamaron del hospital. En ese momento solo se encontraba él en casa y cogió el teléfono. Le comentaron que tenían que ingresarlo pero que llamarían más tarde porque su mujer Encarna y su hija Encarnita se encontraban en el hospital.

Estábamos allí en el hospital de Burjassot, porque yo tenía cita en cardiología para una revisión justo el mismo día que lo llamaron para darle el resultado.

Enrique al recibir la noticia del ingreso se puso muy nervioso. Le detectaron un meningioma, dicho en otras palabras, un tumor en el cerebro. Esa misma tarde a las 17h nuestra hija Encarnita lo llevó al hospital.

Inicialmente, los médicos nos comentaron que no tenía solución que era un hombre de avanzada edad y no creían que pudiera aguantar una operación de ese tipo, pero tras realizarle las pruebas y comprobar que tenía un estado de salud bueno, decidieron operarle.

El 1 de Julio del 2005 le operaron en el hospital la Fe de Valencia. La operación fue compleja pero salió bien. A partir de esa fecha, mi marido y yo dejamos de vivir en nuestra casa y nos mudamos a la casa de nuestra hija Encarnita.

En casa de mi hija Encarnita, (está detrás de su padre). Estábamos celebrando el 81 cumpleaños de Enrique. Al lado de nuestra hija está su hermano mayor Luis, y a su lado, su mujer Josefa.

Afortunadamente Enrique se fue recuperando poco a poco, aunque no recuperó la movilidad al 100% y por ese motivo, se decidió que ya no viviéramos solos, porque necesitábamos ayuda.

Ese mismo año, en septiembre, Enrique sufrió un infarto al corazón del que también se recuperó. Estuvo 8 años más o menos estable pero en febrero del 2013 falleció por una insuficiencia cardiorrespiratoria, en el hospital de Manises.

Lo velamos en casa de mi hija Encarnita. Avisamos a sus familiares y vinieron al entierro desde Ciudad Real, Murcia y Barcelona, algunos de sus hermanos y sobrinos junto con sus hijos y nietos.

Fue incinerado en un acto civil y lo enterramos en el cementerio de Riba-roja. Vivimos un momento muy duro durante el entierro. Se decidió depositar las cenizas de mi marido en la misma tumba de nuestro hijo Ángel. Por ese motivo, tuvimos la oportunidad de sacar al pequeño para enterrarlo junto a su padre. Fue muy emotivo verle junto a los juguetes que sus hermanos depositaron en el féretro. Tenía una pistola de juguete. Su hermano Enrique comentó en ese momento que fue él quien la metió en el ataúd. También había un sonajero.

> **Ahora tengo 95 años y guardo un bonito recuerdo de él. Ha sido el único hombre para mí y siempre hemos estado juntos apoyándonos el uno al otro. Aunque lo echo mucho de menos.**

Después de aquél triste momento, los días pasaban tristemente echándole de menos. Sigo viviendo con mi hija Encarnita, estoy muy a gusto con ella, con mi yerno Lorenzo y con mis nietos... Para ir finalizando esta historia, voy a nombrar a mi familia (hijos, nietos y bisnietos).

Mi marido con mi nuera Trini.

Mi hijo mayor **Luis Oliver** está casado con **Josefa Rodríguez** y tienen tres hijos, **Luis José**, **Inmaculada** y **Raúl**. Mi segundo hijo es **Enrique Oliver** se casó con **Trini Fabuel** tienen tres hijas, **Raquel**, **Verónica** y **Sandra**. Y mi hija **Encarna Oliver**, está casada con **Lorenzo García**, tienen dos hijas, **Mª Ángeles** y **Encarnita**. En total son ocho nietos. Pero no ha quedado ahí la cosa, también tengo ocho biznietos que se llaman **Juan Raúl**, **Lucía**, **Paula**, **Valeria**, **Víctor**, **Neizan**, **Ferrán** y **Vega**. Todos ellos son los que me dan la alegría de vivir. Les estoy muy agradecida porque me cuidan y me miman mucho.

La verdad es que he tenido mucha suerte con los tres hijos que tuve, aunque esté mal que yo lo diga, son muy buenos hijos y unas bellas personas con un gran corazón. Hace años que no salgo a la calle por decisión propia, para qué voy a salir si todo lo que quiero está en casa. Ellos lo asumieron muy bien y sin ningún reproche. Aunque sí que me han animado a salir, pero me acomodé a mi nueva vida y tomé esa decisión. Eso sí, yo seguiré disfrutando de la vida y de los míos el tiempo que me quede, que seguro ¡es mucho!

Bueno, el que sea... no pido más, porque ya he vivido mucho y he pasado por muchas cosas.

Os agradezco a toda la familia que hayáis estado siempre ahí. Os deseo lo mejor.

Besos y abrazos para todos los que estáis y también para los que ya hace tiempo que nos dejasteis, siempre os llevaré en mi corazón.

¡*OS QUIERO!*

Encarna Fúnez Cruz

Árbol Genealógico

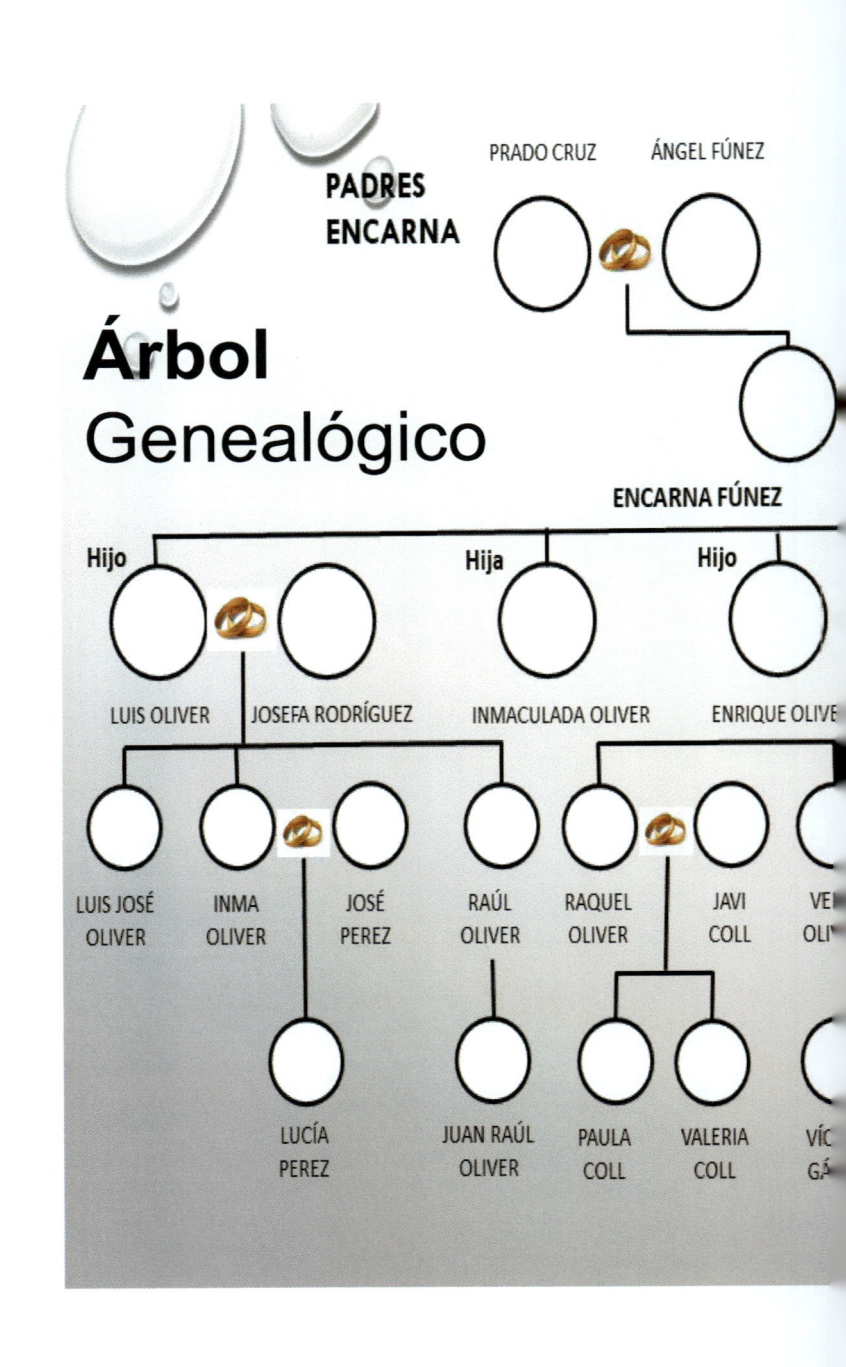

PADRES ENCARNA

PRADO CRUZ — ÁNGEL FÚNEZ

ENCARNA FÚNEZ

- Hijo: LUIS OLIVER — JOSEFA RODRÍGUEZ
- Hija: INMACULADA OLIVER
- Hijo: ENRIQUE OLIVER

Hijos de LUIS OLIVER y JOSEFA RODRÍGUEZ:
- LUIS JOSÉ OLIVER
- INMA OLIVER — JOSÉ PEREZ
- RAÚL OLIVER
- RAQUEL OLIVER — JAVI COLL
- VE... OLI...

- LUCÍA PEREZ (hija de INMA OLIVER y JOSÉ PEREZ)
- JUAN RAÚL OLIVER (hijo de RAÚL OLIVER)
- PAULA COLL, VALERIA COLL (hijas de RAQUEL OLIVER y JAVI COLL)
- VÍC... GÁ...

Familia Fúnez-Oliver

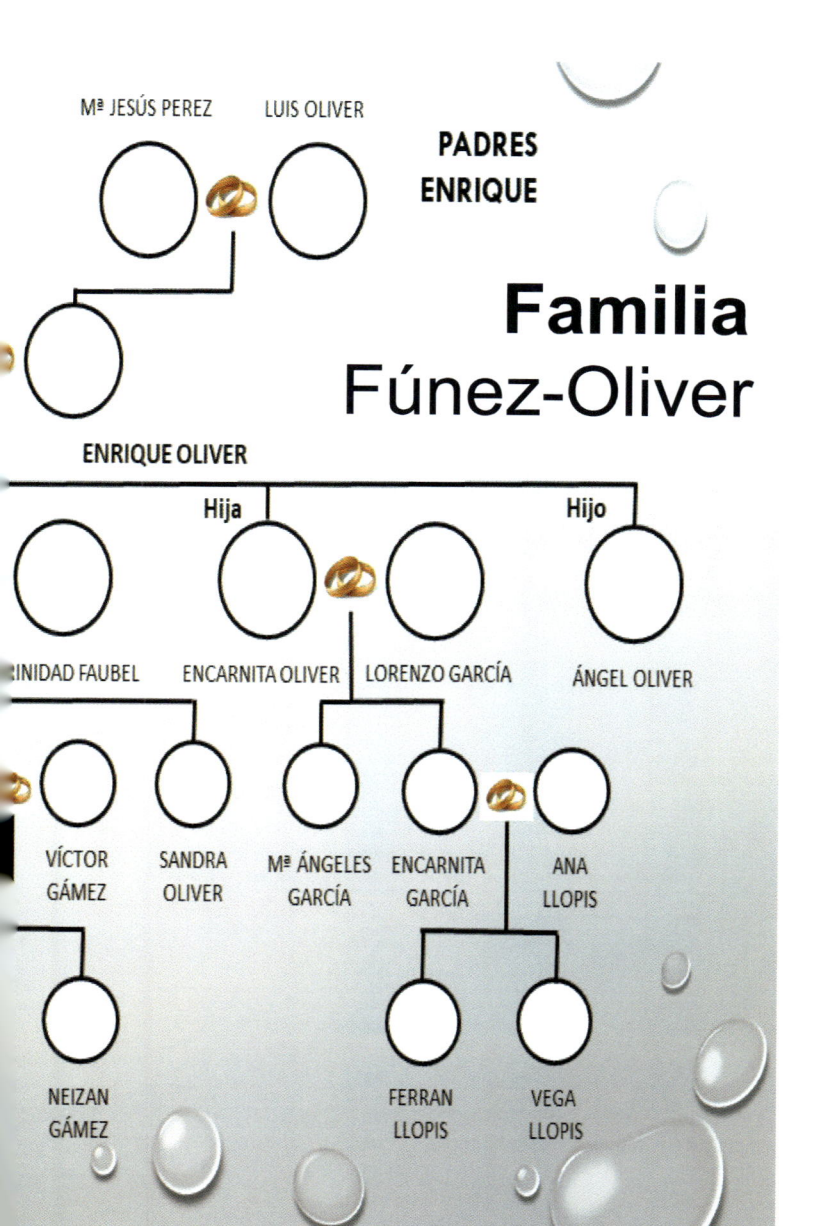

PADRES ENRIQUE

Mª JESÚS PEREZ — LUIS OLIVER

ENRIQUE OLIVER

Hija — Hijo

TRINIDAD FAUBEL — ENCARNITA OLIVER — LORENZO GARCÍA — ÁNGEL OLIVER

VÍCTOR GÁMEZ — SANDRA OLIVER — Mª ÁNGELES GARCÍA — ENCARNITA GARCÍA — ANA LLOPIS

NEIZAN GÁMEZ — FERRAN LLOPIS — VEGA LLOPIS

Esta biografía ha sido una parte de mi historia, porque la vida continúa...

Printed in Great Britain
by Amazon

THE SKYSAGE AFFAIR

An Adam Drake Novel

SCOTT MATTHEWS

Copyright © 2024 by Scott Matthews

Published by Vinci Books

All rights reserved.

No part of this book may be reproduced in any form or by any electronic or mechanical means, including information storage and retrieval systems, without written permission from the author, except for the use of brief quotations in a book review.

Chapter One

THE WIND WAS BLOWING AT fifteen miles per hour and a heavy chop slapped at the bottom of his windsurfing board. Spray was hitting his face, but it couldn't erase his smile. The bright sun made the water ahead a shimmering golden surface and he was flying across it.

Michael Bridge had driven up the Columbia River Gorge Highway from Portland, Oregon, early in the morning to get a feel for the wind conditions that had been blowing all week and were expected to continue through the weekend. He was entered in his first tournament; the Gorge Beach Bash, an International Windsurfing Tour slalom competition at Hood River, Oregon. He intended to win it.

At Stanford University, he'd played water polo and his team had won the NCAA championship, in his junior and senior years. When he was out of eligibility and couldn't continue playing water polo, he'd looked around for a lifetime sport and fell in love with windsurfing.

And when he was offered a job after graduation working for a startup tech company, SkySage, Inc., in Portland, Oregon, just down the Columbia River from the best windsurfing in the world, he'd jumped at the opportunity.

Now he was twenty-eight years old and making good money working for the company that was developing satellite surveillance artificial intelligence for the Pentagon's JEDI cloud program.

Now he was a hundred yards offshore from the Hatchery on the Washington side of the river, on a glorious day. Preparing to carve a jibe to the north, he caught a blur of movement out of the corner of his right eye. He cut hard to his left but wasn't fast enough to keep from slamming into an out-of-control windsurfer.

He looked back over his right shoulder and saw that he'd knocked the other windsurfer off his board, who was bobbing in the water shaking his fist at him.

What was wrong with the guy! He was the one who hadn't looked where he was going!

He didn't remember the guy hitting him hard, but a sharp pain in his chest was suddenly making it hard to breath. He turned into the wind, let go of the sail and sat down on the board to catch his breath.

Pain was spreading along his jawline down into his neck and he felt lightheaded. He looked around to call for help but there was no one close enough to hear him.

Michael Bridge stared at the windsurfers racing back and forth across the water and then slumped forward, as his vision dimmed and he lost consciousness.

THE WINDSURFER in the water watched until he was sure his target was down, before getting back on his board and racing back to shore. He'd waited on the north shore of the river at the launching place called the Hatchery, until he was sure it was Bridge sailing across the river before he went out to intercept him.

The small poison dart from his heart attack gun, a weapon originally developed by the CIA and copied by China, had penetrated the Bridge's neoprene wetsuit, disintegrating as it entered his body.

The man wouldn't have felt anything. If he had, it would have felt like a mosquito bite, nothing more.

When he reached shallow water and dropped sail to walk his rig in, he saw that a river marine patrol boat was speeding across the river. A cluster of windsurfers on the water had gathered around the man lying face forward on his board and must have called for help.

No one looked his way as he pulled his board from the water and left it behind him on the shore. The crowd of spectators were watching the Marine Patrol boat speed to the rescue but let him walk through without saying anything to him. Except for one man who turned and stared at him.

"Aren't you the guy that ran into that windsurfer?" the man asked.

"The other way around, he ran into me."

"Was he hurt?"

"How would I know? He knocked me off my board. I was the one in the water catching my breath, not worrying about that SOB."

He turned his back on the man and walked toward the parking lot.

"You'd better stick around in case the police want to talk to you," the man called after him.

"Just going to my car, I'll be back for my rig."

He had no intention of sticking around to be questioned by the police.

He jogged toward a white Ford Transit van and jumped in. The van and the windsurfing rig were rented with fake ID and he wasn't worried about anyone tracking him down.

He'd be out of the state before the sun went down.

Chapter Two

ADAM DRAKE SPRINTED the last stretch of his five-mile run with his German Shepherd named Lancer running by his side. When they were fifty yards away from the long driveway that led to his newly leased home on Bainbridge Island, Lancer took off like a rocket.

His running buddy was sitting on his haunches next to a white SUV when Drake stopped and leaned down to say, "Next time you leave me for her, there won't be your usual reward for running with me."

"Don't worry, Lancer," he heard a voice call out from the front deck of his log cabin. "Here you go, big boy. I'll take care of you."

Drake turned to see Liz Strobel leaning down with a dog treat in her hand.

"It's not enough that you're turning him against me, you're doing it with something you broke into my place to steal," he chided her with a smile on his face.

"You shouldn't have given me a key if you didn't want me to use it."

"New car?" he asked as he walked to her past the white SUV.

Liz stuck her cheek out for a kiss, "I'll take a hug when you've cooled down. The dealer loaned it to me for the weekend. He's trying to convince me the Cadillac XT5 is better suited to weather in the Northwest than the all-wheel drive CT6-V I was looking at. I'm not convinced."

Drake took her hand and led her off the deck. "Let's walk down to the fire pit on the waterfront and talk while I cool down."

Drake had leased the log cabin for six months on the eastern shore of Bainbridge Island across Puget Sound from Seattle. He'd thought it would the perfect escape from the city when he decided to move north from Oregon to be closer to Liz and Puget Sound Security, where he served as the company's special counsel.

In Oregon, he'd lived on a forty-acre vineyard in the wine country that he loved. The farm, as he preferred to call it because growing grapes was just glorified farming, was on the outskirts of Portland, the state's biggest city. Seattle was a little larger, as the fifteenth largest metropolitan area in America, but to him it seemed twice as big.

Living on Bainbridge Island was meant to be a compromise, between living on the vineyard he loved and the being closer to the woman he loved, but he was beginning to think he'd made a mistake.

A graveled path lined with dark purple rhododendrons crossed a grassy area down to a fire pit at the water's edge and the boat dock he shared with the neighboring property to the south.

"Are you thinking about buying a boat?" Liz asked when they reached the benches around the fire pit.

Drake remained standing, looking across the water to the Seattle skyline. "Liz, do you like it here?"

"Where, here on Bainbridge or here in Seattle?"

"Both, I suppose."

"I grew up on the West Coast and I like it better than living back east. The weather's better in San Diego, but Seattle's nice. I haven't spent enough time on Bainbridge yet to know. Why, are you having second thoughts about moving to Seattle?"

"I'm having second thoughts about living on this island and having a thirty-five-minute ferry ride each day, each way, to work."

"Didn't it take you that long to drive from your farm in Dundee to Portland?"

"That was different. I like to drive."

"You like being in control. I've seen how you fidget in your seat when I'm driving. Maybe you could get them to let you steer the ferry."

"Funny."

"If you don't like it here, where do you think you would like to live?" Liz asked with a note of concern in her voice.

"Not back in Oregon, if that's what you're asking. I just know I'm not as comfortable here as I thought I'd be."

Liz stood and wrapped her arm around his waist. "You can always stay with me until you figure it out."

Drake's phone started playing the opening guitar riff from John Fogerty's "Up Around the Bend", keeping him from having to answer her.

He recognized the caller. "Good morning, Mr. President."

"Do you have a minute, Adam?"

"Fire away."

"I'd like you to look into something for me. A friend of mine is on his way to Portland. His son died windsurfing on the Columbia River and he's being told his son had a heart attack. He doesn't believe it. He's arranged for a private autopsy to be performed tomorrow. I'd like you to attend it with him, if you're available."

"I'm available, but why do you want me there?"

"My friend's son told him he was concerned about China gaining access artificial intelligence software his company was developing. His son works for a subcontractor of Microsoft's on the Pentagon's JEDI contract. They're a client of yours. It seems unlikely, because I know Puget Sound Security did the company's security assessment and you cleared it for JEDI.

"Before I stir things up and tell the Pentagon they might have a problem, I'd like your take on what my friend's telling me. My friend doesn't have your track record trouble shooting problems for us on the q.t."

"I'll do what I can, sir. What's your friend's name and where can I meet him?"

"My friend is Congressman Matthew Bridge. He's staying at the Portland Marriott."

Chapter Three

THEY SPENT the weekend relaxing and shopping. Liz found a boutique she liked and added a weekend outfit to her wardrobe. Drake let her drive him to a marina to look at boats but resisted the best efforts of the salesman to sell him one.

Early Monday morning, they took the ferry back to Seattle. Before Drake left to drive to Portland, he stopped by Mike Casey's office to tell him about the call he received from President Ballard.

He found his friend, the CEO of Puget Sound Security and former Delta Force teammate, in his office talking with someone on the phone. Casey waved him in and motioned for him to sit down in one of the chairs in front of his desk.

"Paul, I'll have Kevin get his best technician on it. I've got to go but don't worry. We'll make sure your research is safe."

Casey put the phone down and let out a deep breath. "That was Bill at Summit Technology. Someone's launched another big phishing attack against them and one of his researchers took the bait and opened an email. He wants to fight back and have us destroy them. You know how Bill gets. How was your weekend?"

"It was okay. Liz is trying to get me to buy a boat."

"Why?"

"We have a dock. I guess she thinks I need a boat tied to it."

"I suspect there's more to it than that."

"There probably is. President Ballard called. He wants me to attend an autopsy in Portland this afternoon with a friend of his."

"Why you and how did his friend die?"

Drake shook his head and laughed. "Sorry, I didn't communicate that very well. His friend is Congressman Bridge from Nebraska. Bridge's son died Saturday windsurfing at Hood River and they're telling him his son had a heart attack. His father doesn't buy it."

"What does the president hope to gain by asking you to attend the son's autopsy with his father? The medical examiner will be able to tell if it was a heart attack or not."

"The Congressman's son worked for one of our clients. He told his father he was worried about China gaining access to what the company was working on. The president wants to know if there's anything to support the son's concerns before he asks the Pentagon to look into it."

"Why didn't the congressman alert someone at the Pentagon himself?"

"I don't know the answer to that. Bridge is on the House Armed Services Committee and its Intelligence and Emerging Threats and Capabilities subcommittee. I would think he'd have someone he could talk to without taking this to the president."

"What company did you say the son worked for?"

"He worked for SkySage, Inc. in Portland" Drake replied.

"SkySage is one of the subcontractors we cleared for Microsoft. They're developing satellite surveillance artificial intelligence software for Microsoft's cloud project for the Pentagon.

"The Pentagon's security requirements for JEDI are hard for a lot of the smaller subcontractors to comply with. SkySage passed with flying colors. Why was the congressman's son worried about China?"

"That's what the president wants to know," Drake said. "I'd better hit the road. I'm meeting Congressman Bridge for lunch."

On the drive from Seattle to Portland, Drake made two phone

calls. The first was to Paul Benning, who was now retained by PSS as its private investigator.

"Good morning, Paul. What does your calendar look like for the week?"

"It has a couple of holes. What do you need?"

"I need you to investigate the death of a windsurfer in Hood River. Do you still have friends in Hood River County Sheriff's Department?"

"Sheriff Wilson's a good friend. What am I looking for?"

"The name of the windsurfer who died is Michael Bridge. Cause of death is reported to be a heart attack. His father doesn't believe it and says his son had no known medical conditions. According to the Hood River News, Bridge collapsed on his board in the middle of the river after colliding with another windsurfer. Find out all you can and talk with any of the eyewitnesses who are still in Hood River."

"How soon do you need this?"

"I'm meeting his father for lunch today. Congressman Bridge has arranged for a private autopsy at OHSU this afternoon, so as soon as you can get up there."

"I can run up there this afternoon. It's only an hour away. Are you sticking around after the autopsy?"

"I haven't decided yet."

"If you do, drop by the office. I'll try to have something for you later today."

"Thanks, Paul. Say hello to Margo for me."

"You got it."

The second call Drake made was to Liz.

"Hello beautiful, how's your morning going?"

"Not as well as yours. I'm in my office and you're on the road driving your 'company car'. You're probably the only man in the country who was given a Porsche Cayman GTS for his company car."

"You're just bitter because you haven't found a way to talk Mike into buying that Cadillac CT6-V you're lusting over."

"The lusting's over. I went ahead and bought one."

"No more lusting, huh?"

"Not over a car, anyway. Will you be back in Seattle tonight?"

"It might be late. Do you have time to do something for me?"

"It depends. Will you be back in Seattle tonight?"

"I will now. Mike told me before I left that we did a security assessment for SkySage, Inc., the company Congressman Bridge's son worked for. Will you review the assessment? I'd like to know who the players are there."

"I'll pull the SkySage assessment report and have a look."

"Call me when you've been through it."

Chapter Four

DRAKE RECOGNIZED Congressman Matthew Bridge (R-Nebr) sitting at a table in the Marriott's Proof ▪ Reader Whisky Bar and Restaurant. He wasn't wearing the confident politician's smile Drake had seen displayed on his website.

The congressman's grief was poorly camouflaged by his tightly pursed lips and clinched jaw muscles.

Bridge had been an All-American wrestler at the University of Nebraska and never lost a match wrestling at 190 pounds. At age fifty-eight, he looked like he was still fit, judging by the broad shoulders and biceps that were stretching the fabric of the black polo shirt he was wearing.

Drake walked to Bridge's table and held out his hand. "Congressman Bridge, I'm Adam Drake."

"Have a seat, Drake," Bridge said, shaking hands. "Would you like a beer? I'm buying lunch."

"I would, thanks. How was your flight?"

"I slept most of the way. We haven't slept much since getting the news about Michael."

"I'm sorry to hear about your son. How's your wife doing?"

"She's taking it hard. Our daughter flew in to stay with her."

The waiter came to their table with menus. "Are you having lunch, gentleman?"

Congressman Bridge nodded and said, "He needs a beer while we look at these."

"What would you like?" the waiter asked Drake.

"A pint of Proofreader Pale Ale, thanks."

"What food's good here?" Bridge asked Drake.

"I like the High Proof Burger and fries."

"That works for me. How long will it take us to get to the Department of Pathology at the Health Sciences University? The autopsy is at two."

"Not long, we can take the aerial tram from OHSU's South Waterfront Campus. It's not far from here."

The waiter returned with Drake's pint and took their orders for burgers and fries.

Congressman Bridge finished his pint of beer and asked, "Why did the president ask you to accompany me to the autopsy? I attended my share of autopsies when I was the County Attorney in Nebraska. You probably did too, when you were a prosecutor. I don't need anyone to hold my hand."

"I don't think that's what the president had in mind."

"Why then?"

"There are probably two reasons," Drake said. "A couple of months ago, I agreed to help him if he ever needed someone outside the government to trouble shoot something for him. The other reason is my company did the facility security assessment for SkySage, to clear it for work on the JEDI project."

"What does that have to do with my son's death?"

"Why do you believe your son didn't have a heart attack?"

"Because he was in perfect health! You don't have a heart attack at his age with his family's clean cardiac history."

"Is that the only reason you're questioning the medical examiner's report?"

Congressman Bridge took a deep breath and started to say something when he saw the waiter returning with their burgers. He waited until the man left before answering.

"You may know that I serve on the House Armed Services Committee. You might not know that I also serve on the Intelligence and Emerging Threats and Capabilities Subcommittee. We have jurisdiction over defense-wide programs related to research, development, testing and development of programs like the JEDI project.

"SkySage is a Microsoft subcontractor working on the JEDI project. My son told me last week he was concerned about China getting access to what the company was working on. I asked him what he was worried about and he said he'd tell me more when he was sure of something. That was two days before he died."

"You think what he was looking into is related to his death. Is that why you requested the autopsy?"

"We know China wants JEDI. It's a game-changer for the next big war. Yes, it's possible that Michael was looking into something that got him killed."

"Did you tell the president what you're telling me?"

"I did. We've been friends since college. I ran his campaign when he ran for the U.S. Senate."

"If this autopsy confirms that your son had a heart attack, what then?"

Congressman Bridge shook his head. "I don't know. I have a hard time letting go of something when my gut tells me something's not right."

Drake nodded his head in agreement. "I know what you mean."

After taking a bite out of his burger, Congressman Bridge put it down and said, "I guess I'm not as hungry as I thought I was. Do you know this pathologist? I was told he was the best pathologist they had available on short notice."

Drake finished the fry and said, "I do know him. Dr. Swanson is the Medical Director of Autopsy Services at OHSU. He's as good as you'll find anywhere in the country."

"You used to have an office here in Portland, didn't you?"

"I still have an office here. I lease it to a private investigator Puget Sound Security has on retainer. His wife was my office manager and legal assistant before I started full time as special counsel for PSS. He's in Hood River right now, investigating your son's death."

"I didn't ask for that. What do you expect him to find out that I didn't get from the medical examiner?"

"Paul was a former detective with the Multnomah County Sheriff's Office here. The sheriff of Hood River County is a friend of his."

"When will you hear from him? I was planning on returning home with Michael tomorrow."

"Paul will be back this afternoon" Drake said. "After the autopsy, I'll stop by the office and talk with him. Why don't we meet for a drink or dinner? I'll tell you then what he was able to find."

"Why don't you bring him along? I'll take you both to dinner, somewhere we can get a good steak." Congressman Bridge looked down at the burger he hadn't finished eating. "I hope I'll have an appetite by then."

Chapter Five

DRAKE RETRIEVED his car from valet parking and drove Congressman Bridge to the South Waterfront Lower Tram Terminal. From there, it was a four-minute scenic ride in the aerial tram up to Marquam Hill and the Oregon Health & Science University campus.

Snow-capped Mount Hood stood tall to the east and the Willamette River wound its way through the city below.

"Quite a sight," Congressman Bridge remarked.

"It gets better on the hospital's viewing terrace where you can see more of the city."

After ten minutes of sightseeing on the terrace, Drake and Congressman Bridge took the elevator down to ground level. From there, it was a short walk to the northwest corner of the OHSU campus and the Richard Jones Hall and Autopsy Services.

Dr. Peter Swanson, M.D., Ph.D., was waiting for them in his office.

In his late sixties, Dr. Swanson had the slight build of a cyclist. With salt and pepper gray hair and silver goatee, he looked every bit the university professor he was as he stood to shake hands with Congressman Bridge and Drake.

"Good to see you again, Adam. I heard you're in Seattle now."

"I am. You look good. Still cycling?"

"Not as many miles as I used to." Dr. Swanson picked up the file on his desk, sat back in his chair and looked at Congressman Bridge. "This is a university hospital, Congressman, and I will have four pathology students assisting me in your son's autopsy. The autopsy will take three to six hours to complete, to allow the pathologists-in-training to be as thorough as possible, with my guidance. The determination of cause of death is made by me, with their assistance in the findings we make. There isn't much that will escape our attention, but I like to know as much as possible about your son before we begin. Can you give me a short account of his medical history?"

"There's not much to tell," Congressman Bridge said. "He had the usual childhood ailments; measles, mumps, colds. He broke his left arm when he took a spill on his bike. He's been involved in sports all his life and played water polo at Stanford. He took up windsurfing when he finished his MBA, but I don't know if he continued running like he did in college. As far as I know, doctor, he was in perfect health."

"Is there a family history of heart disease?"

"Not on either side of the family, going back to his great-grandparents."

Dr. Swanson laid the file down on his desk and stood up. "I'd better get to work, then. If you'll leave a number with my secretary, I'll call you when we finish."

Congressman Bridge got up and turned to leave. "Run every test you can think of, doctor. Look for anything unusual, because this doesn't make any sense. I know you probably hear this a lot, but I have a bad feeling about this. I've learned to trust my gut when it starts churning."

"I'll be very thorough," Dr. Swanson promised.

Congressman Bridge left his card with the doctor's secretary and walked out of the Autopsy Services office with Drake behind him. Out in the hall, he asked Drake, "It looks like I have some time to kill. Any suggestions?"

It was half past two in the afternoon and Drake hadn't heard from Paul Benning yet. "Why don't we drive to SkySage and pick up your son's things from his office? I'd like to know more about what he did there."

"That makes two of us."

SkySage, Inc., according to his Porsche's navigation system, was in Hillsboro, Oregon. The area had been dubbed the "Silicon Forest" because of the sprawling campuses of Intel, Inc., and the other tech companies that were located there.

On the way to SkySage, Drake called Liz using the Porsche's Connect communication system.

"Hi, Liz. I'm in the car with Congressman Bridge on our way to SkySage to pick up his son's things in his office. Did you have a chance to look at the security assessment we did for SkySage?"

"Hello, Congressman Bridge. I'm so sorry to hear about your son."

"Thank you, I appreciate that, Liz. I remember you from a briefing you gave my House subcommittee from the Senate Select Committee on Intelligence. I was sorry to hear you were moving out west."

"It was time for a change," Liz said.

"Liz, did you find anything about a Chinese connection that would have concerned the Congressman's son?" Drake asked.

"There wasn't anything in the assessment report that raised a concern for us. Its IT security met the Pentagon's requirements. There were no security breaches that had been reported. I checked the nationality of their employees and there are no Chinese nationals or even Chinese American citizens working there.

"The only thing I saw was that SkySage got some of its startup funding from an investment firm we looked into before I left Washington. The firm was buying equity positions in U.S. companies that manufactured products with dual-use civilian and military capabilities. I didn't have time yet to check with Senator Hazelton's office. I can call and find out what the Intelligence Committee did with that investigation."

"When you get whatever Senator Hazelton has on this, will you get it over to my office?" Congressman Bridge asked. "My subcommittee has jurisdiction over military programs related to research and development. I'd like to see what the senate committee turned up."

"Be happy to, congressman," Liz said.

'If you get anything in the next half hour, call me," Drake said. "We're almost to SkySage now. If there's anything we need to look for while we're there, call me. It will save me a trip back later."

"I'll call the senator's office as soon as we hang up. Will you be back in Seattle tonight?" she asked.

"Congressman Bridge has invited me to dinner. It might be late."

"Like I said, I'll leave the light on."

Drake didn't need to look to see if the congressman was smiling. He could hear him chuckling softly.

Chapter Six

SKYSAGE, Inc's headquarters were in the industrial corridor between Beaverton, Oregon, and Hillsboro, Oregon, on the tree-lined NE Dawson Creek Drive. The company occupied both floors of a modern-looking brick and glass two-story building.

Intel's corporate offices and campuses were located nearby. Intel had been a high-tech seed planted in the plains west of the Portland metro area that had grown to become the home of Oregon's largest industry.

"What did your son do for SkySage?" Drake asked the congressman as they got out of his Porsche and walked to the entrance of the building.

"He worked with the management team on business development, for the most part. He also worked with the lawyers to negotiate the contract with Microsoft on the JEDI project."

"Do you know anyone here?"

"I spoke briefly with his secretary a couple of times when I called Michael, but that's it."

Drake followed Congressman Bridge to the reception desk, where he introduced himself as Michael Bridge's father.

"I'm here to collect my son's personal things," he told the young receptionist.

"Does Michael know you're here to do that?" she asked with a puzzled look on her face.

"My son is dead, Miss. Apparently you weren't told," Congressman Bridge said sternly.

"OMG! I'm so sorry. I'm so sorry. I didn't know."

"Is there someone who can show me to his office?"

"I'll have to call security to show you the way, Mr. Bridge. Just a moment, please," she said and touched the screen on her console.

Congressman Bridge stepped back and stood beside Drake, while the receptionist summoned someone in hushed tones.

They waited quietly for several minutes before a man in his thirties, wearing jeans and a white polo shirt, walked briskly across the lobby toward them.

Drake couldn't tell from the look on the man's face if he was upset because he'd been called out of a meeting or was upset because, like the receptionist, he hadn't been told Michael Bridge had died.

"Congressman Bridge, I'm Jaron Carhlson, CEO of SkySage," the man said, holding out his hand. "I'm sorry, I didn't know about Michael. Please, come with me."

The CEO turned on his heel and started back across the lobby the way he'd come.

Drake and the congressman exchanged a look and followed him across the lobby and down a short hallway to a conference room adjacent to a large executive office suite.

Carhlson held the door open and waved them in. "Just give me a moment to finish what I was working on," he said. "Would you like some coffee?"

"No thank you," Congressman Bridge said.

Drake shook his head in agreement and entered the conference room behind the congressman.

The conference room was a glass-walled cube with a glass-topped round conference table with eight black leather and chrome chairs around it.

The wall between the conference room and the executive office suite was glass and they saw Carhlson behind his desk talking on the phone.

"I guess I shouldn't have expected them to know Michael had died," Congressman Bridge said.

"No, they wouldn't have had anyway to know, unless someone from SkySage was windsurfing with Michael," Drake said.

"Carhlson's younger than I expected."

"Do you know anything about his background?"

"Michael told me he graduated from Caltech and then worked at Capella Space in Palo Alto, some sort of satellite surveillance company. Michael said his partner is the real brains behind the business."

They saw Carhlson put his phone down and leave his office. Instead of joining them, he walked back to the lobby. Minutes later, he returned and entered the conference room and sat down at the table.

"Michael worked directly with me," Carhlson said. "He was smart and very good at helping grow our company. We'll miss him, congressman. If you don't mind telling me, how did he die?"

"They said he had a heart attack when he was windsurfing. I'm having an autopsy performed. I'm not buying it."

"How did he die, then?"

"You knew my son, Mr. Carhlson. He was healthy, stayed in shape, didn't smoke. There's no family history of heart disease. I don't know how he died, but I will find out. Like I said, I've ordered an autopsy."

Carhlson looked like he was going to say something, when a young woman knocked on the door of the conference and beckoned Carhlson to the door.

"Excuse me or a moment," he said and went to the door. After a whispered exchange with the woman, he returned.

"I forgot about a meeting I need to attend. My assistant will take you to Michael's office, congressman. If there's anything more I can do for you, just let me know."

Carhlson abruptly left the conference room.

His assistant stepped in and said," Mr. Bridge, if you'll follow me, please."

The congressman and Drake were ushered down the hall past two other offices to an open door of an empty office.

"This is Michael's office," the assistant said. "His things are in the box on the desk."

The office wasn't just empty, it had been stripped bare. There was nothing on the walls, nothing on the back bar under the window, nothing on the desk. No computer monitor, no tower under or beside the desk, no phone.

Congressman Bridge walked to the desk and stared into the two-by-two-foot cardboard box.

Drake joined him and saw there were only three things inside; two framed Stanford diplomas and a picture of his Pac 12 championship water polo team.

Congressman Bridge walked around the desk and pulled the drawers open one buy one. "They even cleaned out his desk."

"For them not knowing he was dead when we got here, they certainly cleaned out this office in a hurry," Drake said. "Either they didn't know and they're trying to make things easy for you, or they knew he was dead and they're lying about it."

"They're lying about it," Congressman Bridge said. "The receptionist might not have known, but Carhlson did. I know when someone's lying."

"What now?"

"Let's get out of here. I want to know what Dr. Swanson discovered before I jump to any conclusions."

Chapter Seven

JARON CAHRLSON WATCHED the congressman and his sidekick walk to a metallic gray Porsche Cayman parked in Visitor Parking, get in and drive away. He prayed his reaction to hearing that Michael Bridge was dead had concealed a fear that had roiled his stomach. Had he have something to do with it.

A week ago, he'd learned that Bridge had been staying at night and looking into the company's startup funding he'd received from a private equity firm in San Francisco.

Wayne Berryman received his MBA from Stanford the same year he'd graduated Caltech. He'd met Berryman at a mixer sponsored by an old private equity firm where Berryman had been hired.

Berryman's father, Walter Berryman, was the former governor of California and was serving as the Secretary of the Treasury in the new administration. When Walter Berryman was nominated to his current cabinet position, his son had left the private equity firm where he was working and started his own firm.

He'd been working at NetSuite, the "First Cloud Company" after it was acquired by Oracle, when he met Wayne Berryman again. Berryman had given him, on that occasion, a business card and told him to call if he ever wanted to strike out and start his own company.

Berryman's private equity firm was small, but well-connected, and had been eager to fund his new company. He'd been surprised by the amount of money they had offered to invest and, because of that, he probably hadn't done due diligence before he agreed to Berryman's terms.

He hadn't been bothered that Berryman insisting on a spot on his board of directors. He'd also understood that agreeing to have an intern from Berryman's firm work in his company's finance department, on a rotating basis, was a good faith gesture on his part. It helped Berryman's firm develop new talent and it provided SkySage a recent finance graduate at a reasonable cost.

The interns had always worked out well. Even though it put a spy for Berryman in his company, the information they had access to wasn't anything that Berryman didn't already get as a board member.

But the way Berryman sounded on the phone when he called him four

days ago, and the death of Michael Bridge a day later bothered him.

Berryman had sounded cold and distant. He said he knew that Bridge was digging around and asking questions about his investors. There was nothing to worry about.

It was all a matter of record and Berryman said he'd be glad to answer any questions Bridge had. 'I'll take care of it, Jaron. Relax', were the words he remembered.

Carhlson sat down and leaned back in his chair to think. Michael Bridge's father was right. If his son didn't have any underlying health issues, dying from a sudden heart attack sounded unlikely. The kid ran four miles every day at noon, instead of leaving to eat lunch somewhere.

He opened the laptop on his desk and googled Congressman Matthew Bridge. Five-term congressman from Nebraska. Former Attorney General of Nebraska. Serving on the House Armed Services and the subcommittee on Intelligence and Emerging

Threats and Capabilities. Campaign manager for President Ballard when he'd run for his Senate seat.

If Michael Bridge was looking into Berryman's private equity firm, had he mentioned it to his father? He knew the congressman's subcommittee was involved in overseeing the military's research and development projects, including the JEDI project they were now involved with as a subcontractor. Did that have something to do with the congressman's visit to SkySage today?

Carhlson decided to call Wayne Berryman.

"Wayne, Jaron Carhlson," he said when Berryman answered. "We need to talk."

"I'm heading out for a meeting. Can this wait?"

"The person I called you about last week died this weekend. Did he ever call you?"

"No, why?"

"His father paid me a visit today. He's ordered an autopsy for his son. He's a congressman on the subcommittee that oversees the JEDI project we're working on. I'm curious about what specifically his son was asking about, in case he mentioned it to his father. I'd like to prepare for any questions I might be asked if he comes back."

"Did the father mention my firm? Are you saying there's an investigation or something going on?"

"Why would there be an investigation? You said everything his son was asking about is a matter of record. Is there anything that I should know about? That's all I'm asking?"

After an uncomfortably long silence, Berryman said, "Let me know if you hear anything more from Congressman Bridge or anyone on his behalf. If they want something from me, they know where to find me. Don't worry about this.

"I've answered questions before about my investors and one that involves the Bank of China. I'll answer them again, if anyone asks. And there's nothing about the death of the congressman's son that you need to worry about. Just keep doing what you do best and make us all a lot of money."

Carhlson sat back, drumming his fingers on the arms of his

chair. Berryman's investor with a link to the Bank of China was news to him and it shouldn't have been. He knew better than to get in bed with someone that had any connection with the Bank of China that was owned by China and run by the Chinese Communist Party. Not if you wanted to do any work for the Department of Defense.

Why hadn't Berryman's involvement with the Bank of China been raised when SkySage was vetted for the work they were doing for Microsoft?

Carhlson had a nagging feeling he'd made a mistake when he'd jumped at the chance to land the first big investor that came calling.

Chapter Eight

DRAKE WAS DRIVING BACK to Portland with Congressman Matthews when he got the call that his son's autopsy had been completed and that Dr. Swanson was available to meet with him.

"You can drop me off if you have something else you need to do," Congressman Matthews said.

"I'd like to come hear what Dr. Swanson has to say, if that's okay."

"Sure," the congressman said, staring out the window. "I got used to attending autopsies when I was a prosecutor, feeling sorry for the victims and telling families that I was sorry for their loss. Being on this end of one is certainly different."

"I can only imagine," Drake said.

"He was such a good son."

"Are you a fan of Ruth's Chris Steak House?"

"Never been to one. Is that where I'm buying dinner tonight?"

"If you want a great steak, that's the steakhouse I recommend."

"Sounds good. Want me to call and make a reservation?"

"I'll do it. Call Margo Benning," Drake said, using the Porsche's Bluetooth system to call his former legal assistant and friend.

"Paul Benning Investigations," Margo Benning said, answering the call.

"Hi Margo. Is Paul back from Hood River?"

"He's trying to track down a witness the Sheriff says has a video he wants to see. Do you need to talk with him?"

"Not right now. Congressman Bridge wants to hear what Paul finds out over dinner tonight. Would you make a reservation for the three of us at Ruth's Chris Steak House, say seven o'clock?"

"Consider it done," Margo Benning said. "How are you and Liz getting along?"

"We're good. Let me know when Paul thinks he'll be back."

"I will. Stop by and see me before you leave town."

"Yes, ma'am."

Drake ended the call and heard the congressman chuckling again.

"Your mother?"

"She sounds like she is, doesn't she? Margo was my secretary in the D.A.'s office. She left with me when I opened my law office. She and Paul are family."

"She sounds like a wonderful person."

"She is."

They traveled east for another fifteen minutes without speaking.

Drake took the exit off U.S. 26E and drove up SW Sam Jackson Park Road to the parking lot south of Richard Jones Hall and Autopsy Services. After a short walk to the building, they were ushered to a small conference room down the hall from Dr. Swanson's office. A white thermal coffee carafe and tray of cups were on the conference table.

"Dr. Swanson will be with you shortly," his secretary told them.

Drake held up a cup and Congressman Bridge nodded yes. When they each had their coffee and were seated across the round table from an empty chair on the other side, Dr. Swanson walked in.

"Congressman, Adam, sorry to keep you waiting," Dr. Swanson said and poured himself a cup of coffee.

"As you said, congressman, your son was healthy and fit. The cause of death, however, was sudden cardiac death, or SCD. We found no cardiac abnormalities present, despite histopathologic examination and toxicology screening that could have caused SCD.

"I recommend that you and all of his blood relatives undergo comprehensive cardiac evaluation to determine if there is evidence of hereditary arrhythmogenic syndrome. Fifty percent of the families of individuals who die of SCD have the syndrome."

"Are you saying you don't know what caused my son's death?" Congressman Bridge asked.

"No, don't misunderstand me, congressman. Your son's heart stopped and that caused his death. There are, however, deaths that remain unexplained even after macroscopic, microscopic and laboratory analysis."

Congressman Bridge crossed his arms across his chest and leaned back in his chair. "Are there any other tests that can be done, perhaps tests that can't be done here or ones that require equipment you don't have?"

"Not that I'm aware of, congressman."

"Is there anything I can provide you that will add anything or allow you to interpret your findings differently?"

"If you and his blood relatives undergo the cardiac evaluations I recommend, and we find that his SCD was inherited, that would serve to confirm my conclusion. It wouldn't add to or change my conclusion, however."

"I see," Congressman Bridge said and stood. "Thank you for your time, Dr. Swanson. When will my son be ready to return home with me?"

"Tomorrow, congressman. Just let us know what arrangements you've made."

They shook hands and Drake stopped to tell Dr. Swanson he'd let him know if they learned anything else about the incident at Hood River where Michael Bridge died.

Congressman Bridge was waiting outside Richard Jones Hall, looking up at the sky with his hands on his hips.

When Drake stopped next to him, he said, "Let's go back to that place where we ate lunch. I could use a drink."

"Let's do it," Drake said and put his arm around the congressman's shoulders. "That isn't what I expected we'd hear."

"Neither did I and it's not good enough. If blood relatives could have the same syndrome, why haven't any of us died the same way? We're a large family. I don't get it."

"Come on, let's get that drink you wanted," Drake said and headed to his car.

On the way, Margo Benning called. "Paul's on his way back from Hood River and you have a reservation at Ruth's Chris Steak House at seven."

Drake looked at his watch and saw they had an hour and a half before their reservation. "Margo, the congressman is staying at the Marriott on the waterfront. We're headed to the whiskey bar there. Tell Paul to walk over from the office and join us when he arrives. We can walk to the restaurant from there."

"If you're going to be drinking for the next hour and a half, the walk will do you good," Margo said.

"Thanks, Margo."

"Just make sure my husband gets home tonight, Adam," she admonished.

"I'll make sure he does. Goodbye, Margo."

"That goes for the congressman too."

"Yes, Margo. Goodbye, Margo."

Drake ended the call before she added to the threat he knew was implied by the tone of her voice.

Chapter Nine

DRAKE AND CONGRESSMAN Bridge were enjoying a round of 1792 Full Proof, recommended to them as the 'World's Best Bourbon', and an order of Oregon salt roasted hazelnuts when Paul Benning found them in the whiskey bar.

"Congressman Bridge, this is Paul Benning," Drake said. "Paul, Matthew Bridge."

The congressman brushed the salt off his fingers on his pant leg and shook hands with Benning. "Nice to meet you, Paul. Buy you a drink?"

Benning pulled out a chair and sat down next to Drake. "Sure, whatever you two are having is fine, thanks."

"How was Hood River?" Drake asked.

"Sheriff Jensen made a copy of his report on the accident and the initial autopsy. It took me a while to find the eyewitness."

"What accident?" Congressman Bridge asked.

"It wasn't an 'accident' per se, that's just what they called it in the report," Benning explained. "Just before your son dropped the sail and sat down on his board, he collided with another windsurfer. The other guy was knocked off his board, but they didn't find anything that indicated that your son had been hurt in the collision."

"Did they get a statement from the other guy?" Drake asked.

Benning shook his head. "He came ashore and left. The witness I talked with said he was angry that he'd been knocked off his board. He didn't stick around to talk with the police."

"Do we know who this guy is? Did anyone recognize him?" Congressman Bridge asked. "Seems strange that he'd just up and leave. He'd have seen that Michael wasn't okay."

"No one recognized him, but the witness captured the whole thing on his iPhone. He forwarded the video to me. We know what the man looks like. We don't know who he is or what he was driving when he left the Hatchery. That's a favorite launch spot for windsurfers."

The congressman winched and visibly paled. "You have the whole thing on your phone?"

Benning looked at Drake, who nodded.

"Your son was a hundred yards offshore but you can see what happened. Are you sure you want to look at it?"

Congressman Bridge finished his whiskey and said. "Show me."

Benning took his iPhone out, located the video and handed the phone to the congressman.

Drake got up and stood behind the congressman to watch the video over his shoulder.

The witness wasn't focusing on one windsurfer. The river was a swarm of windsurfers racing over the choppy water, flying up off a swell and crisscrossing in front of one another.

In the middle of it all, two windsurfers collided, knocking one of them in the water. You could see the man in the water shake his fist at the other windsurfer who sailed on for another twenty or thirty yards.

The other windsurfer turned into the wind, dropped his sail in the water and sat down straddling his board. A moment later, he slumped forward and didn't move again.

The video continued, showing other windsurfers coming close to see if he was okay and ultimately, the Sheriff's river patrol boat coming to his rescue.

The last footage of the video showed a man walking out of the water, leaving his windsurfing rig on the shore and walking toward and then past the witness.

He was an Asian man in his twenties, five foot seven or five foot eight, with the build of a gymnast and the walk…of a predator.

Drake asked the congressman for Benning's phone and replayed the video. He knew what he was looking at. He also knew it wouldn't help Congressman Bridge deal with the death of his son to tell him what he was thinking, until he could prove it.

Congressman Bridge was staring into his empty glass, processing what he'd just seen; his son's death windsurfing on the Columbia River.

Drake signaled the waiter and ordered a round for three.

"Paul, is Michael's car still in Hood River?" Drake asked.

"The Sheriff has it in the impound lot."

"Are his things in it, or did they send them here with him?"

"It wasn't mentioned in the report and I didn't ask. Why?"

"We'll need to get his things sent home with the congressman and take care of his car," Drake said. "Congressman, where did your son live?"

"Uh, he leased a condo. I don't remember where it is."

"Would you like us to get his car down from Hood River? We'll take care of the lease on his condo and get his personal belongings sent to you, if that would help."

Congressman Bridge hung his head and let his shoulders slump. "All I could think about was getting an autopsy and having his body sent home. I didn't think about those things."

"You have enough to think about. Let us help."

"I would like to see where he lived, before I leave tomorrow."

"When is that?" Drake asked.

"My reservation is for two o'clock."

"I can help with that," Benning said.

"I appreciate that, Paul. You could come with me to Michael's condo, if you'd like."

"May I come along?" Drake asked.

"I thought someone in Seattle was keeping a light on for you tonight?"

"She is, but she'll understand. There's something I want to look into before I leave."

When their drinks arrived, Congressman Bridge excused himself and headed to the restroom.

"Paul," Drake said, "Let's see if we can enlarge the video of his son colliding with that other windsurfer. I don't think that was an accident."

"What did you see that I didn't?"

"There was just something about the guy he collided with."

"What?"

"The way he walked ashore. He was anxious to get out of there."

Chapter Ten

FRANCIS ZHANG CLOSED the door of his office and unlocked the drawer of his antique Chinese Rosewood writing desk. He kept a phone with a burner app stored there.

The text he'd just received upset him. He needed to know immediately if it also upset their efforts to penetrate the research project the Americans called JEDI.

His call was answered with silence. "His tablet was not in his office. It must be at his condo or in his car. Find it and bring it to me."

"I know where he lived. I don't know where his car is."

"Where did you kill him? Look there. Call me when you have it."

"Yes, sir."

Francis Zhang was an intelligence officer in the Ministry of State Security (MSS), the intelligence, security and secret police agency of the People's Republic of China (PRC).

His primary mission in the United States was recruiting Chinese American university students with a high-tech education and employment potential; students who would have access in the future to intellectual property China would like to "borrow."

A student like the intern he'd been able to place at a company called SkySage, Inc., in Portland, Oregon. Working in the company's finance department, the intern had alerted him to the efforts of the congressman's son who was asking about the source and conditions that were attached to the startup's initial funding that it received from Berryman's private equity firm.

Berryman was the managing partner of the new investment company that was funded in part, by a joint venture that involved the state-owned Bank of China. With the fifteen billion dollars the new investment company had been able to raise, Berryman Private Equity, LLC, had access to unlimited resources to invest in American companies that manufactured products that had both civilian and military applications.

One of the conditions for the startup funding SkySage, Inc., received from Berryman Investments, LLC, was a commitment to allow qualified graduates of a Bay area university to be hired by the firm to gain them experience working there on a two-year rotating intern program.

As the son of the former California governor and current U.S. Secretary of the Treasury, Wayne Berryman's new investment firm had sailed through the initial scrutiny of the American government when it was founded. But when SkySage, Inc., had been awarded the subcontract with Microsoft to work on the Pentagon's JEDI program, his superiors in the Ministry of State Security had become concerned that the Bank of China's involvement with Berryman Investment, LLC, might be looked at more closely.

That concern had risen to a panic level when Berryman's intern had warned him that the son of a United State Congressman, who was on the very subcommittee in the U.S. House of Representatives that had jurisdiction of military research projects like JEDI, was asking to see the files containing the startup's initial funding documents.

Zhang's cover in America was as the owner of a travel agency, Premier Travel and Tours, in San Francisco. In addition to tours of China, it also handled travel to and from China for students studying at universities on the west coast and tours of cities and attractions they might be interested in.

His travel agency had a fleet of tour buses and twenty tour guides. Each tour guide had been sent to him after completion of a course run by the Ministry of State Security. He had designed the course to teach his tour guides the idioms and culture a Chinese American citizen would experience growing up on the west coast. They also came to him with the lethal skills of an assassin, should such skills ever be required of them in the role they played as covert operators for the MSS.

The tour guide he dispatched to eliminate the risk to the SkySage operation was his best operative. As a former commando in the PLA's Navy unit called "Water Dragons", developed to be the equal of the vaunted American Navy's SEALS, he'd been chosen by Zhang for forwarding to the MSS for additional training as a covert operator/ tour guide.

After completing his MSS training, Anthony 'Tony' Lee was positioned in the State of Washington as a tour guide for Premier Travel and Tours. He was also tasked with silencing Chinese traitors, who were discovered after they immigrated to Vancouver, British Columbia, the most Asian city outside of Asia.

To be able to spot talent for Zhang's recruitment efforts, Lee also taught self-defense classes in Wushu Sanda at a Kung-fu club near the University of Washington campus. Wushu Sanda was the unarmed combat fighting system developed by Chinese Elite Forces that combined traditional Kung fu with modern fighting systems. Sanda was China's most popular combat sport and very attractive to Chinese American students of both sexes.

Which was the basis of Zhang's only concern about his best tour guide. Tony Lee was good looking and well-liked by his students, especially students of the female gender. They were a distraction for a soldier, any soldier, and especially one who had to hide his identity and allegiance to a foreign power. If Tony Lee was ever exposed as a spy and assassin for China, it would some woman who caused it.

For the time being, Zhang would overlook Lee's fondness for

beautiful students who wanted to learn his every move, in and out of the Kung-fu club.

If they could find Bridge's tablet, in time to determine that he hadn't found what he was looking for, he'd be able to send Tony Lee back to Seattle without further orders.

If they couldn't, he would have to consider other ways to guarantee that the penetration of SkySage, Inc. wasn't exposed.

Chapter Eleven

DRAKE WALKED down the stairs from the loft in his old law office with his travel duffel over his shoulder. He kept it in the trunk of his Porsche whenever he left town for the occasional layover, like the night before when he decided to stay in Portland.

Paul Benning was in the breakroom loading the coffee maker when he heard Drake on the stairs.

"Margo will be here in a minute," Benning said. "If you're hungry, she's bringing a breakfast frittata she thought you would like."

"I am hungry, surprisingly. After the steak dinner we had with Congressman Bridge last night, I didn't think I'd need to eat again until I got back to Seattle."

"Don't tell Margo what I had to eat, if you don't mind," Benning said. "She has me on a diet again."

"Don't tell Margo what?" she called out from the top of the stairs coming down from the condo above. The property had come as a package when Drake bought the former antique book store for his office that they were now buying from him.

"Morning, Margo. Paul was worried you might not want to hear about the little Weight Watchers Special steak he had, instead of having the big juicy ribeye steak I couldn't talk him into having. He said you didn't want him eating steak at all."

Margo Benning scowled at both men as she walked by them to the conference room with a loaded breakfast tray.

"I know what he ate, Adam. I listened to his stomach complaining all night. Paul, bring the coffee when it's ready. Adam and I are going to have a little talk."

Paul Benning shrugged his shoulders and whispered, "No idea what that's about."

Drake put on a smile and followed Margo to the conference room.

Margo was busy setting out plates and silverware at the head of the conference room table when Drake sat down to her right.

"How have you been, Margo?"

"Will you eat some frittata?"

"Do I need a taster first?"

Margo ignored the remark and handed him a plate with a slice of frittata on it.

Drake smiled and crossed his arms over his chest. "Okay, Margo, what did you want to talk about?"

She put a serving of frittata for her husband across from Drake and sat down at the head of the table.

"Why does Liz think you don't like living in Seattle with her?"

"What?"

"You heard me."

"I don't know where you got the idea Liz thinks I don't like living in Seattle with her."

"Because that's what you told her," Margo said. "That girl moved across the country to be close to you. She deserves more than a six-month trial period with you living on the other side of Puget Sound on that island."

Drake uncrossed his arms and rested his hands on the table. "Margo, I know you mean well. I know you love Liz. I love her too. I have no intention of leaving Liz when the lease on Bainbridge Island is up. I will find a place where I want to live, in time. There's no rush."

"Why don't you want to move in with Liz?" Margo pressed. "She offered."

"Ah, that's what this is about. You think because I didn't tell her I would take her up on her offer, I'm not planning on sticking around in Seattle. Is that it?"

"Why else would you pass up the opportunity?"

Drake swiveled around in his chair to face Margo. "Because I'm not going to live with her until we're married, that's why. Because, I want to find a home we both can feel good about and it's not going to be her condo, that's why. Because...."

Paul Benning came into the conference room with his laptop held out in front of him and said, "You need to see this. I took another look at the video on my laptop while I was waiting for the coffee to finish brewing. Here, let me set it up."

Benning set his laptop down and plugged in the HDMI cable for the large format wall monitor.

When the video the witness gave him that captured Michael Bridge colliding with the other windsurfer started, Benning stopped it when the two windsurfers were seconds away from hitting into each other.

"When I watched this the first couple of times, I thought Bridge might have caused the collision when he turned to the left in front of the other guy. Watch the other guy cut hard to his left."

Benning ran the video a couple of frames and stopped it again. "Watch his left hand. See how he takes it off the boom and reaches down to a pouch strapped to his waist."

"Run that back a couple of frames, Paul. Let me see that again," Drake said.

Benning backed the video up and ran it slowly, frame by frame and then froze it.

"There's something in his hand," Margo said.

Drake got up and walked closer to the monitor. "I can't tell what it is, but there's definitely something in his left hand."

"Now watch," Benning said and advanced the video two more frames.

The windsurfer's left hand snaked out just before impact and struck Bridge's right side a foot below his shoulder, just before being knocked back off his board.

"Until I saw there was something in his hand, I thought he might be reaching out to push off from Bridge to keep from hitting him. He could have dropped his sail to do that, but he didn't. He dropped his left hand off the boom on purpose and it wasn't to push off from Bridge."

Drake turned away from the monitor and stared at the floor with his hands on his hips. "Paul, did the coroner's report in Hood River say anything about the wetsuit Michael Bridge was wearing?"

"It didn't say anything about his personal belongings, why?"

"We need to examine his wetsuit. If I'm right, there will be a tiny puncture in the suit a foot below his right shoulder."

"I don't understand. Bridge wasn't shot, he died of a heart attack," Benning said.

"He did have a heart attack, but I think he was also shot," Drake said. "I remember reading about the Church Committee hearings in 1975 about rogue CIA activities. There was testimony the CIA had developed a small gun that shot a tiny poison dart that penetrated clothing and caused a heart attack. The poison dart completely disintegrated on entering the target's bloodstream and caused a heart attack. The poison was untraceable.

"Other countries, like Russia and China, may have had the same thing. If we examine the wetsuit, I think we'll find evidence of a tiny puncture that could have come from something like the CIA's heart attack gun."

Chapter Twelve

THEY PICKED up Congressman Bridge and left the Marriott in Benning's red Ford F150 Supercab. The condo Michael Bridge leased was in a condominium community called Stonewater in Hillsboro, Oregon.

"Mike was planning on buying the place, if he could persuade the owner to sell," Congressman Bridge said, riding shotgun beside Paul Benning.

Drake was sitting behind him and asked, "Have you been there?"

The congressman shook his head. "I wish now that I had taken the time to come out and visit him. He liked Oregon. I think he was planning on staying in the northwest. He loved the outdoors. He skied, talked about taking up white water kayaking and going on a bicycle ride through the state he called 'The Classic'."

Benning took the exit off NW Sunset Highway onto NE Cornelius Pass Road and followed the route displayed on his navigation system to the Stonewater at Orenco in Hillsboro.

The condo was a two-story buckskin brown duplex with black trim on a standalone corner lot. An upstairs room had a covered private deck with a wood pellet smoker grill on it that Drake recognized. On the deck below, a black mountain bike was chained to the railing next to the front door.

"Your son has good taste," Drake said. "I can see why he wanted to buy the place. Do we have a key to let us in?"

Congressman Bridge opened his door to get out and said, "I know where he hides the key."

In the flower bed next to the steps for the lower deck, Congressman Bridge bent down and picked up a black iron turtle partially hidden under a dark red rhododendron.

"His mother sent it to him when he moved in. It has a hidden compartment. There should be a key in it."

Drake and Benning joined him on the deck and were standing at the front door when a black Camaro roared down a driveway from around back. It shot out onto the street, turned left with its rear tires smoking and accelerated away.

"Did your son ever mention having a reckless neighbor he didn't much care for?" Benning asked.

"I don't know who that was," Congressman Bridge said. "Michael said his neighbors were a quiet married couple in their sixties."

Drake laughed. "Maybe it's true and the sixties are the new thirties. One of them could be late for a Zumba class."

When they walked in and saw the mess inside the condo, another explanation presented itself.

"Looks like we might have scared someone off just now," Benning said.

Cushions were on the floor from a sofa and two chairs in the living area, the cabinet doors in the kitchen were all opened and items from the small pantry were scattered about on the floor.

Congressman Bridge walked down the hall and into an office study. "It's worse in here," he called out.

Drake came behind him and looked in. A bookshelf was swept empty with books and souvenirs laying on the floor. The top drawer of desk was emptied and upside down on the top of the desk.

It was soon evident that the upstairs bedrooms and bathrooms had been searched, as well as the utility room and garage.

When they all met back in the kitchen, Congressman Bridge was furious. "What the hell is going on? It doesn't appear that anything of value was taken."

Drake checked with Benning, who nodded. It was time to tell Michael's father what they suspected.

"We took another look at the video of Michael's accident," Drake said. "It looks like he might have been murdered."

"What are you talking about, Drake?" Congressman Bridge asked. "Dr. Swanson confirmed the coroner's finding, he had a heart attack."

"Have you ever heard of a heart attack gun? The CIA developed one back in the seventies. Other countries probably had something like it. The video shows something in the other windsurfer's hand when he collided with Michael. It's possible that a poison dart fired from whatever was in the guy's hand caused your son's heart attack."

Congressman Bridge grabbed for a stool at the kitchen counter and sat down. "Can we prove it?"

"We might be able to," Drake said. "We need to check Michael's wet suit and see if there's a puncture where the other guy's hand hit him in the side. There wouldn't be any evidence from the poison, if it's what I think it was. We might be able to get the video to show us what was in the guy's hand. That might be as much as we're going to be able to prove at this point."

"Why would anyone want to kill my son?"

"The only thing I can think of is what Michael was concerned about; China and what SkySage is working on."

"If SkySage's work on JEDI is at risk, I need to notify the Pentagon," Congressman Bridge said.

"When we know it's at risk, I agree," Drake said. "Right now, it's just a possibility. My company did the facility security clearance assessment on SkySage and it was solid then. We could test it again and see if it still is. There are other ways China could get access to the work SkySage is doing, however.

"There could be someone at SkySage who's spying for China

and receiving money for the intellectual property they're stealing. That's the usual way China appropriates our technology.

"The artificial intelligence for the cloud SkySage is working on also has dual-use capability, for both civilian and military satellite surveillance programs. It's too early to know what SkySage plans to do with the AI for the cloud after it completes its work for Microsoft, but Michael could have been concerned about the company's future plan for it.

"It could be something else entirely different that Michael wanted to tell you about. We don't have access to the computer or laptop he used at work. SkySage scooped it up before we got there, but they do have proprietary rights to his work product. We didn't find a laptop or computer here, did we?" Drake asked.

"I didn't see one," Benning said.

"I didn't either," Congressman Bridge said. "He had a Surface Pro tablet when he was home for Christmas. I remember because he was trying to get me to buy one. If it isn't here, it could be in his car."

"Maybe that will have something on it that will tell us what he was worried about," Drake said. "Until we know what it was, why don't we keep this to ourselves. Paul will get in touch with Michael's leasing agent to see if he knows where Michael kept the tablet, and we'll see if it's in his car in Hood River. Are you okay with holding off on notifying the Pentagon until we have some evidence to support our suspicions, congressman?"

"If you will promise me one thing; that you'll find evidence my son was murdered and catch the bastard."

Chapter Thirteen

AFTER DROPPING Congressman Bridge off at his hotel, Drake returned to his old office to get his car to drive to Hood River. He had volunteered to make the detour up the Columbia River before returning to Seattle.

Benning had called the Hood River County Sheriff and arranged for him to visit the impound lot and search Michael Bridge's car for the missing tablet.

It was after three in the afternoon by the time Drake left Portland for the Hood River Towing company's impound lot that closed at five. Drake had time to make it before closing, but that left him with a three-hour drive back to Seattle and he promised Liz he'd be back in time to take her to dinner.

"Call Liz," he ordered Bluetooth.

"On your way back, handsome?" Liz asked.

"After a little detour. I should be there by seven thirty."

"Are we still going out to dinner? I'm okay staying in and cooking something for us, if you think you'll be too tired."

"I think I'll have enough energy to eat out."

"If that's all the energy you think you'll have tonight, I'm cooking."

"Too late," Drake laughed. "we have a reservation for eight at that Sichaun seafood restaurant you wanted to try."

"In that case, I might settle for just a good dinner."

Drake laughed again and changed the subject before it cost him. "Mike's case is getting interesting. We might wind up doing a new security assessment of SkySage for Microsoft."

"How are they involved in the congressman's son's death?"

"That's where he worked. I'll tell you all about it tonight."

"Alright, be safe and hurry back."

"I promise."

As much as he wanted to stomp on the gas and get to Hood River sooner than the traffic and speed limit would allow, Drake let his mind downshift to think about a decision he needed to make.

He was still thinking about finding a place to live when he had to slow down to take the exit off I-84 for Hood River.

Hood River Towing impound lot was eight miles south of the city off OR-35S and Drake got there with thirty minutes to spare before it closed.

After satisfying the owner of the towing company that he was the man Congressman Bridge had given permission to search his son's vehicle, he was escorted to a dark green Subaru Outback parked behind the towing company's office.

"The sheriff said you're looking for one of those little tablet things," the owner said. "The car has been locked since I towed it here. I looked through the windows to see if it was in there, but I didn't see one. Maybe you'll have better luck."

When the door was unlocked, the owner stood back and let Drake slide into the driver's seat.

"I need to stay and make sure you only remove the boy's tablet, if you find it. I close the lot at five. I'd appreciate it if you would look for it as quickly as you can. My grandson has a game tonight and I want to be there when he throws the first pitch. It's his first game as the starting pitcher."

"Understood, I'll hurry," Drake said, as he reached under the seat and found nothing. He slid his hand down between the seat and the console with the same result. The driver's side pocket held a pair of Oakley sunglasses in a case and a red and black emergency escape tool, but no Surface Pro tablet.

Drake got out and opened the rear door on the driver's side. The rear seats were folded down and he pulled the left seat upright, and bingo! A black Microsoft Surface Pro tablet was laying on the floor.

He held it out for the towing lot owner to see. "Looks like you're going to get to see his first pitch. Thanks for helping me with this."

"No problem, glad to help. I'll let the sheriff know you found it. You have any idea when someone will come to get the car?"

"A friend of the sheriff's is helping Congressman Bridge take care of his son's affairs. I'll have him call you. His name is Paul Benning."

"Much obliged," owner said and locked the Subaru before heading back to his office.

Drake walked beside him and then peeled off toward his own car. On the way there, he had the feeling that someone was staring at him.

A black Camaro was parked on the other side of the impound lot's twelve-foot-high chain link security fence near the highway. It looked like the black Camaro he'd seen speeding away from Michael Bridge's condo He couldn't be sure it was the same one, but he'd learned a long time ago not to believe anything was a coincidence, until you proved that it was.

The driver's window was down, and the driver turned away when Drake looked at him.

He was an Asian man in his twenties, wearing sunglasses, with a phone held to his ear. He turned his head back to look at Drake for several seconds, and then slowly looked away and continued talking on his phone.

Something about the man set off the alarm system in Drake's brain. It wasn't that he was driving the black Camaro. It was the way the man stared at him.

The way a fighter sized up an opponent before the round began. It was the way you made up your mind about the skill level of your opponent, before you closed on him.

Chapter Fourteen

TONY LEE CLENCHED his fists and cursed his luck. He was waiting for the towing company's impound lot to close for the day. His plan was to cut through the security fence when it was dark and search the car this stranger was walking away from with a computer tablet in his hand.

The guy didn't look like it would be too hard to take the tablet away from him. Six one or two, maybe a hundred and eighty pounds, and fairly fit from what he could tell, but still no match for an elite Water Dragon commando and seventh duan Sanda Blue Dragon fighter.

But Colonel Zhang would be angry, if he attracted attention by snatching the tablet in broad daylight and somehow exposed Operation Yoda, as Zhang called it.

The Star War's Yoda was a Jedi Master and Zhang liked to say that he was going to gain immortality in China by bringing home the technology that would make the country America's equal in any war. Then Zhang would be the Master of JEDI and a hero.

Boldness was the way of the warrior and he was trained to take advantage of any opportunity that presented itself, to complete his mission. He was also trained to obey orders.

Zhang was not directly his superior. He was an intelligence officer for MSS that Lee happened to be seconded to for Zhang's covert operation in America. But Zhang had the authority to send him back to China and Lee was very happy with his life in Seattle.

He took out the burner phone to call Zhang and ask how to proceed. Better to get permission on how Zhang wanted him to recover the tablet, than risk losing his posting in Seattle. There were pleasures there that would be hard to get away with back home in China.

"A man is leaving the impound lot with the tablet. I don't know who he is or why he has the tablet. What do you want me to do?"

"Can you get it without being identified, by him or by anyone else?"

"Not unless I kill him."

"I need to know who he is first. Follow him. If he tries to pass the tablet along to someone else, follow the tablet. I want the tablet, but not if getting it means sacrificing my asset at SkySage. You failed me once, when you didn't search his car and get the tablet after you killed him. Don't fail me a second time."

Lee watched the stranger drive out of the impound lot in his gray Porsche Cayman. As it passed by, he took a picture of its license plate with his phone before it turned onto the highway.

DRAKE WATCHED the Camaro pull away from the security fence and drive onto the highway behind him.

OR-35 heading north was the way back to Hood River and his route back to Seattle on I-84. That the black Camaro was behind him didn't mean he was being followed, or that it was the same Camaro he'd seen at Michael Bridge's condo. But it was becoming more likely that it was.

There was only one reason for it to be here at the impound lot. Someone was looking for the tablet they didn't find in the condo when they searched it. Whoever it was had to be involved in the death of Michael Bridge, in some way.

The SkySage Affair

Whoever it was could even be his killer.

"Call Paul Benning," he directed his Bluetooth-synched iPhone.

"Did you find the tablet?" Benning asked when he answered.

"I did. And now someone's following me from the impound lot. I'm pretty sure it's the same black Camaro we saw racing away from the condo this morning. Do you have someone who can run a trace on a plate for me?"

"Of course."

"Washington BVS 2297. It's a black Camaro ZL1."

"Where are you?"

"Driving back to Hood River. I'll be on I-84 and then I-205 north back to Seattle."

"Give me five minutes."

The Camaro stayed a dozen lengths behind Drake all the way to Hood River. When he approached the interchange with I-84 and curved around on the entrance ramp, the Camaro closed to his bumper and stayed there.

Drake knew about the Camaro ZL1's performance specs. It was a driver's car, a muscle car on steroids. It was fast and the kind of car you'd want to show off.

But Drake wasn't in a hurry.

He accelerated up the ramp to merge with traffic at 65 miles an hour and tapped the brakes to maintain the legal speed limit. He kept his speed at 65 miles an hour to test the patience of the driver of the car with a top speed of 198 miles an hour.

He watched the Camaro fall back a couple of car lengths, where it stayed.

"Call Paul Benning," he said.

"Is he still following you?" Benning asked.

"He is. Did you get a name?"

"The car is registered to a holding company in Hong Kong. There's no way to know who's driving it."

"Not a problem, I'll meet him at some point and introduce myself. He knows I have the tablet."

Chapter Fifteen

DRAKE MADE the drive north to Seattle in less than three hours and the black Camaro followed him all the way. Until he stopped by Puget Sound Security headquarters and dropped off the tablet for Kevin McRoberts to look at and the Camaro drove on past when he turned in.

Drake took a quick shower and still got to Liz's condo in time to keep their reservation seating for eight o'clock that evening.

Her flared white jeans and charcoal sleeveless blouse that complemented her tanned shoulders and arms did nothing to hide Liz's toned figure, when they were escorted to their table. Drake walked behind her and tried not to smile.

Every man's eyes in the softly lighted restaurant followed her as she walked by. The women sitting with them made it obvious they were aware of her, too, by refusing to look her way.

Drake never took her beauty for granted, but seeing other men admiring her reminded him how dangerous it would be if he ever did.

When they were seated and ordered the Spicy and Sour Dumplings Liz wanted to try, she leaned forward with her elbows on the table and asked, "Why do you think we need to take another look at SkySage? Did we miss something?"

"It's possible, or it could be something new that Michael Bridge discovered that got him killed."

"Are we sure that he was killed?"

"The video that Paul got from a witness of his collision windsurfing makes it look that way. If Paul finds that his wetsuit has a puncture, where the other windsurfer poked him with something he had in his hand, there'll be circumstantial evidence that something caused his heart attack."

Liz sat back when their wine and appetizers arrived and waited until the server left before asking, "Have you told his father what you suspect?"

"He's seen the video, but that's all at this point."

Drake served them each a dumpling and raised his glass of wine and touched it gently against her glass. "You look spectacular, if I haven't already told you."

Liz smiled broadly. "You have, but you can keep telling me it as long as you want. Try the dumpling and tell me what you think."

Drake picked a dumpling up and studied it before asking, "I'm guessing that's chili sauce and it's going to be spicy, right?"

"You tell me."

He took a bite and tasted red chile and maybe soy sauce and something else he couldn't place. "It's very good, not too spicy, but definitely Sichuan."

They finished off the dumplings and studied their menus. Liz decided to go bold and chose Prawns in Spicy Gravy, while Drake chose Kung Pao Prawns to keep up with her.

While they waited for their dinners, Drake refilled her glass of wine and casually asked what he'd thinking about while driving back to Seattle. "Liz, where do you think I should look for a place to live?

"Commuting from the island on the ferry sounded romantic, but it ties me to the ferry's schedule. The cabin was nice, and Lancer had freedom to roam around, but it's not the vineyard. I'm not a big city boy. I don't know where to start looking."

Liz sipped her wine and studied his face. "Are you asking me where around Seattle I think you should live? I'm not sure what you're looking for. You know you can stay with me until you find something."

He couldn't tell if she was annoyed because he kept rejecting her offer to stay with her, or because finding a place to live was something he had to figure out for himself.

What he really wanted to ask her was where she wanted to live, if they were married.

"Maybe I should get together with your realtor and start exploring the area."

"I think that's a good idea," she said without smiling.

Way to go, Drake. Awkward and clumsy. Tell her what you really want to say!

He ducked the need to say something when the waiter arrived with their dinners.

"Prawns in Spicy Gravy for you, Miss. Kung Pao Prawns for you, Sir. Will there be anything else?" he asked as he refilled their wine glasses, emptying the bottle.

"Bring another bottle of the pinot gris, if you have it," Drake said.

"Certainly, sir."

He watched Liz expertly lift a prawn out of the gravy with her chopsticks and take a bite. Everything she did, even using chopsticks as if she used them all the time, was beautiful to watch.

"You're going to like your prawns, if they're as good as mine," she said with her eyes smiling.

"Where would you like to live when we're married?" Drake blurted out.

Liz dropped her half-eaten prawn into the spicy gravy and asked softly, "Are you asking me to marry you?"

"Not the way I planned on asking you, but yes, will you marry me, Liz Strobel?"

Tears weren't what he expected.

He waited for her to say something, anything.

"I moved across the country, hoping that I would hear you ask me that one day," she said softly. "Of course, I will marry you, Adam Drake."

Chapter Sixteen

DRAKE MET MIKE CASEY, CEO of Puget Sound Security, the next morning in the hallway walking to his office on the third floor of PSS Headquarters.

"Mike, you have a minute?"

"Sure, your office or mine?"

"Yours will do."

Drake turned and followed his best friend to his corner office. They'd served together in Delta Force and been members of a Joint CIA-JSOC "Hunter/Killer Teams unit. They'd had each other's back in every situation, from fighting in the Middle East to Casey's family home recently when cartel thugs had tried to kidnap Casey's wife and learned the hard way; they were a team you didn't want to take on if you wanted to survive the fight.

They were a team and Drake always involved his friend in every venture he embarked on.

"I need to buy a ring," Drake said as he sat down across the desk from Casey. "Do you know a jeweler?"

Casey sat back in his chair and frowned. "Have you asked her?"

Drake squinted his eyes and just shook his head. "How is that important?"

"Because if you've already asked her, I just lost a hundred dollars."

"You bet on when I would ask Liz to marry me?"

"Office pool. Too much money to pass up," Casey said with an apologetic grin.

"What dates did you pick?"

"We used a random number generator. My dates were in September and December."

"How long has this pool been around?"

"Since the day Liz got here."

"Unbelievable," Drake said and got up to leave.

"Here," Casey said and took an embossed business card from his desk drawer and walked around to hand it to Drake.

"Best hundred dollars I ever lost," Casey said and wrapped his friend in a man hug, pounding his back. "I'm happy for both of you."

"Thanks Mike."

"Before you leave, Kevin got into Michael Bridge's tablet files. He's waiting for you in his office."

Kevin McRoberts was the head of the IT division at PSS. A twenty something former hacker who'd been caught hacking into Microsoft's system while PSS was providing security for its corporate headquarters in Redmond, Washington. He'd been given a chance to exchange his black hat for a white hat working for PSS instead of going to jail. Young McRoberts had chosen wisely and quickly demonstrated himself to be an IT genius and an invaluable asset to the company.

His second-floor glass-fronted office was at the rear corner of the vast IT section. Drake saw Kevin leaning forward, with his elbow on the desktop and his chin cupped in his hand, staring at one of the monitors on his desk, as he walked to his office.

Drake knocked on the open door and was waved into the young man's inner sanctum.

"Good morning Kevin. Mike said you were able to have a look at the files in the tablet I left for you."

"Hi Mr. Drake. It wasn't hard. He used standard Bitlocker

encryption on his Surface Pro. His password wasn't hard to figure out."

"Did you find anything that indicated Michael Bridge was concerned about China for some reason?"

"It's hard to say. He has one file with copies of the original funding documents from a private equity firm in San Francisco. It looks like he was researching a side agreement that involved an intern program. The agreement is pretty lopsided, Mr. Drake, in favor of the equity firm. SkySage agrees to employ an intern for two years from the equity firm's intern program and pay them a ridiculous salary, plus benefits. The only thing I could find that might come close to involving China is a copy of the current intern's payroll sheet. She's a recent MBA from the University of California by the name of Grace Liu."

"What's the name of the private equity firm?" Drake asked.

"Berryman Private Equity, LLC. Wayne Berrryman is the founder and son of Walter Berryman, the former governor of California and now the U.S. Secretary of the Treasury."

"The same Walter Berryman who is handling negotiations with China on a new trade agreement with the U.S." Drake observed. "You mentioned this file had copies of the funding agreement with the equity firm. Is there anything in the file about where the money came from to start this private equity firm?"

"No, but Michael Bridge was trying to find out. He did a search to see if Berryman's firm filed a notice with the Committee on Foreign Investment in the United States, as required if there is foreign capital invested in a U.S. private equity fund. I checked and they didn't, but that only means Berryman and his investors felt they met the conditions for not being within CFIUS jurisdiction."

"And, what a coincidence," Drake snorted, "Walter Berryman, as the Secretary of the Treasury, chairs the federal interagency CFIUS committee and his department handles the day-to-day functions of the committee. I'm beginning to see why Michael Bridge might have been concerned. Wayne Berryman and his Dad would know how to structure a fund with foreign investors and steer clear of government oversight."

"Mr. Drake, I could poke around and find out where Wayne Berryman got the capital for his equity fund, if you want."

"Let's hold off on that for now, Kevin. I know nothing's safe from your prying flying fingers. When we find something that would give Berryman a reason to be involved in Michael Bridge's death, we'll revisit your offer."

"Whatever you want, Mr. Drake."

"Good work Kevin, thanks."

Drake took the stairs to his office thinking about the political minefield he'd wandered into. Matthew Bridge was a powerful congressman whose son was murdered, and he was determined to know why.

The company his son worked for was a part of the most ambitious high-tech project the Pentagon had ever put together. JEDI was a game changer that could make the difference in winning or losing the next big war.

Every enemy of the United States wanted access to the technology that was being developed or would want to see the project sabotaged.

China was an enemy that had been stealing technology for decades and now had the most widespread espionage campaign in the world targeting American technology. Drake knew that half of the FBI's active espionage cases involved China.

But for all of that, what troubled Drake the most was that the Secretary of the Treasury, Walter Berryman, and his son could be helping China steal the technology being developed by the JEDI project.

Chapter Seventeen

FRANCIS ZHANG WALKED SOFTLY BAREFOOT through his house to keep from waking his wife, with a cup of his favorite Dragon Well Tea. It was seven o'clock in the morning and he was returning home at sunrise from practicing tai chi at a nearby park.

Wearing the traditional tangzhaung, or Chinese martial arts suit, consisting of a loose-fitting black pants and a white shirt with a standup collar, his daily routine allowed him to begin each day with a clear mind and relaxed body.

Zhang was fifty-one years old and as fit as a man twenty years younger. You wouldn't know that, however, by looking at him. His hairline had receded to the middle of his head and his wire rim glasses made him a look like one of the professors at the University of California, where his wife taught Art History.

Zhang had entered the country on a temporary business visa in 2009 and became a lawful permanent resident five years later. The company he quickly started, Premier Tour and Travel, and the Chinese student tours his company offered, put him in contact with students at the university where he met his wife, Jennifer Chen.

She was a second generation Chinese American ten years

younger than himself, but their shared love of Chinese art and literature had narrowed the gap of years for them.

With the profit from his business, supported as it was by the MSS, and the salary of a tenured professor at the University of California, the Zhang's lived well. Their home in the Sunset District of San Francisco, purchased for two million seven hundred thousand dollars U.S., and their support of the arts gave them entry into the upper tier of San Francisco society.

It was a privileged life that Zhang despised.

Sitting down in a chair on the rear deck with a commanding view of the city waking up below, it was time to decide what had to be done to protect the work of ten years that it took to penetrate a research company like SkySage.

The problem was, he didn't know what the man who recovered the tablet was up to. There might be nothing on the congressman's son's tablet that would lead anyone to investigate his death. The man could be retrieving the tablet for SkySage. They would have a legitimate reason to want to protect their intellectual property. The man with the tablet could conceivably be working for SkySage.

It was a possibility, but it wasn't one that he was willing to risk taking and being recalled to Beijing for.

The inquiry that had been made in Hong Kong about the ownership of Tony Lee's Camaro indicated someone was suspicious.

Zhang finished drinking his cup of tea and went to his study to call Tony Lee, his agent in Seattle.

Lee didn't answer right away. When he did, he was out of breath.

"Yes?"

"Are you alone?"

"No."

"Call me back in five minutes when you are."

He walked to the kitchen and prepared another cup of tea. His phone vibrated in his hand as he returned to his office and closed to the door.

"What have you learned about the man who has the tablet?"

"His name is Adam Drake. He's a lawyer who works for a large security firm here in Seattle. He's their special counsel, whatever that means. I called our person in the mayor's office and she ran a background check on him. He purchased a commuter card for the ferry that runs from Seattle to Bainbridge Island. He listed a place there as his residence."

"Do you think he has the tablet?"

"I have no way of knowing that."

"I think you do. You have interrogation training. Use it. Follow him to this Island and find out where the tablet is. If he has it, find out if he knows what's on it. When you're finished, make sure his poking around days are over. You're a former Water Dragon, take care of it, unless your whoring around has made you weak. If it has and you fail, you're no longer of any use to me. I think you know what that means."

Zhang waited three seconds for a response and ended the call when he didn't hear one.

He wasn't concerned about his agent's ability to do what he was told to do, but he was concerned about how quickly he was going to do it.

This would be that last chance he would give Tony Lee before he sent him home. Life in America was a distraction that was too much for some men.

Zhang returned to the deck to finish his cup of tea. Looking down on the city that provided the best and the worst that America had to offer, he understood the distraction.

Americans were told they were free to do whatever they felt like doing. They could work or choose to rely on the government to meet their needs. They could take drugs, if they wanted, even if their government knew many of them would become zombies for the rest of their miserable lives. They watched hours of mindless entertainment on their devices, ignored the arts and knew nothing of their country's history or the values that had made it powerful.

China would never let that happen to its people. Soon China would be the most powerful and wealthy country in the world and America would drown in the cesspool it had made of itself.

Chapter Eighteen

DRAKE KNOCKED TWICE on the door of the PSS Vice President of Government Affairs and opened it wide enough to lean in and say hello to his fiancé.

"Get you anything before I settle in next door and get to work?" he asked.

"I'm fine, thanks. Anything you need help with?"

Drake came in and sat down across the desk from her. "Maybe. Kevin got into Michael Bridge's tablet. He found a file Bridge was putting together on where SkySage got its startup money. Turns out it was from Berryman Private Equity, LLC."

"Berryman, as in Secretary of the Treasury Walter Berryman?"

"No, his son Wayne Berryman."

"That's interesting."

"Why?"

"Secretary Berryman is point man on the government's negotiating team for a new trade deal with China. You said Michael Bridge knew SkySage got startup money from Berryman's equity firm. Did he find out who Berryman's investors were?"

"There wasn't anything in the file about Berryman's investors."

"If he was concerned about foreign investors, like China, he could see if Berryman's firm filed a CFIUS notice telling the government a foreign investor is involved."

"There wasn't a CFIUS review."

"Would you like me to find out about Berryman's investors? The Department of Homeland Security is a member of the Committee on Foreign Investments in United States. I still have friends at DHS?"

"Sure, go ahead. We need to know as much about the Berrymans, as well," Drake said. "I'll ask Paul Benning to put together a file on each of them."

"Have you told the president what you've learned about Michael Bridge?"

"Not yet, but if we're going to start asking questions about Berryman Private Equity, LLC, he should be brought up to date," Drake agreed. "I'll call him this morning. Are you sure you don't want another cup of coffee?"

"I'm good. Are you still taking me to lunch?"

'I thought we'd swing by your condo, get Lancer and go to a park. We can get something from that deli, you like. I want to take Lancer to the cabin tonight. Would you like to come with us?"

Liz gave him a thumbs up. "Count me in."

Drake walked twenty feet down the hall to his office and closed the door. Before he went any further investigating the death of Michael, he needed to clear it with the president.

President Ben Ballard's personal secretary told him the president would take his call in ten minutes when his meeting ended. The president answered him in five minutes.

"Thanks for giving me a reason to get out that meeting."

"Glad to help, Mr. President."

"It's Ben, Adam."

"Yes, sir. I thought you would like to know what I've learned about Michael Bridge's death. It looks like he was murdered."

Drake heard the president sigh. "Matthew was right, then. He didn't have a heart attack?"

"He did have a heart attack, but there's evidence someone

caused him to have the heart attack. Another windsurfer ran into him with something in his hand that resembles the heart attack gun the CIA developed years ago."

"Can we prove it?"

"We're checking the wetsuit he was wearing to see if it has a puncture in the area where the other windsurfer made contact with him."

"Have you been able to find out anything about why he was concerned about China?"

"That's where this is becomes a little sensitive. Michael Bridge has a file on his tablet that we were able to locate and open. He was looking into the startup funding for SkySage. It came from Berryman Private Equity, LLC, in San Francisco."

"Any relation to my Secretary of the Treasury, Walter Berryman?"

"His son, Wayne Berryman started and runs the equity firm."

"I understand why you said this has become sensitive," President Ballard said. "Is Berryman's firm the reason Michael Bridge was concerned about China?"

"I don't know. We're looking into any foreign investors who might be involved with SkySage. China might be one of them."

The president took a deep breath and let it out slowly through his mouth. "If any of this involves Berryman or his son, it couldn't come at a worse time. My opposition is already leaking information about the trade agreement with China, saying we're caving to China's demands. We're not, but if you repeat the lie often enough, the media's coverage will convince a lot of people that we are. And the mid-year election is right around the corner."

"How would you like me to proceed, sir?"

"Do we know if SkySage submitted a CFIUS notice?"

"It didn't. Liz is reaching out to friends at DHS to find out why. We thought asking Treasury might draw unwanted attention to the Secretary and his son's firm."

"Good thinking. If I ask for the information, the same thing would happen. Why don't you ask your farther-in-law and his friends to poke around and see what they can come up with?"

"Will do. How much of this do you want me to share with Congressman Bridge. He might feel obligated to have his committee investigate SkySage and its investors."

"I'll talk with Matthew," President Ballard said. "Keep doing what you're doing. Call me when you learn more."

Chapter Nineteen

AFTER TAKING a long picnic lunch at the park on Lake Washington with Lancer, Drake and Liz worked late at PSS and ate Chinese takeout for dinner in their offices.

When it was time to catch the eight fifteen ferry to Bainbridge Island, they stopped by Liz's condo and then drove to the terminal in her new white Cadillac CT6-V, with Lancer riding proudly in the back.

Their ferry was the M/V Wenatchee, a Jumbo Mark II-class ferry. It was four hundred and twenty feet long, with a maximum passenger load of two thousand, four hundred and ninety passengers and two hundred and two vehicles.

Theirs was one of the last cars that drove onto the ferry. As the ferry pulled away from its birth, Drake stood at the back of the Cadillac, with Liz on his right and Lancer on a leash to his left. He was admiring the Seattle skyline with a towering snow-capped Mount Rainier glowing a soft pink in the background.

"Lancer has to stay on the exterior of the ferry, but have you seen the Native American artwork on the Wenatchee? It's worth a look," Drake said.

Liz slipped her arm through his. "Let's stay outside and go to the viewing deck. I love the mountains you can see from there."

"The viewing deck it is," he said and turned her around to walk to the stairs. On the way there, a red BMW R 1250 RT touring motorcycle caught his eye three cars ahead and to the right. Its rider, wearing jeans and a gray leather jacket, was studying a map and turned to look at him.

"Nice bike," Drake called over to him.

The rider nodded and looked back at his map.

Drake noticed that the rider hadn't raised the drop-down visor on his helmet. Even with the visor down, he sensed that the man was following him with his eyes as they walked past. Either that, or he was staring at Liz, which was more likely.

They stood at the aft rail of the ferry and watched Seattle recede in the distance.

"I called Pam, my realtor," Liz said. "She said to call her whenever you're ready."

"Maybe this weekend. Did she have any suggestions?"

She nudged her elbow in his side. "She needs to know what you're looking for first."

"That's the problem, I don't know myself and you're no help."

"There's no rush. Just give her some idea to get her started."

"Where would you like to live?"

"With you."

Drake laughed. "Like I said, you're no help."

"We'll figure it out."

They felt the ferry begin to slow and turn to port as it approached the Bainbridge ferry terminal. Passengers were heading for the stairs and elevators down to their vehicles and they followed the movement.

When they reached the lower deck and walked back to Liz's CT6-V, Drake saw the motorcyclist was sitting on his BMW, still with his visor down, ready to motor off the ferry.

The sun was low in the sky to the west, with the sunset a few minutes away, when Liz drove off the ferry and headed north from the terminal on State Highway 305 NE.

By the time she took the exit onto NE Day Road, they were two miles from the cabin and the sun had set on the other side of the island. There was a chill in the night air as the evening cooled when Drake lowered his window.

"Would you like a fire tonight?" he asked, when she turned onto to the long drive leading to the cabin.

"If it's not too much trouble."

As soon as she stopped the car on the gravel turnaround in front of the cabin, Drake got out and opened the rear door to let Lancer out.

"Go ahead, scout the place for us," he said and waved his dog away. Lancer took off at full speed and ran down the path to the firepit on the waterfront. In ten seconds, he was back with his tail swinging widely from side to side.

"That's one of the things I know I want, a place where Lancer won't have to be cooped up," Drake said.

"Top of the list," Liz said and popped the trunk as she got out. "I'll bring our bags while you get wood for the fire."

"Roger that, mi capitán!" Drake said and tossed the keys to the cabin over the top of the car to her.

Drake walked around the cabin to the wood storage locker on the rear deck. There was half a cord of split dry oak firewood in the locker when he'd leased the place. He hadn't used much of it. He rarely started a fire when Liz wasn't there.

When he had an arm full of wood and started toward the back door, he noticed that Lancer was standing with his ears alert, staring into the wall of foliage that surrounded the cabin to the north and west.

"What's out there, Lancer? One of those squirrels that harass you?"

Drake left Lancer on the deck and knocked on the back door for Liz to let him in.

The lights were on and the cabin was lit with a soft light reflecting off the varnished cedar logs,

"Would you like me to fix you a drink while you get the fire started?" Liz asked.

Drake knelt in front of the river rock fireplace and dropped his armload of firewood in the brass bin on the hearth. "A glass of Pendleton would be great. You know where the wine is," he said over his shoulder.

With a couple of wadded up pages of newspaper and kindling for a base, Drake laid a couple of the split firewood pieces down and lit the paper with a wooden match from the bin.

He stood back and watched as the fire caught and the kindling began popping.

Liz walked over and handed him his glass of whisky.

"Salud," she said and touched her glass of red wine to his glass.

"Here's to a quiet night away from the city," he said and took a sip of the amber liquid.

As the whisky burned down the back of his throat, he jerked his head around to the window.

"Did you hear that?" Drake asked. "Sounded like a shotgun. I'd better call Lancer in."

Chapter Twenty

DRAKE WENT OUT to the front deck and whistled for Lancer. The only sound he heard was a soft wind rustling leaves in the treetops.

"He'd heard something at the edge of the property out in the trees" he told Liz when she joined him. "I'll search there. See if he's somewhere down the driveway. He likes to chase squirrels here when they tease him."

Liz jumped down from the deck and started walking down the long curving driveway, calling for Lancer

Drake walked to the edge of the Shore Pines twenty yards away and stopped to listen. The pines were a visual barrier between the log cabin and the neighboring property. With their low canopy reaching down several feet from the ground, he couldn't see into the dark pines very far.

He squatted down and listened. Ahead and to the left, he heard rapid panting.

He swept aside branches and crashed through the thick growth of mature pines. Three more steps and he saw the dark shape of his dog on the ground.

Drake kneeled next to Lancer. "What happened, boy?" he asked as he ran his hand gently down Lancer's head to his neck...where he felt wet hot blood gushing from a wound.

"Liz," he yelled, "Over here. Get the first aid kit from my go-bag in the front closet and a flashlight. Lancer's hurt."

"Coming," he heard her yell.

"Easy, boy," he said to calm Lancer. "We'll get you fixed up and to the vet as soon as we can."

Lancer's eyes were open, but he didn't move his head in response.

Drake had seen war dogs injured in Afghanistan and Iraq. He remembered the emergency treatment their handlers had given them. Stop the bleeding. Cover the wound. Keep your dog calm and get him to a medic as soon as possible.

"Where are you?" Liz yelled.

"Here," he replied. "Give me the packet of QuikClot gauze pads and a sterile bandage to cover the wound."

"What happened?"

"I don't know. We've got to get him to the animal hospital. We drove by it when you turned off the highway onto Day Road."

Drake held his small tactical flashlight in his teeth and gently applied the QuikClot gauge pad with its clotting agent to stop the bleeding. When he had the sterile bandage in place over it, he called out to Liz.

"Open the rear door. I'll sit in back with Lancer."

Drake slipped his arms under Lancer's body and stood slowly, holding him firmly to his chest. Backing out of the pines, he stepped onto the gravel path and turned to walk to the driveway and Liz's CT6-V fifteen feet away.

He slid carefully into the back seat and nodded for Liz to shut the door.

The Day Road Animal Hospital was a mile away. Liz stopped out front and ran to the front door. The hospital was closed for the night, but Drake saw her speaking to someone on an intercom and run back to open his rear door.

"There's a vet on emergency call," Liz said. "She lives nearby, and she'll be here in five minutes. How is he?"

"His pulse is weak. and his heart rate is faster than normal, but he's still with us. It looks like he's been stabbed."

"Oh my God," Liz said. "There was someone out there in the trees?"

"My guess is he confronted someone and was stabbed. He wouldn't have done that, without being told to attack, unless he saw that we were in imminent danger."

Drake was speaking softly to Lancer and stroking his head, when a Subaru Outback pulled up behind Liz's car. A young woman got out and hurried to Liz.

"I'm Mary Olivera," she said and held out her hand. "Is this Lancer in the car?"

"Drake thinks he's been stabbed."

"Let's get him inside. Do you need help with him?" she asked Drake.

Drake swung his legs out and stood with Lancer in his arms. "I'm good. I used a QuikClot gauze pad to stop the bleeding. His pulse is weak and his heart is racing."

"Follow me," the veterinarian said and marched to the front door.

Drake followed her into the waiting area and down a hallway to a room, where she turned on the overhead lighting and pointed to an operating table.

"Put him there." She took out blue disposal latex gloves and a surgical mask from a storage cabinet and said, "Let's take a look."

She carefully removed the sterile bandage and lifted the Quik-Clot gauze pad to inspect the wound.

"I can't tell how deep these wounds are. They look like stab wounds. A thin knife, maybe a one-inch wide blade. How long ago did this happen?"

"Twenty minutes ago," Drake said. "I heard a shot close by and went looking for him. We brought him directly here."

"You thought he'd been shot, Mr...?"

"Drake. I didn't know what had happened. I went out to call him in and found him in on the ground. His name is Lancer. He's five years old."

"I need to call my assistant to help me with this. Keep him calm, I'll be right back."

Dr. Olivera left and Liz joined Drake speaking softly to Lancer and petting his head.

"He's going to be all right, Adam."

Drake clenched his jaw and stared down at his best friend. "Someone is going to pay dearly for this."

Dr. Olivera returned and began preparing for emergency surgery. "He's lost a lot of blood. He'll need a transfusion to stabilize him. Then we'll see how bad his injuries are. You can stay, if you want, but when my assistant gets here, I'll have to ask you wait outside."

"Of course," Drake said. "We'll stay."

Chapter Twenty-One

IT WAS midnight by the time Drake and Liz got back to the cabin. Lancer was going to be okay, they were told, but his recovery following a transfusion and emergency surgery was going to take a while.

Lancer had been stabbed twice in the neck. One of the wounds hadn't been very deep, after glancing off his collar. The second, however, was deep and had just missed slicing through his jugular vein.

He'd lost a lot of blood, but the clotting agent had kept the loss from being as bad as it could have been. The veterinarian had told Drake Lancer was lucky to have an owner familiar with QuikClot who knew how to quickly apply it.

Drake hadn't been able to sleep. He was standing down on the dock, with a cup of coffee in his hand, when Liz found him watching the sun rising over the mountains east of the city.

"You okay?" she asked, wrapping her arms around his waist and pressing her forehead into his back.

"Why was someone hiding in the trees? Lancer knew someone was there when I was getting firewood. Why didn't he just bark and let me know?"

"Maybe the man who stabbed him left and then came back," Liz said. "Maybe it was a burglar and he was waiting for us to go to bed."

"If a burglar was out there and didn't expect us last night, he would have left and tried again when we weren't home. I don't think it was a burglar."

Liz gave him a hug and came around to stand beside him. "If it wasn't a burglar, who was it then?"

"I don't know, but I'm going to find out. Let's go see if there's any evidence that will help in the pines."

Drake led the way up the dock and along the gravel path to the edge of the deck where Lancer had been standing.

"He was looking in this direction," Drake said, pointing at a spot at eleven o'clock in the trees. "Let's start there."

Drake started across the gravel path that wrapped around the cabin and stopped. Dark Hemlock mulch covered the ground from there to the edge of the trees. A small nonorganic thing was out of place laying there at the edge of the tree line.

He leaned down to study it. A round yellow plug, with a diameter about the size of a .410 shotgun, was attached by two thin wires to a cylinder two inches long with the same diameter. Three small plastic stabilizing wings extended from the sides of the projectile.

Drake knew what he was looking at. Lancer didn't bark because he'd been hit by a small version of Taser's **XREP** (Extended Range Electronic Projectile). Originally fired from a twelve-gauge shotgun shell, the **XREP** projectile could reach out and taser a target ninety feet away.

Like this scaled-down version of the **XREP**, a self-contained taser was housed in a specially designed shotgun shell that used a small charge of gunpowder to launch the projectile.

As soon as it left the end of the shotgun's barrel, a ripcord connecting the projectile to the shell snaps, activating its battery and sending a high-voltage charge to the electrode prongs in the projectile's nose. Impact with a target's clothing, and then his skin, would brake pins connecting the nose to the base of the projectile, causing it to swing free, still connected to the nose by the thin wires.

The XREP had proved to be too expensive for Taser to manufacture, but someone had developed a smaller version that copied the original design.

If Lancer had been tasered, it would explain why they hadn't heard him bark. But why had he been stabbed?

Drake pointed to the mini-EREP on the ground and told Liz to have a look.

"Lancer was tasered but recovered and still attacked the person who stabbed him. Let's see where that took place," he said.

With the sun still low in the morning sky, it was dark in the pines where the canopy of leaves reached down to a couple of feet above the ground. Drake walked into the pines and leaned down to search among the carpet of pine needles. Moving forward slowly, he found the blood where he'd found Lancer.

A foot beyond the blood, pine needles were scraped back and dark earth exposed. A heel of a boot or shoe had been drug backwards, leaving a narrow trench an inch deep.

"Liz, come see this. This is where Lancer fought his attacker."

She moved beside him and studied the area around the dried pool of blood. Farther back in the pines, she spotted something laying at the foot of a tree. When she went forward to see what it was, she saw that it was a ragged patch of gray leather.

"Adam, over here. Lancer got a piece of him."

Drake moved to her side and squatted down to see what she had found. When he reached down to pick up the patch of leather, Liz grabbed his arm to stop him. "Shouldn't we leave it for the police?"

"They can investigate Lancer's stabbing, but they wouldn't know what to do with this scrap of leather. I do."

"What does that mean?"

"I know who stabbed Lancer. Remember the man sitting on the red BMW motorcycle on the ferry? He was wearing a leather jacket, gray just like this piece Lancer tore off."

Drake stood and turned to walk back out of the stand of pines. "Let's go inside. I'll see if Kevin can access the surveillance footage from the security cameras on the ferry. WSDOT runs the ferries and tries to identify everyone loading and unloading a ferry. If nothing else, they'll have the license number of his motorcycle."

Chapter Twenty-Two

SITTING at the breakfast bar in the kitchen, Drake started to call Kevin McRoberts at PSS headquarters and realized it was still early. Kevin was a video gamer and often played in tournaments around the world all night long. He worked long hours at PSS, but those hours didn't start at eight o'clock in the morning.

The CEO of PSS, however, did start his day early.

"Good morning, Adam. What gets you up this early?"

"I never went to sleep last night. Someone stabbed Lancer at the cabin. He's resting at the animal hospital after a transfusion and emergency surgery."

"Is he okay?"

"The vet says he should make a full recovery, in time."

"I'm sorry, Adam. I know how you love that dog. Do you know who did it?"

"Not yet," Drake said. "That's why I'm calling. When Kevin gets in, will you have him access last night's surveillance footage from the security cameras on the M/V Wenatchee, the eight fifteen ferry from Seattle to Bainbridge? Have him look for a guy on a red BMW R 1250 RT motorcycle. He was wearing a gray leather jacket, jeans and a black helmet. He kept the visor down when I noticed him, but we might get lucky."

"You think this is the guy who stabbed Lancer?"

"Lancer tore a patch of gray leather from his jacket. It's him."

"Any idea what he was doing at your cabin?"

"He must have followed us from the ferry, but I don't have a clue why."

"Could this have anything to do with what you've been doing for the president?"

Drake took the new cup of coffee Liz handed to him and thought for a moment. "I don't see how it could. I guess it's possible, but why would they come after me."

"Will you be back in the office or do you want Kevin to call you?"

"We're going to stay here until we know how Lancer is doing. I've got my laptop. I can work from here on a couple of things."

"Stay safe and let me know how Lancer's doing. If you need anything, call me," Casey said.

"I will. Thanks Mike."

Liz leaned down across from him and rested her elbows on the breakfast bar. "What now?"

"We wait to see if Kevin can identify our guy," Drake said and started drumming the fingers of his left hand on the breakfast bar. "Mike suggested last night could have something to do with me helping Congressman Bridge, although I can't see how."

"What about his son's tablet you brought back from Hood River? If someone killed him to stop him from finding something at SkySage, maybe his killer doesn't want anyone else to find out what that was. He'd want to know what was on his tablet?"

"You mean his concern about China? Killing him about that just points the finger at China. None of the FBI cases involving Chinese industrial espionage, that I know of, have included murder or wet work."

"By making it look like Michael Bridge had a heart attack, the FBI's case wouldn't have involved murder this time, either," she pointed out. "Was Paul able to confirm the wetsuit was punctured, that it was murder?"

"I haven't heard. I'll call him later and find out. Even if we prove it was murder, there's no evidence it had anything to do with China."

"Unless we prove his killer was working for China…"

Drake nodded his agreement and got up. "Let's go check on Lancer. By the time we get back, Kevin might have something for us."

Dr. Olivera was still at the animal hospital and met them in the reception area.

"Lancer's doing fine," she told them. "I'll keep him over the weekend, to make sure he doesn't have a reaction to the transfusion or need further treatment."

"Can we see him?" Drake asked.

"Certainly," Dr. Olivera said and led them through the hospital to a recovery room with a window. Lancer was lying on his side in a kennel with a large area of his neck shaved around the wounds.

"He's not fully awake yet," the veterinarian said. "We check his vitals every hour. When he's ready to be moved, he'll have his own kennel in the dog ward. It he has a favorite blanket or bedding, having it will allow him to rest better. When he's ready to leave, we'll give you instructions on how you can take care of him at home."

She walked them back to the reception area, shook their hands. "We'll call you this afternoon to update you on Lancer's condition."

Liz slipped her arm through his as they left the clinic and walked out to her car. "You okay?"

"Relieved to know I didn't lose him. Furious that someone tried to kill him. Can't wait to get my hands on the SOB that did it," Drake said.

When they were seated in Liz's car, Drake took out his phone to call Kevin McRoberts at PSS headquarters.

"Have any luck?" he asked his young hacker extraordinaire.

"I found him on the surveillance videos, but he never took his helmet off," Kevin said. "The red BMW is registered to a holding company in Hong Kong, but I was able to identify the person riding it. Well, sort of."

"What does 'sort of' mean?"

"I accessed the WSDOT ticketing information for the ferry you took to Bainbridge. He purchased the ticket online, but the name, address, phone and email address he used is bogus. A person by that name doesn't exist, the address is on a street that doesn't exist, and the phone and email address don't check out."

"So, we don't know who he is?"

"Actually, I think we might. He used a debit card from an online bank account. That account was opened, using the same information he used when he bought the ferry ticket. When I looked at the transactions in his account, I found a check deposited every month from a Kung fu club near the University of Washington for Wushu Sanda instruction. He's a Chinese martial arts instructor there."

Wushu Sanda was a form of martial arts developed by the Chinese military, combining traditional Kung fu with modern fighting techniques.

"Send me the address of the Kung fu club, Kevin, then treat yourself to lunch anywhere you choose. I'm buying. You are the man."

His phone had been on speaker.

"Sounds like we might have the China connection we we're looking for," Liz said.

"Let's find out."

Chapter Twenty-Three

THE KUNG FU club met in a martial arts studio on Greenwood Avenue North in the University District. It met off campus because "there were no facilities available that didn't adversely impact existing university recreation programs", according to the club's website.

Drake thought there were other reasons a club would not want to be restricted by the university's club rules, but reserved judgment on the matter until he knew more about the club.

They returned to Seattle on the ferry and parked Liz's Cadillac CT6-V on the street, half a block from the studio, after following the car's GPS instructions across the city

University Martial Arts was located at one end of a small marketplace that housed an acupuncture and massage clinic, a coffee shop and neighborhood organic foods market.

They walked hand in hand up the sidewalk to the studio and stopped to look in the storefront windows. The interior was dark, but there was enough ambient light to provide a view inside of a large hardwood floor practice area and black walls with bright-colored banners on them.

"Looks like we're here between classes," Liz said.

"There might be someone in that office at the back."

Drake walked to the front door and found that it was open.

"If our guy is here, he'll recognize us from the ferry," Drake said. "Hang back a bit when we get to the office and cover me."

With Lancer being tasered and stabbed, Drake and Liz were both armed. Liz carried her Glock 19M in a tan leather crossbody concealed carry purse that complemented the tangerine polo and white jeans she was wearing. Drake's Kimber Ultra Carry II was riding in a saddle leather belt holster hidden under his untucked black polo.

As they approached the door with "*Office*" painted on it, they heard music playing on the other side.

Liz stepped back and to the left of the door, as Drake knocked twice and stepped to the right.

The music stopped and the door opened to let a young woman walk out.

"Hi, may I help you?"

"Your website says you offer instruction in Wushu Sanda," Drake said. "I'd like to know more about it, see if it's something I might be interested in."

"Have you studied any of the martial arts?"

"Some close quarter combat when I was in the army, but that's it."

"No problem, we have an excellent instructor for Wushu Sanda," she said and smiled. "He'll interview you and decide what class would be best for you. Why are you interested in Wushu Sanda, if you don't mind me asking?"

"I've always been interested in Kung fu. I read that Wushu Sanda combines traditional Chinese Kung fu with more modern martial arts. I thought that might be a good place to start."

"Are you interested in taking a class with your husband?" she asked Liz.

"I don't think so. I'll watch and see how he does."

"Is the Wushu Sanda instructor here, by any chance?" Drake asked.

"I'm sorry, Tony is in California at a corporate retreat that starts this weekend. Let me get you a brochure. It has a number where you can reach him when he gets back next week."

"Thanks," Drake said.

Liz had wandered away to look at a display of the pictures of the University Martial Arts instructors.

Drake waited for his brochure and then joined her.

She pointed to the picture of a Chinese man with piercing light green eyes, who looked to be in his mid-to-late twenties, by the name of Tony Lee.

Drake stepped closer to study his adversary. Slim build, five nine, maybe a hundred and sixty pounds, like the guy they saw on the ferry on the red BMW.

He took his iPhone out and took a picture of Tony Lee and each of the other five instructors.

"Guess I'm going to have to brush up on my fighting skills, in case I have the pleasure of meeting Mr. Lee," Drake said and turned to leave.

"You could just shoot him," Liz suggested.

"Not until I ask him why he came after me and who he works for. Then, maybe I'll shoot him or let Lancer have a go at him."

They left and walked back to Liz's CT6-V.

"Where to?" she asked.

"Let's stop at headquarters before we catch a ferry back to Bainbridge. I need to let Mike know what's going on."

Liz drove them across the Evergreen Point Floating Bridge to Kirkland and parked next to Drake's gray Porsche Cayman GTS in the PSS Headquarters underground parking.

While Liz went to her office to check with her contact in Homeland Security to ask why Berryman Private Equity, LLC didn't make a CFIUS filing, Drake went looking for Mike Casey.

He found him with the PSS armorer inspecting a Kalashnikov KP-9 SBR, the Russian version of the Heckler & Koch MP5K.

"When you get a chance, you need to spend some time with this baby," Casey said. "9mm, fun to shoot, cheaper than the MP5K and made in the USA."

"Are you thinking of buying some?" Drake asked.

"Nah, they're still Kalashnikovs," Casey said, shaking his head. "I have too many memories of dodging bullets from AK-47s. How's Lancer?"

"I'll know more tonight. We're going back to Bainbridge. Before I leave, we need to talk. I think we've found something that may support Michael Bridge's concern about China and SkySage."

"Does this have something to do with what Kevin dug up on the guy on the ferry?"

"He might be the guy who killed Bridge. He was at the impound lot in Hood River when I went there for the tablet. The black Camaro he was driving is registered to a holding company in Hong Kong, just like the red BMW motorcycle he was riding on the ferry.

"I think he came after me because he thought I might have the tablet. It's all connected in some way. We need to find out how."

Chapter Twenty-Four

ON THEIR WAY upstairs to their offices, Casey asked Drake if he was hungry.

"We had an early breakfast, but sure, I could eat," Drake said. "What did you have in mind?"

"I'm hungry for Southern barbeque."

"At that place you like with the hot sauce?"

"No, Dixie's Barbeque closed last year. There's a food truck that's almost as good. Why don't you see if Liz would like to join us? I'll check their website and see where they're located today."

Drake turned right at the top of the stairs and walked down the hall to Liz's office.

She was on the phone, so he opened the door wider and whispered that Mike wanted to go for barbeque, did she want to go? She shook her head no and mouthed "thanks".

Drake waited for Casey at the stairs and followed him down to underground parking. He could tell his friend was already savoring a side of baby back ribs by the way he was skipping down the steps.

Casey was already buckling in when Drake opened the door of the black Range Rover that dwarfed his gray Porsche Cayman next to it.

"You ever think of getting something a little smaller?" he asked, as Casey backed up and drove up the ramp from underground parking.

"I'm still thinking of getting a boat, after all the fun we had in Costa Rica. I'll need something this big to haul it around. You should get a boat. You wouldn't have to take the ferry all the time."

"I'm not staying on Bainbridge," Drake said. "Liz's realtor is putting together a list of properties for me to see."

"Did you get the ring yet?"

"Haven't had time."

"Do it by next Wednesday. There's another office pool. I'd like to win this time."

Drake shook his head and laughed. "Who organizes these pools? Who has time?"

When Casey didn't answer, Drake turned and asked, "You?"

Casey smiled. "It's good for morale. Besides, it gives me a chance to win back that Benjamin you cost me."

"That's why you want me to use your jeweler! So, you can call him and find out when I buy the ring?"

"How can you think such a thing? Now, what was it you're wanting to do about Michael Bridge and SkySage?"

Drake took a deep breath before saying, "Before last night, I just wanted to do what the president asked me to do; find out if there was anything that supported Michael Bridge's concern about SkySage and China. When they, whoever they are, came after me and damn near killed Lancer, it became personal. But I'm afraid this is too big for us to continue."

"That hasn't stopped us before."

"Before, there wasn't the possibility of a superpower like China being involved. Before, we didn't have two of our biggest clients, Microsoft and SkySage, involved. If China is behind the murder of a congressman's son and whatever's going on at SkySage, this could start a war."

"Then, let's find out what we can and let the president handle it. If the guy who came after you is working for China, he'll get what's coming to him. If he isn't, then we'll take care of it."

Casey pointed ahead to a white food truck in the parking lot of the Kirkland Brewing Company.

"Get ready for some finger-lickin-good wood-smoked barbeque," he said and jumped out of his SUV to get in line and place his order.

Drake followed behind. It always amused him to watch his friend satisfy his hunger for food of every kind and in great quantities. Tall, at six foot seven, and thin, Mike Casey was never bothered by the calories he inhaled and never seemed to gain a pound.

With Casey's side of ribs and Drake's pulled pork sandwich in hand, they walked to a vacant picnic table in the shade and sat down across from each other.

Casey started in on his ribs and waited, with raised eyebrows, for Drake to try his sandwich.

"It's good," Drake said, licking barbeque sauce from his lips.

They ate without talking, until Casey finished his ribs and sat back with a satisfied smile.

"Okay, now that I can concentrate," Casey said, "How to you want to proceed? The only connection to China, and it's a remote one, is a black Camaro and the BMW on the ferry that are both registered to a holding company in Hong Kong. Suspicious, but what you lawyers call circumstantial evidence."

"There is the concern Michael Bridge expressed to his father about China," Drake offered. "If that was a legitimate concern, it would be a motive for murder if someone wanted to stop him from asking questions."

"Possible murder. Has Paul Benning been able to confirm that his wetsuit was punctured?"

"I haven't heard from Paul, yet."

"Then what we have is a possible connection to a possible murder that centers around Michael Bridge and SkySage. Start there."

Drake thought for a moment. "We did the initial security assessment for SkySage and their facility security clearance. We're still the security consultants they use.

"We could meet with the facility security officer (FSO) at

SkySage, tell him there's reason to believe Michael Bridge was murdered, and does he need our help with the reports he'll need to file to maintain their facility security clearance."

"That's what any good security consulting firm would offer to do," Casey agreed. "Sounds like we have a plan."

Chapter Twenty-Five

WHEN HE RETURNED FROM LUNCH, Drake stopped at Liz's closed office door and knocked.

"Come in."

There was an empty Chobani Nonfat Greek Yogurt container and a granola bar wrapper on the desk next to her laptop.

"You missed out on some good barbeque."

"I was waiting for my friend at DHS to come on the line," she said, "Otherwise, I would have joined you."

"Did you learn anything about SkySage?"

"Quite a lot. Berryman Private Equity, LLC, was formed three years ago. That was when Wayne Berryman's father became the Secretary of the U.S. Treasury. No CFIUS notice was filed because Berryman Private Equity, LLC was a new entity and considered to be a "greenfield" investment."

"And the Committee on Foreign Investment only has jurisdiction over existing U.S. companies, if there's foreign investment," Drake added. "Do we know anything about where Wayne Berryman got the money to start his equity firm?"

"Ahh, that's where it gets interesting. Wayne Berryman has a foreign investor, a Hong Kong holding company. That holding company has a limited partner that just happens to be a Chinese private equity firm, with eighty percent of its shares owned by the Bank of China."

"And the Bank of China means the People's Republic of China and the Chinese Communist Party. So, there is a China connection to SkySage."

"Well, there's a China connection to Berryman Private Equity, LLC, but it's a passive investment," Liz said. "Wayne Berryman is the CEO and runs the company. The holding company doesn't have any control over what he does and wouldn't have access to any of the intellectual property being developed by SkySage."

"But Wayne Berryman does. He sits on the SkySage board of directors."

"He wouldn't be stupid enough to pass anything along to his foreign investor. Economic espionage carries with it a potential fine of five million dollars and fifteen years in prison."

"That assumes the Justice Department is willing to prosecute someone like Wayne Berryman, the son of a cabinet member," Drake said and stood up, shaking his head. "Maybe he thinks he doesn't have anything to worry about. Maybe we should give him a reason to consider the possibilities."

"How would we do that?" Liz asked.

"Let me work on that," Drake said and left.

In his office next door, he sat down to pull up information on CFIUS and think.

The Foreign Investment and National Security Act of 2007 (FINSA) authorized the President of the United States, when there wasn't a CFIUS clearance for an investment, to impose adverse conditions on a company or even require divestiture of its interests in the U.S. company.

He didn't know anything about the relationship between the SkySage CEO and Wayne Berryman. But if he met with the CEO to let him know that he'd heard from a reliable source that the Committee on Foreign Investment was preparing to review a foreign investor's position in Berryman Private Equity, LLC.

That would certainly give the SkySage CEO a reason to call

Berryman and give Berryman something to worry about. Shaking the tree to see what Berryman might do was a long shot, but it might tell them something about Berryman and his foreign investor's interest in SkySage.

Before he had a chance to tell Liz what he was thinking of doing, Paul Benning called.

"I thought you should know that Michael Bridge's wetsuit does have a small puncture, right where the video shows the other windsurfer making contact with his body," Benning said. "It took a couple of days for the sheriff in Hood River to find the wetsuit and call me to come and look at it."

"Did you tell the sheriff that we believe Michael Bridge was murdered?"

"I did, and he's opening an investigation and keeping the wetsuit as evidence."

"Good work, Paul. Have you told Congressman Bridge what you found?"

"No, I thought you might want to tell him."

"Okay, I will. One other thing, will you give Kevin McRoberts a call and give him the information you have on the Hong Kong holding company that the black Camaro is registered to?"

"Sure."

"A guy riding a red BMW came after me out on Bainbridge Island. Kevin was able to access the ferry security footage and we have the license on the bike and the identity of guy riding it. It's also registered to a Hong Kong holding company. I need to know if it's the same holding company."

"I'm sure it is. Margo called Liz and I know about Lancer. Sorry, Adam. How's he doing?"

"He's spending the weekend at the animal hospital. The vet says he should make a full recovery."

"That's good news. Will you be down our way anytime soon?"

"I haven't told Liz, but I'm planning on driving down tomorrow to visit SkySage."

"Stop by and see us. Margo wants to give you a hug."

"What for?"

"To apologize for her attitude and thanking you for finally asking Liz to marry you. By the way, have you bought her a ring yet?"

"Are you in the office pool?"

"Isn't everybody?"

"Tell Margo we'll see her tomorrow," Drake said and hung up.

He wasn't sure if he should be angry or pleased that everyone was so interested in when he gave Liz her ring. But he was relieved that Margo was going to lighten up on him a bit.

Drake checked the Omega Seamaster chronometer Liz had given him and saw that he had time to slip out and visit the jeweler Casey had recommended. If anyone was going to win the office pool, it might as well be his best friend.

Chapter Twenty-Six

PICKING out the perfect ring took longer than Drake thought it would. It was a quarter to five in the afternoon when he slipped into his office and locked the ring in the secure document storage drawer of his credenza.

Before meeting with Casey to discuss what he'd learned about the wetsuit, he decided to call Congressman Bridge first.

"Congressman, did I catch you at a bad time?"

"No, Adam, now's as good a time as any to talk."

"How are you?"

"Tired, depressed, mad as hell. Planning a funeral for your only child is a rotten thing for parents to have to do."

"I can only imagine. When is Mike's funeral?"

"We're delaying it for another week, to give his friends from Stanford to arrange to get here."

"Please let me know the date." Drake said. "Liz and I would like to attend, if that's all right?"

"I would like that. Have you found anything more about how he died?"

"Paul Benning called me a little while ago. He was able to

inspect Mike's wetsuit. It has a puncture where the other windsurfer's left hand struck him."

Drake heard the congressman take a quick deep breath and waited for him to say something.

"Paul told the sheriff in Hood River about the puncture and showed him the video from the eyewitness," Drake continued. "The sheriff is opening a criminal investigation, with the wetsuit as evidence."

"Thank Paul for me. None of this would have happened if he hadn't gone the extra mile."

"I will."

"Have you learned anything else about what Mike was concerned about?"

"We're following up on a couple of things. I'll let you know when we have something solid to report."

"If there's anything I can help with from here, let me know."

Drake said that he would and ended the call.

He sat back and closed his eyes. He'd told Mike's father that he could only imagine what he was feeling, but that wasn't true. He remembered the numbness and fog he'd been in when his wife, Kay, had died. He was useless helping her parents with her funeral arrangements and even now, thinking about it, made him ache inside.

Kay had slipped away from him quickly, dying just months after her aggressive form of breast cancer had been diagnosed. Sitting at her bedside, day after day, holding her hand to try and keep her from leaving him, was the worst time of his life.

Knowing that Matthew Bridge was experiencing the same grief saddened him. It also made him angry. Unlike his wife's death, Michael Bridge's murder could be avenged.

Drake left his office with a deeper resolve to find out who was responsible for the young man's murder.

He stopped at Liz's office and asked if she wanted to come with him to Casey's office.

"Did you think of a way to make Wayne Berryman worry?" she asked.

"I think so. Let's run it by Mike and tell me what you think."

They found the PSS CEO sitting behind his desk face-timing with his wife, Megan.

"Just tell the girls that Dad has an adventure planned for us this weekend," he said, as he waved them in. "I want it to be a surprise."

"Alright, if you're sure you want to do this," Megan said.

"I'm sure. I'll be home in an hour."

Drake sat in one of the black leather chairs in front of Casey's desk and asked, "What sort of adventure?"

"I leased a boat. We're going to explore the San Juan Islands."

"That's great," Liz said.

"He had too much fun driving that yacht in Costa Rica," Drake said. "We might not see him in the office very often this summer."

"Oh, I'll be around. Someone needs to keep an eye on you two. What's the latest on SkySage?"

"That's why we're here," Drake said. "First, Paul Benning inspected the wetsuit. It has a puncture and the sheriff is opening a homicide investigation.

"Second, we identified the guy who stabbed Lancer. His motorcycle is registered to a Hong Kong holding company, just like the black Camaro that followed me from Hood River."

"The same holding company for both vehicles?" Casey asked.

"Probably, we haven't confirmed that yet. Third, we might not have found a China connection to SkySage but we have found one to Berryman Private Equity, LLC. A Hong Kong holding company was the source of the startup money for Berryman's new firm. That holding company has a limited partner. Eighty percent of the limited partner's shares is owned by the Bank of China."

"A Chinese company that answers to the Bank of China that answers to the Chinese Communist Party. What a coincidence."

"My friend at DHS is trying to find out what she can about the limited partner," Liz said. "China's securities laws and regulations aren't as transparent as ours."

"Fourth, there's no China connection to SkySage, other that Wayne Berryman, who sits on the board of directors of SkySage,"

Drake ended with. "I'd like to shake Berryman's tree and see what falls out."

"How?" Casey asked.

"By going to SkySage tomorrow to advise them we're going to recommend an updated security assessment be provided to our client, Microsoft, in light of Michael Bridge's murder," Drake explained.

"The facility security officer at SkySage will do everything he can to make sure the company continues to be "eligible for access" and continue working for Microsoft on the JEDI project. When I start asking if the FSO had any reason to be concerned about Michael's top-secret security clearance, we'll get Berryman's attention when he hears about it."

"How will that get Berryman's attention," Casey asked.

"Because I'm going to ask if the FSO had any knowledge of anyone connected to the company having any foreign contacts or foreign influences that would raise a red flag. When he asks why, I'm going to tell him that Congressman Bridge is going to ask his friend, the president, to conduct a CFIUS review of SkySage and Berryman Private Equity, LLC, because Congressman Bridge suspects China was involved in his son's murder."

"Is Congressman Bridge going to do that?" Liz asked.

Drake turned to her and smiled. "No, but Berryman won't know that when he hears about it."

Chapter Twenty-Seven

SIX HUNDRED AND forty-eight miles south of Seattle, Washington, Francis Zhang stared at the fog surrounding a nearby mountain peak while he waited for a call from his contact in Hong Kong.

He was in the main house of a martial arts and meditation retreat center the Ministry of State Security (MSS) had purchased three years ago. It was used for meeting with its agents in America, who could attend classes and demonstrations there, and be hidden among martial arts students from around the world.

Secluded on a mountain peak on California's Redwood Coast in Humboldt County, the two hundred thirty-acre property included a main house, guest cabins, an indoor training hall and a two-mile fitness trail and obstacle course.

Just four hours from San Francisco by car, it was the perfect place to meet privately with his Premier Travel and Tour guides, especially when one of them needed to be reminded of the consequences of failure.

The call he was waiting for would likely determine the future of his tour guide, Tony Lee.

His caller, Peter Cheng, was the head of HK Capital, LLC, and didn't waste time with idle chatter. His raspy smoker's voice grated on Zhang's ear like a piano needing to be tuned.

"Is our problem solved?"

"Not yet."

"Why is that?"

"The target was guarded by a war dog. He shook off the effects of a taser sooner than could have been anticipated."

"Do you know if there is anything on the tablet that will jeopardize your operation?"

"I don't know. I didn't want to take a chance there might be."

Cheng said softly, "And now this man has been given a reason to think just that."

"Perhaps, but he's done nothing that indicates he knows anything."

"Perhaps you should continue to follow him. Make sure he doesn't interfere any more than he already has."

"What do they want me to do about our Water Dragon?"

"You know how to deal with failure. Is he any use to you now?"

This is what Zhang had expected. The MSS didn't tolerate failure, and that included failure from men in his position as well. Any appearance of weakness on his part, would be viewed as a failure of his leadership.

On the other hand, Tony Lee was the best man he had and already knew where the man lived and worked.

"It would be most efficient to keep our dragon in the water for the time being. He knows the man."

"It's your call. Just make sure it's the right one," Cheng said and ended the call.

Zhang watched the fog drift away from the mountain peak across the small valley. His instructions were clear; keep the lawyer in Seattle from knowing what they were up to.

He saw that his twenty tour guides were running up the fitness trail toward the training gym and he decided to join them. Tony Lee's punishment for failing to secure the tablet didn't need to be terminal, but it needed to be something he would remember.

He left the main house and walked briskly down the cinder trail to the training gym in the cool late afternoon air. At fifteen hundred feet altitude, the temperature dropped quickly when the sun began to set.

The training hall was a long building with a gym at one end and a hardwood floor for practice and competition at the other end. The white walls displayed stylized depictions of great battles fought by Shaolin warrior monks.

Zhang's twenty tour guides were standing around in the gym, wiping sweat from their bodies with clean white towels and drinking from water bottles that had been floating in a tub of ice water.

He walked to the edge of the gym and waited for them to turn toward him. When he had their attention, he turned and walked the length of the training hall to the practice floor.

"Line up facing me," he told them. "I have learned that some of you no longer believe Mr. Lee is as good as he once was. So I will give you the opportunity to find out."

Tony Lee glared at Zhang but said nothing.

"You may use the broad sword, the staff and the twin sticks to challenge him. If anyone defeats him, they will be excused from tomorrow's activities," Zhang said.

Lee turned his back on his challengers and walked to the gym at the other end of the training hall. When he got there, he took his shoes off and did five minutes of warmup; jumping rope, followed by a shortened stretching routine. When he finished preparing for the nineteen matches to come, he stood quietly with his eyes closed.

After a minute, with every eye in the hall watching him, he took three running steps and unleashed a flying tornado kick at the top of the hanging heavy bag. His right foot thudded into the bag ten feet above the floor.

Landing softly on his feet, he turned and walked slowly back to the practice floor.

They came at him one at a time, with their weapon of choice. When Zhang clapped for the next challenger to enter, the defeated comrade would acknowledge his failure with a bow to Lee and retreat to watch the next match.

After thirty minutes watching Lee dispatch every challenger with lightning fast blows and powerful kicks that a Shaolin warrior monk would applaud, Zhang dismissed the humiliated tour guides.

"Why?" Lee asked when Zhang approached him.

"To remind you that failure has consequences. Go cool down and then meet me in my office. The attorney you failed to kill came looking for you at your kung fu studio. Follow him and find out what he's up to."

Chapter Twenty-Eight

A LOW-PRESSURE FRONT was moving south off the coast of Alaska Friday morning, bringing with it dark clouds and the possibility of a wet drive down I-5.

Drake and Liz left Seattle in her Cadillac CT6-V on what promised to be, for Drake, a boring drive. The CT6-V only had six hundred miles on its odometer and was still in break-in mode for another nine hundred miles. No full throttle starts, no exceeding four thousand rpms and constantly varying speeds for three long hours. Five hundred and fifty horsepower wasted and another three hours to endure on the drive back to Seattle.

Fortunately, Drake loved spending time with his fiancé.

Before he left PSS yesterday, he'd made an appointment to meet the Facility Security Officer at SkySage to discuss the need for an updated security assessment. The FSO had asked why one was needed, and Drake had brusquely told the man it was necessary, if SkySage wanted to keep from having its JEDI contract cancelled.

"I didn't mean to scare the guy," Drake said, recounting the conversation to Liz. "His voice was barely audible for the rest of the call. It'll be interesting to see if he tries to handle this on his own or if he mentioned our appointment to anyone else. I wouldn't be surprised to see the CEO sitting in on our meeting."

"Security is his job, but if SkySage loses its security clearance on his watch, he'll never work as a security officer again," Liz said. "You should feel sorry for him."

"We'll see how good a job he's been doing. If he's not involved in any way, I'll make sure he's protected."

"Do Paul and Margo know we're coming to Portland?"

"You would know better than I do," Drake said with a smile.

"How would I know?"

"Because I suspect you get a call from Margo just about every day."

"What makes you think that?"

"Having Paul congratulate me for proposing to you before I told him anything. You wouldn't have mentioned it to Margo, by any chance?"

Liz kept her twinkling eyes on the road ahead and shrugged. "I have felt it necessary to maintain a close relationship with the person who seems to know more about you than anyone else."

"That would be Margo. Do they know we're on our way to Portland?"

"I haven't talked to Margo in days."

"Would you like to see them?"

"I'd love to."

Drake took his phone out and called Margo.

"Are you and Paul available for dinner tonight," he asked.

"Will Liz be with you?"

"Is that a requirement now? What about just having dinner with your old friend and former boss?"

"There's something I want to see and she's the one who can show it to me. Will she be with you?"

Drake knew what Margo was referring to, but he wasn't going to be rushed into giving Liz her engagement ring. He had a plan and Margo wasn't going to force his hand.

"Is Paul there, Margo?"

"Why?"

"Because if you don't want to have dinner with me, maybe he does."

Drake heard the phone go silent. He'd been put on hold. He looked over at Liz, who was frowning at him.

"Something wrong?"

Paul came on the line and kept him from saying something he'd probably regret.

"I'm afraid to ask what you and Margo were talking about," Benning said.

"Ask her. I have a favor to ask. I'm meeting with SkySage this afternoon. I may want you to do some surveillance work, if you're available?"

"When?"

"Probably this weekend."

"Sure, I can handle that."

"Good. I'll call you after my meeting with SkySage."

Drake put his phone away and turned to look at Liz.

"After we see the SkySage FSO, I'd like to swing by the vineyard. If you're okay with a late lunch, we'll pick up something in Dundee and have a picnic on the farm. That sound okay?"

Liz nodded, "Sounds great."

Giving Liz her ring today wasn't what he'd planned, but sometimes you have to be flexible to keep the women in your life happy.

"I've been thinking about ways to make sure that Berryman hears about our recommending a review of our security assessment," Drake said. "When we ask about any foreign contacts that may have raised a red flag, what about asking him about Grace Liu, the Berryman intern?

"She's Chinese American, and technically not a foreign contact. But with the way China has been recruiting university students to spy for them, he should be keeping an eye on her."

"If he hasn't been keeping an eye on her, or wants to keep our recommendation to himself, that might not be enough," Liz said. "What if I ask him where I can find her, that I'd like to meet her?"

"That should get someone's attention other than the FSO's," Drake said. "If you get to meet her, just tell her we need to under-

stand Berryman's intern program for our security assessment review, since she's really not a SkySage
employee."

"And that's true, we do want to know about the intern program. I hope we won't get her fired by questioning the arrangement."

"She'll be okay. Berryman could find a place for her with another of the companies he invests in. If she is at SkySage to spy for China, they won't keep her there for long. They'll hide her until they can get her out of the country."

"Has anyone told SkySage there's evidence Michael Bridge was murdered?" Liz asked.

"We'll let the FSO tell him them that's why we're recommending a review of our security assessment. If I'm right, as soon as the CEO hears it, he'll call Berryman. I want to know how Berryman reacts to the news. That's why I'm going to ask Paul to fly to San Francisco and keep an eye on Berryman."

Chapter Twenty-Nine

AFTER GETTING their visitor badges from the receptionist at SkySage, Drake and Liz were escorted to the FSO's office in the administrative wing of the building.

Drake knew that Tim Benjamin was thirty-seven years old, a 2005 graduate of Boise State University with a Bachelor of Science degree in Business. A former captain in the Idaho National Guard, he'd been deployed to Afghanistan in 2012, where he served as a military intelligence officer.

When Benjamin returned home, he'd completed an online course at Colorado State University to earn a Masters Degree in Management (MiM), while working for an Idaho aerospace company. Using what he'd learned in the Army National Guard, he then completed a course to qualify for work as a Facility Security Officer and went to work for SkySage as its first FSO.

Benjamin was standing in front of his desk waiting for them when they arrived at his office.

Drake shook his hand and introduced himself and Liz.

"I'm Adam Drake, special counsel for Puget Sound Security, and this is Elizabeth Strobel, our vice president for government relations."

Benjamin shook hands with Liz with a concerned look on his face. "Have we met?" he asked her. "You look familiar."

"I don't believe we've met, Mr. Benjamin. You make have seen me at one of the security conferences we hosted when I was at the Department of Homeland Security."

"Call me Tim," he smiled. "You were the Secretary's executive assistant. I thought I recognized you. Please, have a seat."

When they were sitting in front of his desk, Drake spotted an orange and blue Broncos football coffee mug on the credenza behind him.

"Boise State?" Drake asked. "Did you play football?"

"Wide receiver. You?"

"Middle linebacker, Oregon. I hated playing on that blue turf you guys had."

Benjamin laughed. "It's still there. That's pretty much what all of our opponents say."

Drake liked the FSO but it was time to get down to business.

"Tim, Michael Bridge was murdered. That's why we're here."

"We heard he had a heart attack."

"Did you know him?"

"I handled his background investigation and helped him get his security clearance."

"Tim, there's evidence his heart attack was caused by caused by a substance injected into his body" Drake said. "He collided with another windsurfer moments before he collapsed. There's a puncture in his wetsuit where the other windsurfer reached out and touched him."

"Is there a murder investigation?"

"There is. The Hood River County Sheriff has opened the investigation. You'll probably be contacted by his department any day now."

"How does this relate to the security assessment review you mentioned?"

Drake turned to Liz to let her explain.

"Before he died, he told his father, Congressman Matthew

Bridge, that he was concerned about China gaining access to the JEDI project you're working on," Liz explained.

Benjamin shook his head vigorously. "I don't believe that! He'd been through our security training. He knew he was supposed to come to me with any concerns he had."

"Do you have knowledge of any of your employees having foreign contacts or gaining access to classified areas of information without a need to know?" she asked. "Are there any employees with foreign travel that you're aware of, say to China?"

"Not that's been reported to me," Benjamin said. "I do monthly security audits that would reveal foreign travel."

"What about Grace Liu, the intern from Berryman Private Equity, LLC? She's Chinese American. Has she been to China since she started her internship? Has she had any foreign contact with anyone from China, family or relatives, perhaps?"

"Grace was born here, she's a U.S. citizen and her family lives in San Francisco. She hasn't reported any foreign contacts or foreign travel and she does not have access to classified information. She was fully vetted before she began as an intern and Berryman Private Equity, LLC, vetted her as well before she came to us.

"I'd like to meet her," Liz said. "Would you arrange that before we leave today?"

"No problem," Benjamin said and punched a button on the black intercom console on his desk. "Patricia, would you escort Ms. Strobel to the conference room and take Grace Liu in to see her?"

"Yes. Sir," was the reply.

"You mentioned Berryman Private Equity, LLC," Drake said. "Is Grace Liu your employee or Berryman's?"

Benjamin swiveled in his chair from side to side several times before answering. "She's on our payroll, but technically she's Berryman's employee."

"Isn't that a rather strange arrangement?"

"I was told the arrangement was part of the agreement SkySage made with Berryman. Berryman uses the companies he invests in to provide on-the-job experience for interns he's considering for a position with his firm."

Drake studied Benjamin for a moment. The FSO didn't seem to be nervous when asked about the intern program. Maybe because there was nothing to be nervous about.

He wasn't sure that was true for Berryman's firm and decided to see if the FSO felt the same way.

"Did you know that Berryman got his money from a holding company in Hong Kong? Have you investigated Berryman Private Equity, LLC, for the ties it has with China?"

"I'm not sure what you're getting at."

"Wayne Berryman sits on your board of directors," Drake said. "Could he be the reason Michael Bridge was concerned about China?"

Benjamin blinked twice quickly and sat back in his chair. "Are you saying that my duties as a facility security officer should include investigating and doing background checks on our board of directors."

"Don't you think it should?"

"The CEO would have to approve it. I couldn't do it on my own."

"Then perhaps you should recommend it to him and get his approval."

Benjamin crossed his arms over his chest and stared at a spot on the wall over Drake's shoulder.

"You said you're recommending a review of our facility clearance because Michael Bridge was murdered. Are you suggesting that Bridge was murdered because he was concerned that Wayne Berryman is providing China with access to our intellectual property?"

"It's a theory that has to be considered."

"What do you want me to do about it?"

Drake stood and reached across the desk with a business card. "If I were you, I would make sure Wayne Berryman isn't a security risk before we come back to conduct our review. Call me if you have any luck."

Chapter Thirty

DRAKE WAITED for Liz in the reception area while she met with Grace Liu. He was imagining the trepidation FSO Benjamin was feeling about a meeting with the CEO to recommend an investigation of a member of the board of directors, when Liz walked in.

He asked if she was ready for a picnic as they walked arm-in-arm to the door and left the building.

"Ready and hungry," she said. "What are we having?"

"I called the Dundee Bistro and ordered a charcuterie plate and a bottle of pinot gris. We'll pick it up on the way. How was your meeting with Grace Liu?"

"She's smart, a little reserved. She confirmed what the FSO told us. I ask her if she wanted to visit China and she said that with the stories her parents told her, China was the last place she ever wanted to go. I believed her."

Drake held the door of her CT6-V open for her and asked, "Are you ever going to get me drive this?"

"Maybe when she's good and broken in," she smiled.

When he was sitting beside her as she drove out of the SkySage parking lot, she asked, "What did the FSO have to say after I left?"

"He didn't appear to know anything about Berryman's Hong

Kong investor, but he was quick to put two and two together. He asked if I was suggesting that Michael Bridge was murdered because he was concerned about Wayne Berryman providing China access to their intellectual property."

"What did you say?"

"I told him it was a theory that he should investigate."

"Do you think he will?"

"He said the CEO would have to authorize it. I think he'll get his courage up and meet with the CEO. I told him it would look good for him, if he did it before we came back for our review."

"Now we wait."

"Now we wait."

Thirty minutes later driving down OR 219, a route Drake had driven hundreds of times, they stopped at the bistro to pick up his to-go order.

"Is this going to be hard for you?" she asked when he got back in the car.

"What, coming back? No, I love this place, but it's a chapter that had to be closed. I couldn't stay here with you living in Seattle. It'll be good to see how the vineyard's doing."

Liz drove slowly up SW 9th Street and then onto NE Worden Hill Road. They passed vineyards on both sides of the road and four wineries, before they approached the Arterberry Maresh winery and tasting room at the Red Barn.

"That was the first vineyard on Worden Hill Road and the fifth oldest vineyard in the state," Drake pointed out. "They had two ninety-six-point pinot noirs in 2017. Up ahead is the Erath winery. It had Dundee Hills first official wine production in 1972."

Liz slowed down as Worden Road curved north and headed up the hill. Drake's vineyard was on the left with a sliding driveway gate to keep out unwanted visitors and foraging deer.

Drake jumped out and walked to the keypad to open the gate. As it slid back, he stood with his hands on his hips, admiring the rows of newly planted pinot noir vines that crossed the property, from the bottom of the southeast facing slope to the old stone farmhouse at the top.

Each vine in each row was encased in a white grow tube that made him think of rows of white crosses at Arlington Cemetery, in the nation's capital, and the contrast between a beginning and an ending.

Liz drove through the opening and rolled down the window. "It's beautiful, Adam."

"Yes, it is," he said as he started walking up the driveway.

She drove slowly along beside him, knowing that he was thinking about the promise he'd made to his wife before she died that he'd restore the old vineyard.

When they reached the top of the property, Liz parked her car behind the farmhouse while Drake unlocked the back door before returning to get their picnic lunch.

The stone farmhouse was cool and quiet inside. Drake set the charcuterie plate and the bottle of wine on the counter.

"I'm going to open the windows to get some fresh air in here," he said. "Would you mind getting out a couple of plates and wine glasses? I thought we'd picnic on the front porch."

Drake went from room to room opening windows and returned to open the bottle of pinot gris.

Liz had taken their lunch out to the front porch and was waiting there, giving him time to slip out the back door to her car to get a small black velvet box from his laptop shoulder bag.

She was sitting in one of the Adirondack chairs, when he walked out onto the porch and set the bottle of wine on the table between the chairs.

Getting down on a knee in front of her, Drake reached for her left hand with his right hand and took the black box out of his pocket with his left hand.

"Would you do me the honor of wearing this ring, so everyone will know you really did say yes?" he asked.

Liz let him slip the ring on her finger and leaned forward to kiss him.

"You mean so Margo will know tonight that you really did propose to me?" she said softly just before their lips met.

Chapter Thirty-One

JARON CARHLSON, the CEO of SkySage, Inc., stormed back to his office after meeting with his FSO and slammed the door.

The work they were doing for Microsoft had propelled SkySage into an elite group of artificial intelligence companies in the world. Now it could all be flushed down the drain because he'd trusted Wayne Berryman.

"Damn you, Berryman," he said out loud on the way to his desk.

He used his iPhone to call Berryman, instead of the phone on his desk, to preserve what little privacy still existed these days. He didn't need someone in his own company to listen in on what he was going to be talking about.

"I'm sorry," the operator said, "Mr. Berryman had left for the weekend. Would you like to leave him a message?"

"Can you reach him?"

"Mr. Berryman doesn't like to be called when he's out of town at his villa."

"Miss, I really don't give a damn what Wayne likes or doesn't like. If you have his number, you tell him to call Jaron Carhlson immediately. If I learn that you didn't make the call, I'll make sure that he fires you!"

Was Berryman stupid enough to have been involved in killing Michael Bridge? Of course, he was. He was the epitome of entitlement and privilege, using his father's position and wealth to get whatever he wanted. A million-dollar condo in the city, a vineyard estate in Napa, and an investment firm with a fifteen-billion-dollar portfolio.

Was killing a sitting congressman's son, who happened to be a close friend of the President of the United States, what Berryman had meant when he said he'd take care of their problem?

He flinched when his phone started crab-walking across his desk.

"What is it now, Carhlson?" Berryman asked.

"Did you have Michael Bridge killed?"

"What are you talking about? Why would I have him killed?"

"Because he was concerned about you being on our board of directors, with access to JEDI project information that you might share with China."

"Carhlson, listen to me! I did not have anything to do with that boy's death! You told me he had a heart attack. How could I have had anything to do with that? And I would never give anything to China. Just because an investor of mine is a holding company in Hong Kong, it doesn't make me a spy for the Chicoms."

"You better be telling me the truth, Berryman. They've opened a homicide investigation and the company Microsoft used to make sure we got our facility security clearance is coming back to review its assessment of our security. If we lose our facility clearance, we lose our contract with Microsoft and you can kiss your investment goodbye."

———

WAYNE BERRYMAN TOOK the three-hundred-fifty-dollar bottle of 2015 Louis Martini 'Lot 1' Cabernet Sauvignon he'd just opened and a wine glass onto the balcony of his master bedroom.

The sun was setting, casting shadows over the fifty-two acres of his vineyard. It was a sight that put his mind at ease whenever he managed to get out of the city for a weekend. Except for tonight.

He stared into the dark ruby red wine swirling in his glass and wondered if there was really anything to the saying, "in vino veritas", because he needed to know the truth about his foreign investor. Maybe by the time he finished the bottle of cabernet, he would know.

He'd met Peter Cheng on a trip to Hong Kong with his father when he was the governor of California. Cheng had listened patiently one night in the bar of their hotel, over several rounds of scotch, while he discussed his plans for starting his own investment firm when he completed his MBA. Cheng had given him a business card for his holding company, wished him well, and said goodnight.

A week after getting his MBA, Cheng had called him and said he was in town and would he like to take him to dinner. Before Cheng returned to Hong Kong later that week, he had the money to start his own.

Had he made a deal with the devil? Had he neglected the due diligence he'd been taught to do before any entering into any business deal? His father had vouched for Cheng, surely that was all that was required.

There was only one way to find out was to call Cheng.

Hong Kong was fifteen hours ahead of San Francisco, making it eleven in the morning in Hong Kong. Cheng would be in his office, even on a Saturday morning.

"Mr. Berryman, how are things in San Francisco?" Cheng asked.

"Not as well as I would like them to be, I'm afraid."

"I'm sorry to hear that. Is there anything I can do to make things better?"

"I've just learned that a company I invested in may be involved in a criminal investigation," Berryman explained. "One of its employees who was killed was apparently concerned about my involvement with you, as a foreign investor. It's possible the criminal investigation may extend to you and your relationship with the CCP."

"That would be unfortunate, wouldn't it? This investigation could also be interested in knowing if you are involved in economic espionage, I suppose. We both know that you are not, but such an investigation would harm both of our interests. What would you like to do about this?"

"I'm not sure."

"Why don't you let me look into this and see if there's anything I can do. Give me a day or two and we'll talk again.

———

FRANKLIN ZHANG WAS ATTENDING a reception with his wife at the Chinese consulate in San Francisco when his phone vibrated in his pocket. He excused himself and left the room to read the text message.

YOUR BIRD MUST LEAVE ITS NEST AND NOT RETURN. CONFIRM ASAP.

Chapter Thirty-Two

TONY LEE WATCHED the foursome sitting at a sidewalk table at the Coquine restaurant on SE Belmont Street. The attorney and his woman were with another couple, a man and a woman in their fifties. They were having dinner outside despite the cool summer night temperature.

He'd been keeping an eye on the attorney and reporting on his movements since arriving in Portland that morning. After renting a red Subaru WRX at the airport, he'd been able to establish visual contact on the attorney by early afternoon by locating the white Cadillac in the parking lot of SkySage, Inc., in Hillsboro.

Fortunately for him, the woman sitting with the attorney was still driving the white Cadillac with the GPS tracker he'd planted on it, when they took the ferry from Seattle to Bainbridge Island.

Thinking about that night when he'd followed the attorney to the log cabin, reminded him of his throbbing left forearm from being bitten by the man's dog. He was still taking pain pills to manage the pain, and when he got the chance, he vowed to make the man suffer more pain than he was feeling now.

His phone vibrated and he saw that Zhang was calling him.

"Where are you?"

"Sitting in a car watching the attorney having dinner with his woman and another couple."

"Leave them and drive to the address I'll send you. There's a young Chinese woman in an apartment that can't be around to see the sun rise tomorrow. She doesn't date and binge watches sci fi on television all weekend, smoking marijuana and drinking wine. Make it look like suicide. This is a chance to redeem yourself."

"Who is she?"

"Does it matter? Call me when it's finished."

Lee waited for the woman's address to arrive, entered it on the Subaru's GPS navigation screen and pulled away from the curb. He was ten feet away from the attorney as he drove past and resisted the temptation to wave goodbye.

On the twenty-minute drive to Hillsboro on Highway 26, Lee planned the kill. The obvious choice for a young woman living alone, smoking marijuana and drinking wine, was an overdose.

He took the bottle of Oxycontin he'd been prescribed for his forearm lacerations out of his courier bag and saw that it was less than half full. To be safe, he needed more than he had and would need to stop at an all-night pharmacy to refill his prescription.

"Siri, is there an all-night pharmacy in Hillsboro, Oregon?" he asked his smartphone.

"Here's what I found," Siri replied. He saw there was a twenty-four-hour pharmacy in a mall he'd driven past, following the attorney on the way to SkySage, Inc.

Retracing his earlier route, he exited onto NW 185th Avenue and then turned west on NE Evergreen Parkway. He parked the Subaru and thirty minutes later, returned with a full bottle of OxyContin in a generic pill bottle. It had only cost a hundred dollars to keep it from being traceable to his prescription.

Finding the woman's apartment took considerably more time. Orenco Station was a high-density community, with an urban town center and light rail access. The Hillsboro neighborhood was situated in the heart of the Silicon Forest, where Oregon's high-tech companies, like Intel Corporation with its four campuses, were located.

The planned community was designed to be pedestrian-friendly and beginning-the-weekend revelers were everywhere, when he parked two blocks away from the woman's apartment complex. If he was going to gain entrance and not be seen, his approach would have to be later that night.

Lee got out and walked toward her apartment. The complex consisted of two five-story buildings facing each other across a large swimming pool and lawn area that was surrounded by a six-foot tall wrought iron railing. Judging by the street number on the side of the building, the woman's apartment was in the second building.

As he walked past the first building, he saw a woman using a key fob to open the front door of the building and walk inside to the elevator.

Lee walked on past the second building and returned to his car, a plan beginning to take shape in his mind.

Opening his iPhone, he asked Siri for pizza restaurants nearby and found that Schmizza Public House wasn't far away. Five minutes later, he was parked at the curb on Orenco Station Parkway watching for a Grubhub driver to leave the restaurant with a pizza to deliver.

The first Grubhub driver's car was parked right in front of the restaurant and the driver was inside and pulling away before Lee had a chance to act.

The next Grubhub driver to leave with a pizza, however, was parked back down the street behind Lee. When he walked past the red Subaru, Lee slipped out and followed him.

When the driver started fumbling with his keys beside a gray Honda Civic, Lee closed the ten-foot gap between them and delivered a vagus nerve strike to the driver's neck with the heel of his right hand.

Lee kept the unconscious driver from falling, by wrapping his right arm around his body, while grabbing the pizza box with his left hand.

He lowered the driver to the grass along the curb behind a bushy tree, checked to see if anyone had seen him take the driver down, and unlocked the passenger-side door of the Honda with the keys he'd taken from the driver's tightly-clenched fist.

Opening the passenger-side door, he lifted the driver into the seat, carried the pizza box around the car and got behind the wheel.

Lee took the driver's Grubhub hat and stripped off his Grubhub shirt and now had a way in.

The rest was easy. He waited in his car until he saw a couple walking to the front door of the second apartment and ran to slip in behind them.

When the elevator door closed to take them wherever they were going, Lee checked the directory that indicated Grace Liu's apartment, No. 127, was down the hall to the left of the lobby.

Liu opened the door when he knocked and started to say she didn't order pizza, when Lee pushed her back inside and spun her around to apply a gentle choke hold.

When she was positioned on her sofa, slouched down with her head thrown back, Lee forced half of the OxyContin pills down her throat and poured what was left of a glass of Rosé in her mouth.

As her apartment door was closing behind him, he stripped off his surgical gloves in the hallway and left with the pizza box under his arm and the sound of a sci-fi movie playing on the television.

Chapter Thirty-Three

DRAKE AND LIZ were back in Seattle by noon on Saturday. They had decided to get a room in the Portland Marriott Downtown Waterfront Hotel Friday night, instead of driving back to Seattle, after Margo Benning had insisted on ordering champagne to celebrate Liz's ring at dinner after a bottle of wine.

While Liz arranged a tour of homes with her realtor, Drake picked up his car at PSS Headquarters and took the 2:10 pm ferry to Bainbridge Island to check on Lancer.

The veterinarian on duty wasn't the one who had operated on Lancer, but she reassured Drake that Lancer was recuperating nicely.

"We had to keep him sedated for an extra day. He wasn't happy about being here," she explained as she led him to Lancer's room. "He's better now, but you're going to have quite a time keeping him down when he leaves here."

"When will that be?" Drake asked.

"We'll check his stitches tomorrow. He should be ready for checkout Monday."

When she opened the door of the recovery room, Lancer lifted his head when he saw who it was and started to get up.

Drake raised his hand, with his palm toward Lancer, signaling him to stay.

"You've trained him well, I see," the veterinarian said.

Drake knelt and stroked Lancer's head. "How are you doing, Lancer? I'll bet you're sore, aren't you? Good boy, Lancer. Good boy. You rest for another day or so and we'll get you home. I've got to go now. Do what they tell you, Lancer. Good boy, Lancer. Good boy."

He gave Lancer one more pet on his head and stood to leave with his teeth clenched.

There will be a day of reckoning, he promised his dog, *and I pray that it's soon.*

Sitting in his Porsche on the ferry ride back to Seattle, he called Liz. "Are we good to go?"

"She has three areas she wants us to tour to get a better idea of what we're looking for. How was Lancer?"

Drake smiled, knowing that she meant what he was looking for. "He's ready to come home. I think they'll release him Monday. Do you want me to meet you and the realtor somewhere?"

"She's picking us up at my condo when I call her and tell her you're back."

"Your place it is. I've got to go, Liz, someone's calling me."

Drake didn't recognize the caller's number.

"That you Drake?"

"Who's asking?"

"The guy who has to clean up the mess you created for me, Tim Benjamin."

"What mess did I create?"

"Grace Liu is dead," the SkySage FSO said. "She committed suicide last night. Any idea why she would do something like that after meeting with Ms. Strobel?"

"I have no idea. Liz thought Grace Liu wasn't a security risk and believed her about not having unreported foreign contacts or travel. How did she die?"

"Opioid overdose."

"Did she have a prescription for opioids?"

"She didn't report having an opioid prescription, as she was required to," Benjamin said.

"Did she have a random or scheduled drug test?"

"She passed both of them."

"Did you have any reason to believe she might be using drugs?"

"No, but that doesn't mean she wasn't provoked into getting some and killing herself."

Drake considered the possibility for a moment. "An innocent person doesn't kill herself because she didn't report something."

"Are you suggesting she wasn't innocent?"

"I'm saying suicide is an overreaction to being asked routine security questions. Are the police convinced it was a suicide?"

"They say they are," Benjamin said. "The detective who called me did say there was one thing that didn't fit a suicide. The neighbor who called the manager to open her apartment when she didn't answer, was there to go running with her that morning. They found running clothes and shoes laid out on the foot of her bed."

"That doesn't fit," Drake said. "You said you had a mess to clean up. I agree. Two people at SkySage have died in one week under suspicious circumstances. You need to find out if that's a coincidence, or if there connected in some way we don't know about."

"How do I do that? I'm not a detective."

"Would you like to have one to work and find out?"

"I don't have the authority to hire one, if that's what you're suggesting."

"But I do," Drake said. "It'll be part of our review of your security assessment. His name is Paul Benning. I'll have him call you. He's a private investigator on retainer to Puget Sound Security. For the time being, let's keep his involvement to ourselves. No reason to make your CEO think you're going behind his back to investigate Grace Liu's death, when the police aren't."

"All right, but don't get me fired, Drake. If that happens, you'd better be prepared to make room at PSS for a new hire."

"If it comes to that, I'd consider it."

Drake felt the ferry slowing on its approach to the Seattle

terminal and knew there were a couple of things he had to do before he went house hunting.

He needed to call Paul Benning and get him touch with the SkySage FSO.

And he needed to let the president and his father-in-law what he was thinking of doing.

Chapter Thirty-Four

WHEN DRAKE GOT to Liz's condo, he gave her a kiss and told her about the call from the SkySage FSO.

"She didn't appear to be upset when I asked her about any foreign contacts or travel," Liz said.

"I have a feeling she didn't kill herself. The detective who called the FSO said it looked like she was planning to go running with a neighbor the next morning. Her running stuff was laid out on her bed."

"First Michael Bridge and now Grace Liu. Were they seeing each other, by any chance?"

"We need to find out. Before you call your realtor, I'd like to make two calls out on your balcony, it you don't mind?"

"Sure," Liz said and pulled back the sliding balcony door for him.

Benning was happy for Drake's call. "Margo is painting our bedroom. I'm taping it off and could use a break. Thanks again for dinner last night."

"It was worth it. Margo seems to like me again."

Benning chuckled. "As long as you two worked together, I'm surprised you let her get under your skin."

"She has a way."

"Don't I know it. What's on your mind, Adam?"

"Berryman's intern at SkySage committed suicide last night. I'd like you to get in contact with the FSO there, Tim Benjamin. Let him know you're investigating Grace Liu's death on our behalf. See if you agree with the police in Hillsboro that she killed herself. Ask if she was seeing anyone. Start your clock whenever you want, but the sooner the better."

"How about right now?"

"It's your marriage."

"That it is," Benning said. "I guess I should keep it that way, for as long as I can. I'll call you Monday."

Drake leaned against the balcony railing and looked at the Seattle skyline to the west, while he thought about what he wanted to tell the president.

The president asked him to look into the death of Michael Bridge because it was a delicate matter. It involved the death of a friend's son, employed by a defense contractor working on a top-secret DOJ project. The president wanted to help his friend, who couldn't accept that he'd had a heart attack.

The president also wanted to protect the whole JEDI project. An official inquiry that was launched, because of what Michael Bridge had told his father before he died, would call into question the security of the JEDI project, the Pentagon's ability to protect top-secret projects and his administration's ability to keep America safe.

Drake's plan to find and question Wayne Berryman, the son of the president's Secretary of the Treasury and member of his cabinet, could very quickly turn an off-the-books unofficial inquiry into a messy official investigation.

Would the president trust him to do what he was thinking of doing and do it discretely?

Time to find out.

"Mr. President, do you have a minute?" Drake asked when the president answered his call.

"You're never going to call me Ben, are you?"

"Probably not, sir."

"What have you found out?"

"Quite a bit," Drake said. "First, Michael Bridge was murdered. The sheriff in Hood River has opened a homicide investigation."

"Does his father know that?"

"Yes, I told him. We also learned this morning that an intern at SkySage committed suicide last night. The suicide part is questionable and we're looking into it.

"She worked at SkySage, but she was an intern from Wayne Berryman's equity firm. That's what Michael Bridge was looking into, where SkySage got its start up money and why they had an intern program," Drake said.

"Why was Michael Bridge concerned about SkySage's startup money or the intern program?"

"Both, I think, for two reasons," Drake said. "Grace Liu was Chinese American and a recent University of California IT graduate. That's the type of university student we know China likes to recruit for economic espionage.

"The other reason is that Wayne Berryman's private equity fund got its money from a Hong Kong holding company that has a limited partner with eighty percent of its shares owned by the Bank of China. As far as we can tell, Michael Bridge hadn't learned that yet, but that's what he was trying to find out."

"And you think that's what got him killed?"

"It's possible, but it might be more," Drake added. "If China had a spy in place, like this intern, they would have kept her there to get as much information as they could until she was arrested. That's been what they've done in the other economic espionage cases the FBI has prosecuted.

"The fact that Berryman Private Equity, LLC, has a foreign investor isn't enough reason to have Michael Bridge killed either. Having a foreign investor isn't against the law."

"What's the rest of it, then?" the president asked.

"To cover up the fact that Wayne Berryman was loaned fifteen billion dollars from the Bank of China the same year that his father became your Secretary of the Treasury."

Drake waited for the president to say something.

"Unfortunately, enriching family members of high-ranking government officials isn't new," President Ballard acknowledged. "If China loaned Wayne Berryman fifteen billion dollars to get his father to play ball with them, they made a bad investment. Walter Berryman is aggressively negotiating a trade deal for us that doesn't favor China."

"I don't know that influencing Secretary Berryman was the reason his son got the big investment for his firm. I think it had to do with getting Wayne Berryman on the board of directors at SkySage and his interns working there."

"Do you think Wayne Berryman is working for China?"

"I have no way of knowing, but I'd like to find out," Drake answered.

"How do you intend to do that?"

"By showing up at his villa in Napa and asking him."

"When?"

"Tomorrow."

"If you do, I can't authorize your visit."

"I'm not asking you to, Mr. President. I'll be asking him about his foreign investor as part of the security assessment review at SkySage that's been necessitated by the murder of Michael Bridge. I'm just doing what any good security consultant would do for its client."

Drake made two more quick phone calls before returning inside from the balcony of Liz's condo. The first was to ask Mike Casey, who was out on a power cruiser motoring around the San Juan Islands, if he could use the PSS Gulfstream to visit Wayne Berryman in California. The second was to ask Kevin McRoberts to track down where he might find Wayne Berryman.

Then he was off for an afternoon of house hunting with Liz and her realtor.

Chapter Thirty-Five

THE PSS GULFSTREAM G-650 touched down at the Napa County Airport at ten o'clock Sunday morning.

Drake had talked Steve Carson, the PSS pilot, into giving up his Sunday to fly he and Liz to California to talk with Wayne Berryman. To make up for the last-minute assignment, Drake surprised the pilot with a rented Ferrari from Go Rentals to use until they returned to Seattle later in the day.

"That's some perk," Carson said over his shoulder to Drake, as he took the keys from a smiling and attractive female car rental employee.

"I thought a single man, loose in Napa for the day, needed a proper ride," Drake said. "I don't know how long we'll be, Steve. Let's plan on meeting back here at five o'clock."

"Roger that," Carson said and gave him a two-fingered salute.

Drake turned to see Liz leaning against the side of the Audi A5 Cabriolet convertible he'd rented for them to drive. She was dangling the car's keys from her fingers and grinning.

"Do you mind?" she asked.

He faked a frown and said, "I'm sorry Liz, I forgot to list you as a driver when I rented it. Maybe next time."

"You didn't forget, but that's okay. The rental agreement is right here. I'll call and have them add my name. You're not in any hurry, are you?"

Drake shook his head and laughed. "I can see this relationship has a few kinks to work out. Go ahead and call the rental agency. You can drive after we find someplace to have lunch."

Liz tossed him the keys and walked around to the passenger side door. "I know a place. My boyfriend used to take me there."

He smiled as he slid in and got behind the wheel. He started the engine but didn't take the bait, as he opened the GPS navigation screen. "What's the name of this place?"

"The Farm at Carneros."

Liz's selection proved to be all she promised it would be. They pulled into the Carneros Spa and Resort in time for Sunday Brunch at the Farm Restaurant. They ordered Eggs Benedict and agreed they were the best they'd ever eaten and that the Farm's cranberry Mimosas were a tart delight.

Liz drove away in the Audi to search for Wayne Berryman's villa, with her auburn hair flying in the wind and a broad smile on her face.

They found the secluded villa located to the east of the historic two-lane country road known as the Silverado Trail that connected the towns of Napa and Calistoga.

A long gravel driveway curved uphill from the road and then leveled off to run through the center of a vineyard. On the far side of the vineyard was a Mediterranean-style villa.

"Berryman lives well, if this is his vacation home," Drake said.

"I never thought he wouldn't," Liz said as she slowed to let a vineyard worker cross the driveway when he walked out from between a trellised row of grape vines. "He's the entitled son of our ruling class."

"That's cynical."

"I worked in Washington and met too many of them."

She parked the Audi on the circular driveway in front of the villa and looked around. There was a guest house to the right of the villa's main building, with a stone walkway connecting the two. To the left, was an expanse of green lawn with a large above-ground pool and a stone pool house at the far end.

The grounds surrounding the villa were beautifully landscaped with olive trees, lemon and lime trees and red roses.

Drake got out and started toward the front door. "Time to meet Wayne Berryman."

"I think he's out by the pool," Liz said. "I hear voices."

Drake followed her to a stone walkway along the side of the villa that was bordered with purple flowering bushes on the right and delicate pink roses on the left.

They found Wayne Berryman standing behind a young woman in a skimpy bikini, getting ready to roll a bocce ball across the grass. It was obvious that he was admiring more than just the form she used as she leaned forward and released her throw.

Drake clapped when the ball she had thrown knocked Berryman's blue ball away, leaving her red ball an inch away from the pallina they were using as a target.

The sound startled Berryman and he spun around to glare at Drake.

"What the hell are you doing here? This is private property."

Drake walked forward with his hand extended. "We're here to ask you about an intern of yours who just committed suicide. My name is Adam Drake. I'm special counsel for Puget Sound Security. This is Liz Strobel, the vice present for government affairs of our company."

Berryman ignored Drake's outstretched hand. "What does that have to do with me and who the hell is Puget Sound Security?"

"Puget Sound Security is the company that will determine if a company you're invested in gets to keep its security clearance for access to classified information," Drake said. "The intern you placed at SkySage, Inc., is the young woman who committed suicide."

Berryman frowned and checked the thin gold watch on a leather band on his left wrist. "I have company arriving soon. How long will this take?"

"It shouldn't take long," Drake said.

Berryman dismissed the young woman with a wave of his hand and pointed toward an outdoor fireplace beside the pool with chairs and two red sofas around it.

"Over there," he said.

When Drake and Liz were sitting on one of the sofas facing him in one of the chairs, Berryman asked, "Why would this woman's suicide involve the security clearance at SkySage?"

"Her name is Grace Liu," Liz said. "She is Chinese American and she's the second person to die last week who worked for SkySage. I met with her two days ago to ask about her foreign contacts, or recent foreign travel. She committed suicide that night."

"A number of the interns in our program are Chinese. What does that have to do with anything?"

"I think you know why it's important, Berryman," Drake said. "One of your investors in Hong Kong has a limited partner owned largely by the Bank of China the CCP."

Berryman stood and pointed down the driveway to the road. "You can leave now. I've been through all of this before."

Drake stood but Liz stayed seated. "Sit down, Berryman and tell us how you find the people for your intern program."

Chapter Thirty-Six

BERRYMAN REMAINED STANDING, blinking twice, and sat down. His left hand was resting on the left knee, tapping it with his index finger.

"I don't have to tell you anything about the way I conduct my business," he said, "But I will, if it will help SkySage with its security clearance. What do you want to know?"

"What purpose does it serve?" Drake asked. "Grace Liu worked in the finance department at SkySage. How does that benefit your private equity firm?"

"Each intern works at a company I've invested in for two years. With the experience they gain, they're ready to work for me or find work elsewhere. It's purely philanthropic."

"You don't expect us to believe that, do you?" Drake asked. "You're placing people with companies so they'll help you find ones to invest in. They're spying for you, aren't they?"

Berryman smiled. "Everyone participates in industrial espionage, in one way or another, Drake. Surely you know that in your line of work."

"You mean like the kind of industrial espionage China engages in?' Drake asked. "Except then, the industrial espionage is a crime if it's being done for a foreign country."

"You're getting awfully close to slandering me," Drake. "Keep this up and you'll being hearing from my lawyer."

"How do you find your interns?" Liz asked.

"They find me. We have information posted about the opportunity at most of the universities in the Bay area. I look for people with advanced degrees in areas that will land them in the types of companies I invest in."

"Is that the way you found Grace Liu for your intern program?"

"No, she was referred to me by someone. I donate to the arts. An acquaintance who teaches art history at her university gave her my name."

Drake exchanged a look with Liz and said, "One last question. How did you find Hong Kong Capital, LLC? Did you find them, or did they find you?"

Berryman stood quickly and pointed to the road again. "That's it! Get off my property before I call the police."

Drake smiled at him and stood as well. "We'll talk again, I'm sure. But thanks for talking with us today, Wayne. It's been enlightening."

They walked backed to their car down the stone walkway, where Drake stopped to pick a pink rose and hand it to Liz.

"Did you notice his red face after I asked him about the holding company?" Drake asked. "I think I hit a nerve."

"You think China sought him out because they wanted someone who could buy access to American companies for them? Or, because they wanted access to his father through him?"

"Both, I think. With his dad's position, foreign investment in his new firm wasn't going to be thoroughly investigated. If it was, it would be by CFIUS and the Treasury."

Drake held the door of the Audi A5 open for her. As she slid into the seat, she asked, "Did we learn anything or just shake the tree?"

He walked around the rear of the car and got in. "We learned that a professor at one of the universities that supports the arts sent

Grace Liu to him. When we find the art history professor at the university Grace attended, we might find out who's behind this."

WAYNE BERRYMAN POURED himself three fingers of fifteen-year-old scotch from a bottle at the outdoor kitchen bar and sat down to think.

He hoped his reactions to the questions the attorney asked him didn't reveal how shaken he'd been when he heard that his intern was dead.

Peter Cheng said to give him a day or two to see what he could do about their problem at SkySage. Was Grace Liu's death Cheng's doing? If so, did that mean he'd helped to place someone at SkySage who was a spy for China? That's what the attorney was suggesting.

He was also suggesting that Hong Kong Capital may have chosen to help him get his firm started for nefarious reason, which was nonsense. China got nothing in return from him except a nice profit.

That fact didn't seem to register with the attorney, if he even considered it at all. Or the fact that his intern committed suicide, for that matter. She wasn't murdered. What did her death have to do with the facility security clearance at SkySage?

This attorney was barking up the wrong tree and had to be stopped before his investment in SkySage was put at risk. The question was how to do that.

Berryman checked the time and saw that it was two thirty in the afternoon, which made it three thirty in the morning in Hong Kong. Peter Cheng needed to know about his conversation with the attorney but he would have to wait to call him.

The only other thing he could think of doing was to call his father. As the Secretary of the Treasury, he chaired the Committee on Foreign Investment in the U.S. He would know if there was a way to get the attorney to back off from interfering with the facility security clearance at SkySage.

Berryman got up to refill his glass and chuckled as he thought of one way to get the attorney off his game. Nothing interfered with a man's work more that an IRS tax audit. As special counsel for the company he worked for, an IRS field audit of the business would require his attention. Maybe a personal audit of the attorney, as well.

His father had joked about using an IRS audit against political enemies who were threats. It was worth a try to see if his father would do the same thing for his son and Berryman Private Equity, LLC, when they were being threatened.

Chapter Thirty-Seven

DRAKE CAUGHT the 7:55 a.m. ferry to Bainbridge Island Monday morning to bring Lancer home. He was driving Liz's Cadillac CT6-V because it had a rear seat that Lancer would be comfortable on.

The veterinarian had called on their flight back to Seattle the night before to let him know that Lancer was ready to come home. He needed to rest in a familiar place and Liz's condo had seemed the best choice.

Paul Benning called him on the way to Bainbridge Island to report what he'd learned about Grace Liu's death. The Hillsboro Police were comfortable with its conclusion that she was just another person who died from an OxyContin overdose. Benning didn't buy it.

"She had running shoes and outfit laid out at the foot of her bed," Benning said. "Her running partner called her around nine o'clock the night she died. Liu told her she was looking forward to running the next morning. There was a single empty bottle of rosé in her apartment. That's not enough alcohol to cause an accidental overdose from mixing oxy with it.

"But that's not the reason I don't think she committed suicide. Her drug of choice was marijuana and she'd been smoking it. No one the police interviewed said she used any drug other than marijuana which is legal here. But the bottle of OxyContin they found didn't have a prescription label on it. That's the way you'd expect illegal oxy to be packaged if you were using it without a prescription."

"Did you talk with FSO at SkySage?" Drake asked. "What did he think about it not being suicide?"

"He doesn't think she would use illegal drugs like oxy. She was extremely intelligent and focused on her work. She had a B.S. in Computer Science, a minor in Art History at the UC Berkeley. She told me that she was the first person in her family with a university education and would do everything she could to make them proud of her.

"She volunteered to help with the company's blood drive and its United Way program and stayed late if she was ever asked to. He says she was the least likely person at SkySage, in his opinion, to commit suicide."

"She sounds like she's too good to be true," Drake said. "And that makes me a little suspicious of her. Did she have access to classified information?"

"She worked in the finance department. I suppose she had access to their IT system. But SkySage would limit access to classified information to people who needed it for their work and had the required security clearance."

"Ask the FSO is she had that kind of access. Also ask him what he knows about her family. Do they have extended family in China? China is known to force college students to spy for them by threatening their families back in China."

"If she didn't have access, do you still want me to find out about her family?"

"Yes, we'll need as much information as we can find for the security assessment review we're doing."

"I'm on it," Benning said.

Drake started to put his phone away and go to the upper deck of the ferry to a cup of coffee but decided to call Kevin McRoberts at PSS before he did.

"Good morning, Mr. Drake."

"Kevin, I have something I'd like you to do for me. There's a young woman at SkySage that died Saturday night. Her name is Grace Liu. She attended UC Berkeley and had a B.S. in Computer Science. She also minored in Art History. Find out who her Art History professors were."

"All of them?"

"I'm just looking for one," Drake said. "She got her job at SkySage when her art professor and patron of the arts referred her to Wayne Berryman for an intern position. See if there's one that she might have been close to."

"Okay, Mr. Drake, you got it."

Drake waited for the cars in front of him to drive off the ferry and followed them through the Bainbridge Island terminal. He continued on to the northern end of the island, stopping at his cabin to pick up Lancer's bed, his food and his stainless steel food and water bowls.

He waited patiently at the animal hospital, as the veterinarian explained Lancer's current condition and how to care for him at home, before taking him to see his dog.

Lancer's wagging tail signaled that he was not only glad to see him but that he was glad to leave.

Drake knelt and pulled his head close to his own. "Let's get you home, Lancer. Proud of you, partner. You're a warrior, Lancer. You'll be chasing those squirrels in no time."

Lancer didn't need a leash, but Drake put one on him to comply with the hospital's rule and led him slowly out of the animal hospital to Liz's car.

Drake helped Lancer get into the back seat and made sure he was comfortable. As they headed out of the parking lot, Drake turned back to see that Lancer's eyes were closed.

"Don't worry, Lancer," he said under his breath, "I'll find the coward who stabbed you."

Chapter Thirty-Eight

PETER CHENG LEFT Hong Kong and drove to his home on Deep Water Bay on the south shore of Hong Kong Island.

In the middle of his lunch with a wealthy business client, Wayne Berryman had called with information that alarmed him.

Deep Water Bay, called by Forbes the "wealthiest neighborhood in the world", was a place of tranquility where he could be alone and think. His role in what the Ministry of State Security called Operation Yoda was supposed to have been limited.

He'd been instructed to find a way to get Wayne Berryman to take the money he needed to start his private equity firm, with certain conditions. He was also instructed to coordinate with an MSS agent in San Francisco to get a student spy employed at SkySage, the company working on a piece of the Pentagon's JEDI Project.

He'd done what the CCP wanted. He'd also been reminded, more than once, that every Chinese citizen and corporation had a duty to conduct espionage for the state under Beijing's National Intelligence Law.

Since being ordered to work with the MSS his role for the CCP had grown to include making tactical decisions for the operation, like the one he was about to make.

Berryman called to let him know that the attorney from Seattle had ambushed him at his villa, asking questions about whether he'd found his foreign investor in Hong Kong or had the investor found him.

That wasn't a problem. Private capital firms were always looking for new startups to invest in. Meeting Wayne Berryman initially had resulted from a legitimate meeting with his father, the Secretary of the Treasury. Following up with his son after he graduated with his MBA is what any good equity firm would be expected to do.

What had alarmed him was Berryman mentioning that the attorney had also asked about his intern that died and how he had found her for his intern program. Berryman had stupidly mentioned that her Art History professor had introduced her to him.

Her Art History professor was Franklin Zhang's wife who acted as his "spotter" on campus to find and recruit university students to spy for China.

If the attorney from Seattle continued investigating the death of the congressman's son, he would eventually identify and want to talk with Jennifer Chen, Zhang's wife. That could not be allowed to happen.

The problem was how to prevent the attorney from talking with her?

The MSS could have the attorney killed. Zhang had already tried that. Zhang could try again, but a second attempt was risky. Even if they were successful, his death would surely be investigated, just as the congressman's son's death was now being investigated.

He didn't like ordering someone's death, but when it was a matter of someone else facing the consequence for failing the MSS or himself, he would do whatever was necessary to stay alive and remain as the manager of his firm.

And that meant considering the other possibility to keep the attorney from questioning Jennifer Chen; Zhang would have to kill his wife or have someone else do it for him.

Jennifer Chen hadn't known that Zhang was an officer in the

MSS when she married him. When it was revealed to her, she had reluctantly agreed to identify Chinese American students she thought could be persuaded to spy for China.

Zhang had also known when the MSS agreed to allow the marriage that he was putting her at risk. No individual life was more important than the state and each citizen had a duty to make whatever sacrifice was required of them. It was just unfortunate that it was Jennifer Chen's time to make her sacrifice.

By the time he drove his Bentley Continental GT into the garage of his home on Deep Water Bay Road, he'd made up his mind.

It was eleven thirty in the evening in San Francisco when he made the call from the office in his home.

"Yes?" Franklin Zhang asked.

"We have a problem to discuss with you. Wayne Berryman called me half an hour ago. The attorney your man failed to deal with visited him at his villa. He was asked how our little bird came to be his intern. Berryman unfortunately told him her Art History professor had referred her to him."

"That is unfortunate."

"We can't let the attorney get to you through your wife."

Zhang was silent.

"There are two ways to make sure that doesn't happen. I think you know what they are."

"Both of them have risk. The one sure way to keep the attorney from identifying me is to stop him from trying."

"You tried that. The other way has less risk."

"Not necessarily. If Berryman has mentioned my wife, her disappearance would surely lead the police and ultimately the attorney to my door. The safest way is to eliminate the attorney."

"If we fail again, the consequence will be unpleasant for both of us. Can you guarantee success this time?"

"No man can escape a well-designed plan that's backed with all the resources the plan requires. Can you guarantee that I will have whatever resources I may require?"

"You have the manpower. What else will you need," Cheng asked.

"Let me develop a plan and I'll let you know."

"Do it quickly. We don't know how fast the attorney will move on this."

"I will call you tomorrow."

Cheng ended the call and walked to the picture window that provided a view of people walking on the beach below and swimming in Deep Water Bay.

The waters of the bay were protected by shark nets. Swimming there was one of his favorite things but he wondered how much longer it would be a pleasure he would get to enjoy.

Chapter Thirty-Nine

WHEN LANCER WAS RESTING in Liz's condo, Drake returned to PSS headquarters. Liz was looking at something on the screen of her laptop and writing on a legal pad when he knocked on her door.

"Lancer's okay and resting at the moment," Drake said. "Keeping him that way is going to be a chore.

"That's a good sign, isn't it?"

"It is, if we don't let him overdo it. I need to find someone to check in on him when we're gone. Do you think your neighbor would be willing to help out?"

"She loves Lancer. I'll ask her. Did you have a chance to talk with your father-in-law?" she asked, waving him in.

"I called him at the terminal while I waited to board the ferry. He's getting together with the committee to see what they can dig up on Secretary Berryman and his China connections. He said there are whispers in Washington that he's promising future concessions the U.S. might be willing to make with China, if they play ball in the short term. He's not telling anyone what he's promising, he says, because he doesn't want anything leaked to the press. Some people are very uncomfortable with that."

"Berryman's not stupid enough to go behind the president's back on something this important."

"Senator Hazelton thinks Berryman wants to be president. Maybe he's promising concessions he'll make when he's the man in the White House."

Liz shook her head. "He can't win a national election. He's not well known outside of California and he's not that loved even there."

"He's getting a lot of exposure as the president's lead negotiator. With enough money, anything's possible, I guess."

Liz put her pen down and leaned back in her chair. "Has Paul gotten back to you about the intern's suicide?"

Drake sat down in the chair in front of her desk and said, "He doesn't believe it was suicide. The FSO at SkySage doesn't either. Paul's running a complete background check on Grace Liu. I asked Kevin to find out who her Art History professor was at Berkeley."

"Do you think Berryman was telling us the truth."

He shrugged his shoulders. "I think he was, but we'll see." He started to stand up, when his phone vibrated in his pocket.

He didn't recognize the number and pointed to his office. "I'll take this and be right back."

"Yes," he said.

"Is this Mr. Drake?" the caller said.

"It is."

"You visited our Kung fu studio and said you were interested in taking lessons from our Wushu Sanda instructor. He's available to interview you tonight at eight o'clock at our studio, if you can make it."

"Excellent," Drake said.

"Mr. Lee just wants to make sure you're prepared to devote the time it requires to learn Wushu Sanda. You won't be starting lessons tonight."

"I understand. I'll be there at eight o'clock."

When he returned to Liz's office, she saw the grin on his face and asked, "Who was that?"

"The woman we met at the Kung fu studio. She wanted to know if I wanted to meet with their Wushu Sanda instructor tonight."

"I don't have a good feeling about this, Adam. If he is the one who came after us on Bainbridge, meeting him on his turf at night doesn't sound like a great idea."

"He doesn't know that we know who he is."

"Oh, he knows. We went to his place looking for him."

"We were going to meet him sometime. This gives us a chance to be prepared when we do. Besides, I won't be alone."

"He might not be alone either."

"It won't matter. I know a couple of guys who will be interested in Wushu Sanda. They'll be going with me."

"Guys? Don't even think of leaving me out of this!"

"Relax, Liz, I wasn't thinking of leaving you out. We'll go with a band of brothers for backup. We'll go in, like we did the first time, just you and me. The others will be there, if we need them."

"And who is this band of brothers?"

"I thought I'd ask Dan Norris, Marco Morales and a couple of guys in Dan's Hostage Rescue Team. I think a former FBI HRT commander, the best Ranger recon soldier the Army ever had, and two former special ops guys can handle whatever this guy has in mind."

"Are you going to tell Mike what you're planning?"

"I'm in charge of special projects. Helping Congressman Bridge and the president is a special project. Besides, if I tell him, he'll want to come along. I'd like for him sit this one out."

"He's not going to like it."

"I know, but it's in his best interest. He's not as young as he used to be."

"Neither are you! He definitely won't like it, if he hears that's the reason you didn't include him."

Drake smiled and winked. "Only two people know that's my reason and they're sitting in this room. Should I be worried?"

"That's not the real reason, is it?"

Drake knew she remembered that Mike's wife, Megan, still blamed him for her husband being paralyzed and in a hospital in

San Francisco. The international model and assassin had been in his hotel to kill him and Mike had gotten in her way.

Since then, he had tried to keep his friend out of the action, as often as possible. He hadn't succeeded in keeping his Delta Force partner behind his desk, but he'd tried. He hoped Megan understood that.

Drake tilted his head back and took a deep breath. "We both know Mike can take care of himself, but I promised Megan I wouldn't let him take unnecessary risks. I'm the one who has a score to settle this time.. If I want to keep the promise I made to Megan, I need to keep him running the company and letting me do what I signed on for as often as possible.

"The Special Projects division of Puget Sound Security was my idea. When your former boss, the Secretary of Homeland Security, and my father-in-law asked me to be a trouble shooter for the government, from time to time, I agreed. Mike supported the idea.

"He's backed me with the full resources of PSS, without hesitation, every time I've asked him to. He knows we can't pass up this opportunity to find out why Michael Bridge was killed. And he knows they made this personal when they hurt Lancer. So he might grumble about not being asked to go with us, but he knows how hard I try to keep my promise to Megan. He'll be okay."

"He's your best friend and you know him better than I do," Liz said. "I just hope you're right about this."

Chapter Forty

AFTER DRAKE MET WITH MARCO, Dan and the two Hostage Rescue Team members, Drake and Liz left PSS Headquarters for his meeting at the Kung fu studio. They stopped to pick up a takeout order from Liz's favorite sushi restaurant and rushed home to get ready.

Their reserve force would meet at headquarters at seven o'clock and leave immediately to recon the studio. Marco would go in on foot and find locations from where the team, in two PSS SUV's, could rapidly respond to a call from Drake or Liz.

The call for backup would be communicated over a two-way system that consisted of a nearly invisible earbud and a neck-loop coil that Drake and Liz would wear under their shirts. The neck-loop coil served as a covert microphone that converted sounds within a twenty perimeter and would be monitored by a team member for each of them.

Drake and Liz were dressing casually, with body armor concealed under loose-fitting clothes, along with their favorite handguns; a Kimber Ultra Carry II for him and a Glock 19 for her.

The backup team would be wearing blue jackets over body armor, jeans and a blue cap with white lettering that identified them as PSS security. They had debated about the weaponry they would carry and decided on tactical flashlights, twenty-one-inch expandable batons carried in belt scabbards and Sig Sauer P320 X5 Legion pistols.

If they encountered the unexpected, each SUV would also carry a Mossberg 930 SPX tactical shotgun and a Sig MPX Copperhead submachine gun. While it was unlikely that they would need the two guns, the recent street violence in the city made it a prudent choice.

The four men from PSS were in position by seven thirty that evening. The Kung fu studio was housed in one of two buildings on the south side of NE 72nd Street. The two buildings were separated by a small parking lot. A brew pub was on the other side of the parking lot, facing the back of a Chinese restaurant across the parking lot that was next to the Kung fu studio.

To the west of the studio, across Green Lake Drive North that intersected with NE 72nd Street, was a wooded area and park. To have sight lines to the studio and the west and east along NE 72nd Street, Marco Morales stationed the two SUV's at each end of the street.

At five minutes to eight o'clock, Drake and Liz were two blocks from the Kung fu studio when Dan Norris called Drake.

"Comm check, Adam," Norris said.

"Good here," Drake said.

"Comm check, Liz," Norris said.

"Hear you fine, Dan," Liz said.

Norris called Drake back.

"We're parked at each end of the street across from the studio. No sign of anyone at the studio. Marco's closest to you, in the brew pub across the parking lot. Open parking spaces in front of the studio."

"Roger that," Drake responded.

A minute later, Drake turned onto NE 72nd Street from East Green Lake Drive North in his Porsche Cayman. In the middle of the street, he turned right again and entered the small parking lot.

There were no cars parked in front of the Kung fu studio, but all the parking spaces in front of the brew pub were occupied.

Drake pulled into an empty parking space in front of the studio and turned off the engine. They sat silently, listening for any noise coming from the studio. The only noise they heard aside from traffic noise was the ticking sound of the Porsche's engine cooling.

"Wait a minute before you go in," Norris told Drake. "Two groups moving toward us. One is coming from the park across the way and the other from down the street from the east. It looks like our peaceful protestors slash Antifa."

"Roger that," Drake replied, and took his Kimber out of the holster on his belt.

"Dan says there might be trouble headed our way," he told Liz. "Antifa protestors."

"We're trapped in here, if they are," Liz said.

"Dan, if they're coming from both ends of this street, we're getting out and taking cover," Drake said and opened his car door.

Liz followed him out and drew her weapon.

"Black jackets with hoods, ski masks and goggles, gloves and shields," Norris reported as the mobs closed on them. "Steel pipes and...oh, shit! Four guys up front with machetes."

Morales came running across the parking lot and got behind the Porsche with Drake and Liz. "This little thing car of yours isn't much cover. Let's move to those dumpsters behind the restaurant."

The three of them turned and sprinted to three dumpsters lined up outside a back door of the restaurant.

On the way, Drake called out to Norris. "Sit rep?"

"Twenty-five to thirty of them gathering across from your parking lot. You should be able to see them now."

"We were set up," Drake declared.

"Looks like it. How do you want to handle this?"

"Let's see if we can persuade them to leave. You're behind them. Wait for my signal and then come out with the Mossberg and Copperhead. Let them see you. We'll come toward you down each side of the parking lot. When they see they're caught in a crossfire, they might leave."

"If they don't?"

"We defend ourselves. Give us a minute to get in place."

Drake turned to Marco and Liz. "Marco, cross the parking lot and move down the side of the building. Get as close as you can to the street. We'll do the same on this side."

"Roger that," Morales said. "Keep an eye on the door of the studio, in case your guy's in there."

"If this is his doing, he won't be here. Move out," Drake said and ran out from behind the dumpster.

Chapter Forty-One

DRAKE AND LIZ ducked into the studio's front door alcove, twenty-five feet from the street.

The mob was crowding around four men, listening to one of them who appeared to be the leader. The four in the center of the mob were the ones with the machetes, not steel pipes.

In unison, the mob turned and faced the parking lot, searching for them.

"Dan," Drake said softly, "All of the PSS vehicles have Viper alarm and security systems. When I turn trigger mine, do the same with both SUVs. The alarms and flashing lights will let them know you're behind them and we're not alone."

"Roger that," Norris said.

Drake took his phone out of his pocket and hit the Viper SmartKey app and triggered his car's alarm. The 120-decibel siren blared and the lights in the Porsche started flashing. A moment later, the sirens and lights in both PSS SUVs across the street joined in.

Men spun around and saw Norris holding a tactical shotgun beside his SUV. Down the street, two other men were standing beside another SUV holding weapons in their hands.

Before the mob had time to decide what they were going to do,

Drake stepped out of the alcove and signaled both SUVs to shut their alarms off. He waited until they did and then shut off the Porsche's alarm.

When the the mob turned back and stared at him, Drake lowered his pistol to his side and said, "Leave and no one will get hurt."

"Don't think so," the leader stepped forward and said. "You're outnumbered."

"And you're surrounded by men with enough firepower to make sure that doesn't matter," Drake said calmly.

The sound of sirens growing louder in the distance appeared to agitate the mob, waiting for the leader to make his decision. When he hesitated, the mob began moving away from him and the other three men with the machetes.

With the wailing sirens closing on them from two directions, the mob broke up and fled down the street toward the cover of the nearby park.

Drake watched as the leader in the street held a phone to his ear. He nodded once, said something to the other men and then ran after the disappearing mob.

Liz stepped out of the alcove and stood beside him. "Whoever called them off must have been watching."

"I'm thinking the same thing," Drake said and scanned the roofline and the dark windows of the buildings across the street for a lookout.

Morales ran across the parking lot and said, "That was weird. I thought we might have a little fun tonight."

"Not sure it would have been fun," Drake said. "The four guys with the machetes are ex-military, the way they waited for the order to retreat."

Dan Norris jogged across the street and joined them. "Want us to stick around?"

"No," Drake said. "You four leave. We'll stick around and talk to the police. We'll meet you back at headquarters."

"See you there," Norris said and jogged back to his SUV with Morales at his side.

Drake turned around and studied the front of the Kung fu studio. Hanging from the top of the alcove was a single wireless CCTV camera.

He pointed to the camera. "He could be inside watching. When the police leave, we're going in."

Two dark blue Ford Police Interceptors arrived with sirens wailing and lights flashing and blocked off the street at each end of the block. When they saw the street empty and Drake and Liz standing on the sidewalk waving at them, they killed the lights and sirens.

One officer from each Interceptor got out and walked toward them.

"Are you two all right?" Officer Montgomery asked. "A mob of protestors were reported harassing you."

"We're fine, officer," Drake said. "They took off running to the park over there when I set off the alarm siren in my car."

"Were any of them armed?" the second officer asked.

"Four of them had machetes," Liz said. "Most of the rest had steel pipes and shields."

"How long ago did they run off?" Officer Montgomery asked.

"Three or four minutes ago," Drake said.

"If you're sure you're all right, we'll see if we can catch up with them," Officer Montgomery said.

"We're fine," Liz assured him.

They watched the two men jog to their Interceptors, get in and drive away.

"Let's see if Mr. Kung fu is here," Drake said and walked back to the front door alcove of the studio.

The front door had a gray metal frame with upper and lower glass-pane window, separated by a black metal bar at waist height. At the end of the bar was a Schlage numbered keypad door lock.

"Now what?" Liz asked.

Drake stepped back and studied the door. Even if he had a black light and ultraviolet googles to see fingerprints on the keypad, he didn't have time to figure out the sequence of numbers and unlock the door.

Both sides of the alcove, however, consisted of floor to ceiling pane glass panels.

Drake went to his car parked in front of the studio and retrieved the red emergency hammer and seat belt cutter tool he kept inside.

"You sure you want to do this?" Liz asked.

"Do I have a choice? I have to know if he's in there?"

A voice from the outdoor security camera above the door startled them.

"Don't waste your time. I'm not in there."

"That's a shame," Drake said. "I looked forward to meeting you."

"You will, but not today."

"You can count on it, Lee."

Chapter Forty-Two

FRANCIS ZHANG RECEIVED the news stoically that his plan had failed; the attorney was still alive.

He had been too clever, trying to hide his four men in an Antifa mob to conceal their identity. For all the bravado of the black clad anarchists, they had cut and run and left his men exposed and outnumbered.

They could have charged in and killed the attorney, of course, but Lee had made the right choice by calling them off and preventing them from being killed or captured. It wouldn't have taken the authorities long to find out they were trained soldiers in the U.S. illegally, posing as tour guides for his travel agency.

Zhang left his study with a Cohiba Robustos Supremos cigar in hand and went out to the rear deck of his house to smoke. He brought a supply of the Cuban cigars home with him, whenever he traveled to China, but he only smoked one when his wife was out of the house.

She was out tonight, attending a lecture at the university. It saddened him to think about living alone, even if it meant smoking a cigar whenever he wanted to, but he knew it was inevitable. He'd been given a chance to avoid having his wife killed, but he had failed.

Peter Cheng had made it clear they would not be allowed to fail in the greater mission, penetrating the Pentagon's JEDI project, and getting the AI being developed for it at SkySage.

He stood at the railing of the rear deck and stared at the lights of the city in the distance. His wife's death would have to be viewed as a random act of violence, somewhere on the university campus, something consistent with other acts of violence occurring there.

Rapes were common there, he knew. He had often cautioned Jennifer to be careful when she was on campus, especially at night. But the victims usually survived, albeit scarred for life.

Muggings happened frequently, most often in darkened public areas, with severe injury occurring infrequently.

Then Zhang remembered a Cal student had been killed walking near the campus earlier in the year. He'd been shot in the head from behind, at close range. No suspects had been identified, according to news reports, and the investigation was ongoing.

A copycat murder on the campus was a possibility.

It would be a quick death and Jennifer wouldn't have to suffer.

Zhang stayed out on the deck for another twenty minutes to finish his cigar before returning to his study. It was nine thirty in the evening, and he knew where the man was who would be ordered to murder of his wife.

Tony Lee was in Seattle, where he'd been monitoring the failed attempt to kill the attorney from his apartment. The WIFI security camera at the Kung fu studio could be accessed remotely and there had been no need for Lee to be at the studio.

Lee answered Zhang's call and was heard telling someone he'd be right back, that he'd take the call in the other room, and continue watching the movie.

"Your alibi?" Zhang asked.

"Yes."

"Fly here tomorrow. I have something I want you to do for me."

"All right."

"Let me know when you'll arrive. I'll come and get you."

"Anything else?"

"No, that's all."

He would have liked to tell Lee to bring the 3D printed pistol he'd been issued, but Zhang knew the plastic pistols could be detected by TSA airport security, if they were paying attention.

Lee would have to use one of the ghost guns he kept in the small armory at his travel agency for his "tour guides".

He wondered how Lee would react when he was told to kill his wife. He'd been trained as an assassin, according to his file MSS he was given when Lee had been assigned to him, but he'd never been ordered to kill someone before.

Zhang had. It had been part of his final training in the MSS before he'd been sent to America. She had been a young dissident at Tsinghua University in Beijing.

There is an expression in China, "Kill the chicken before the monkey" meaning target the weak to frighten the strong and the many. The woman had been too vocal in her opposition to the party's leaders on campus and needed to be silenced. Her death was a warning to the other students that there was not going to be another Tiananmen Square for the world to see.

Zhang had cut her throat in broad daylight, as she walked across the campus, and been left to bleed out for all to see.

His wife's murder would have to be less spectacular, but without her killer being identified. If Lee was identified, he would be returned to China before he could be arrested. His fate there would likely be the same as his wife's, a bullet in the back of his head.

Or, if Lee was close to being arrested, Zhang would be ordered to make sure that he never was.

There were things that had to be done, and done quickly, before the damned attorney came to San Francisco to find Grace Liu's Art History professor. This time his plan had to succeed

Chapter Forty-Three

THE MORNING after the encounter with the Antifa mob Drake's day started badly. He found a note on his desk at PSS headquarters that summoned him to a meeting in the CEO's office.

Liz was right, I should have told his Mike about being invited to an interview at the Kung fu studio, he thought on his way down the hall to Casey's office.

Casey was on the phone when Drake opened the door of his office and was waved in.

"How bad is it?" he heard Casey ask.

Drake sat down and studied his friend's face for a sign of what was to come.

"When do we have to be there?" Casey continued with a frown on his face. "Both of us, the day after tomorrow? That can't be right."

Casey was shaking his head as he listened and then slammed the phone down. "You may have crossed the line this time."

"How's that?"

"I received a notification of an audit from the IRS. They're conducting an office audit of the company about the fringe benefits we provide you. I had my tax attorney, Martin Olsen, call to find out what this is all about. He was told a special audit team has been dispatched from IRS headquarters to conduct the audit. They'll be here Thursday and require our presence at eight o'clock sharp, in their office."

"How did I cross the line?" Drake asked.

"I think we can guess. Martin said his IRS friend remarked that we must have ruffled someone's feathers at the Treasury. That's where the order for the office audit originated."

"Oh, I see. I visit Wayne Berryman on his vineyard. Two days later his father, the Secretary of the Treasury, orders an IRS audit of my fringe benefits."

"Martin said you should be prepared to be audited personally, going back a minimum of three years, maybe for a maximum of six years."

"What an abuse of power," Drake said, standing up to leave. "This will involve my law practice in Portland, the vineyard, everything! I'll be tied up for years with this nonsense!"

"Maybe that's what this is all about, keeping you distracted and off Wayne Berryman's back for a while."

Drake turned in the doorway and smiled, "That's not going to happen. I'll request a postponement of the audit. I'll need time to retain legal representation. You should do the same. And just so you know, I'm moving back to Oregon. It's too far away from the Seattle IRS office, so I need a change of venue."

"Are you really moving back to Oregon?"

Drake winked. "The lease on the cabin on Bainbridge is only for six months. Where else would I go?"

On the way back to his office at the other end of the hallway, Drake stopped to tell Liz about the IRS audit.

"Why would his father order an audit, if he wasn't trying to keep us from looking into his son's involvement with China?" Liz asked.

"Or maybe his own involvement with China," Drake offered. "FYI, Mike didn't say anything about last night."

"That doesn't mean he didn't hear about it."

"No, it doesn't. But it might mean he doesn't have a problem with what we did."

Liz pointed her finger at Drake. "You mean what you did. I just went along to make sure you didn't get in trouble."

"Right," Drake said and closed her door.

In his office next door, he called his tax attorney in Portland, Oregon, and asked him to call the Seattle IRS office to request a postponement and change of venue.

His next call was to his father-in-law's senate office to talk with the senator.

"Adam, I was getting ready to call you," Senator Hazelton said. "Are you calling about Secretary Berryman?"

"Yes, for a couple of reasons. I'm pretty sure he's responsible for an IRS audit I just learned about."

"Your own?"

"PSS at this time, regarding my fringe benefits. I'm sure a personal audit will follow."

"Why do you think Berryman's responsible?"

"Two days ago, I paid his son a visit at his villa in Napa. He didn't like being questioned about an intern who was recently murdered. She was his intern at SkySage."

"And you think his son asked him to send an audit your way because of that?"

"I do. A friend in the Seattle IRS office told Mike Casey's tax attorney the order for the audit originated in the Treasury Department, not in the IRS."

"I'm surprised Walter Berryman would do something like that. Maybe I shouldn't be," Senator Hazelton said. "I met with our friends on the committee over the weekend. There are some in the intelligence community who are concerned he's too friendly with a member of the Chinese team negotiating the new trade deal."

"Do we know who he is?"

"You mean who she is."

"Is he compromised?"

"He might be, although he's known to play around from time to time. So far, all we have are rumors about a couple of dinners where they appeared to be overly friendly."

"Is there anything involving any financial entanglement?" Drake asked.

"Only his son's foreign investor in Hong Kong. There's nothing to show Berryman's benefiting from it in any way."

'No, not at this time, anyway. Do you think I should let the president know about the coincidence of this IRS audit and my questioning Berryman's son?"

"That's your call. From what I hear, there's an obvious tension between the president and the secretary during cabinet meetings. It might not serve a purpose right now, with the China trade deal the president wants wrapped up as quickly as possible."

"Understood, I'll hold off. Say hello to Mom for me."

"I will Adam. Good luck with the IRS. I wish I could help."

"I do too."

Chapter Forty-Four

FRANCIS ZHANG PULLED to the curb at Terminal Two of the San Francisco International Airport and waited for Tony Lee outside Alaska Airlines' baggage claim exit doors.

Lee had used the Inflight Internet service to text him thirty minutes before he was due to land, giving him ample time to drive to the airport to pick up his agent.

He flashed his lights twice when Lee walked out pulling a black rolling duffel bag. He watched his young Water Dragon move through the crowd that parted before him, as if it sensed his predatory nature.

Zhang popped the trunk of his gray Mercedes E 450 sedan and waited for Lee to stow his duffel bag and sit beside him.

"I reserved a room for you at the Double Tree at the Berkeley Marina in the name of Tom Leman. The keys for a silver Chevrolet Malibu are in the blue courier bag you saw in the trunk, along with a CZ-P10C pistol and suppressor.

"My wife is giving a lecture tonight at the Doe Memorial Library at seven o'clock. I've traced her likely route from the library to the Great China restaurant nearby, where she's meeting me at nine o'clock.

"I will send you a photo of her, from this morning when she left for work, wearing the clothes she'll be wearing tonight. The map has red dots marking the places where I think you'll have the best chances of not being seen, with escape routes if you need one.

"This needs to look like a copycat murder, like one that happened on campus several months ago. Come from behind, shoot her once in the head and walk away.

"Tomorrow, come to the travel agency at nine o'clock in the morning. We'll turn in your rental car, go to another car rental agency to get you another. Stay out of sight for a day or so and then call me.

"Do you understand what you are to do?"

Lee turned to look at Zhang and asked, "I understand what you want me to do. I don't understand why?"

Zhang didn't turn to look Lee's way and said, "The man you failed to kill the other night may come to see her. I can't allow that to happen."

"It was your plan that failed, not mine."

"That's enough! You have your orders. Follow them."

Zhang didn't speak again until they arrived at Lee's hotel. "If anything goes wrong, you cannot be arrested. Do you understand?"

Lee opened his door without answering and went to the rear of the Mercedes to get his duffel bag and blue courier bag. He stood there, waiting for the trunk to open. When it didn't, he saw that Zhang was watching him in the rearview mirror.

"Yes, I understand," Lee said loudly enough for Zhang to hear

I hope you do, Zhang thought, watching Lee walk away pulling his rolling duffel bag with the courier bag hanging from his shoulder.

LEE LOWERED the window shades in his hotel room and opened the courier bag on the bed.

He was familiar with the pistol. It was a Chinese clone of the Czech CZ P-10C that had been upgraded with a threaded barrel for a suppressor. He'd trained with it on the mountain-top retreat with Zhang's other tour guides.

The suppressor was a SilencerCo Osprey 9, reputed to be the quietest of the 9mm silencers. He hadn't used this suppressor, but at the close range he expected to be firing from, it wouldn't matter.

He picked up the magazine and slid out a bullet. A 9mm +P Speer hollow-point. One would to the job, but it was nice to have sixteen other rounds in case he needed them.

With eleven hours to kill before Jennifer Chen left the library to meet her husband for dinner, Lee put the Malibu keyless remote fob in his pocket and left the room with the courier bag to explore the university campus.

In light mid-morning traffic, it took Lee twenty minutes to drive east on University and Hearst Avenues to the UC Berkeley campus. He parked the Malibu in the Stadium Parking garage and followed the campus map app he'd downloaded to the Doe Memorial Library.

The massive old library building was located south of an open green space called the Memorial Glade. He stopped at the bottom of the steps of the main entrance to take a picture with his phone, before walking west along a path and turning south on the sidewalk along Sather Road.

The west side of the library was lined with trees that provided a half a dozen places where he could wait for Zhang's wife to pass by without being seen.

He continued walking south and found the Sather Gate, with its ornate bronze grillwork spanning across two pillars, providing a choke point and cover along the path Zhang said his wife would likely follow.

Lee continued past the gate and turned to take a picture back along the path to the library he'd just covered. Tonight, would be a walk in the park, as Americans liked to say.

His stomach growled and reminded him he needed to find a place to eat before returning to his hotel room, until it was time for his second assassination on foreign soil.

Chapter Forty-Five

WHEN DRAKE'S tax attorney confirmed that his IRS office audit was postponed, he flew to San Francisco Wednesday morning on Alaska Airlines to talk with Jennifer Chen, Grace Liu's art history professor.

Tony Lee had cancelled his Wushu Sanda classes for the rest of the month and the Kung fu studio didn't know if he would be returning as an instructor. That left the professor as his last source of information for learning how Grace Liu became an intern at SkySage, Inc.

Drake walked into the Doe Memorial Library at one o'clock in the afternoon, after landing at the San Francisco International Airport and taking a cab over the Bay Bridge to the University of California campus.

He stood in line at the reference desk and asked for directions to the Art History Department, when it was his turn.

The attendant frowned and took off her black horn rim glasses. "Are you a reporter?"

"No, why do you ask?"

"The Art History Department is closed for the day. You'll have to come back tomorrow."

"That doesn't explain why you asked me if I'm a reporter."

"Because I've been told to direct all reporters to the Chancellor's Office, where the Director of Public Affairs is handling inquiries about Professor Chen."

"I'm sorry, I don't understand?"

The student standing behind Drake leaned forward and said, "Professor Chen was murdered last night, that's why."

"Professor Jennifer Chen?" Drake asked.

"Yes, Professor Jennifer Chen," the student said impatiently. "Here, take my copy of the Daily Californian, if you want to read about it."

Drake took the newspaper and stepped out of the line to read it. A bold black headline reported, **"PROFFESOR GUNNED DOWN OUTSIDE LIBRARY!"**

He picked up a map of the library on the reference desk and found there was a reading room with current periodicals on the second floor.

When he had copies of the San Francisco Chronicle and San Francisco Examiner in hand, to add to the information in the student newspaper story, he sat down in a comfortable chair in the reading room and began reading.

Jennifer Chen, 47 years old, had been found the night before at Sather Gate, bleeding from a single gunshot to the back of her head. She was pronounced dead by EMT paramedics, who arrived on scene at eight forty-five that evening. Pacific Daylight Time. There were no witnesses to the murder and no one had reported hearing the shot.

Professor Chen was survived by her husband, Francis Zhang, the owner of Premier Travel and Tours in San Francisco, and by her parents, Arthur and Nian Chen, of Los Angeles, California.

The three newspapers' stories repeated the same facts provided by the Berkeley Police Department at its news conference, with one additional fact that was mentioned in the Daily Californian. A month before Professor Chen's murder, a student had been killed in similar fashion, less than a mile from campus. The student reporter wondered if Professor Chen's murder was committed by the same person, or if it was a copycat murder.

Drake folded the newspapers on his lap and sat back in his chair. Was it a matter of bad timing, or just a coincidence, that the Art History professor who introduced Grace Liu to Wayne Berryman was murdered the night before he flew to San Francisco?

He knew better than to believe it was a coincidence. No one knew he was coming to San Francisco, except Liz and Mike Casey, because he'd made his reservation online.

That thought made him think of Professor Chen's husband, who owned a travel agency. Wayne Berryman said he was introduced to Grace Liu by an Art History professor at some art function. Jennifer Chen was that art history professor and might have been accompanied by her husband at the time.

Was it worth his time to talk with the husband? Even it was, the day after his wife was murdered was not the time to ask for a meeting.

Drake returned the two newspapers to the newspaper rack and left the library. Not knowing what he might learn from Professor Chen, he hadn't bought a two-way ticket to return to Seattle or reserved a room for the night.

Shrugging his shoulders, he decided to stay for the night. Tomorrow, if it felt right, he'd visit the Art History Department and ask about Grace Liu, the professor's student. He was focusing on the professor, who had introduced Liu to Wayne Berryman, but It might have been Grace Liu who had arranged the introduction.

If she had, what was she involved with on campus? Was she a campus activist, a vocal supporter of China and its rulers? Was she one of the Chinese/American students that China used to spy in the U.S., by threatening family members still living in China to get them to cooperate?

Drake was walking along with a group of students, not paying attention to where he was going, when he noticed yellow tape up ahead, marking off a crime scene. It was under the ornate bronze metalwork supported by two columns he recognized as the iconic Sather Gate on the Berkeley campus.

It was where he'd read that they found Professor Chen's body the night before.

Standing inside the taped-off crime scene were three men, two of them in uniforms and one in plain clothes, a detective in the San Francisco Police Department he knew by the name of Cabrillo.

Drake stopped outside the taped off area and waited for Detective Cabrillo to look his way.

Detective Cabrillo finally did and walked over.

"What's a San Francisco detective doing in Berkeley?" Drake asked.

"Trying to solve a murder, what else?" Cabrillo said and held out his hand. "What brings you here, business?"

"I flew down this morning to talk with Professor Chen. I was a day late."

"Really," the detective said with raised eyebrows. "Then we need to talk."

Chapter Forty-Six

ON THE WAY to Detective Cabrillo's unmarked gray Ford, he asked Drake if he was hungry.

"Sure, are you buying lunch?"

"On my lowly cop's salary? I thought I'd let a rich lawyer buy today."

Cabrillo motioned for Drake to get into his Crown Vic sedan. "There's a great Cajun place over on Shattuck Avenue. It's not far, but I'm not leaving my car here on campus."

"Sounds like you know your way around this side of the Bay," Drake said.

"I grew up in Oakland. My mother lives here and I have friends at both Oakland and Berkeley Police Departments. So, yeah, I get over here from time to time."

Cabrillo skirted the campus, drove the short distance to Shattuck Avenue and parked in front of Angeline's Louisiana Kitchen.

Drake watched him jump out and lead the way to an outside patio. "Have you ever had alligator?" Cabrillo asked over his shoulder.

"I've eaten some strange things in the Middle East, but I've never had alligator."

"Try it sometime."

Drake looked at his menu when they were seated and asked, "What else is good?"

"Everything's good. I like the Voo Doo Shrimp and the Shrimp Creole."

When two shrimp orders were in the way to the kitchen and they were waiting for a server to bring them glasses of iced tea, Cabrillo started in. "Why did you come to Berkeley, Drake?"

"Like I said, to talk with Professor Chen?"

"About what?"

"She introduced one of her students to someone involved in a security clearance we're reviewing."

"What kind of security clearance?"

"The kind of clearance that allows a defense contractor to work on top secret projects for the Pentagon."

Drake could see the wheels whirling behind Cabrillo's eyes.

"Is that connected to her murder in some way?"

"I don't know."

"Is it possible?"

Drake waited for the server to set their glasses of iced tea down and leave before asking, "How are you involved with Professor Chen's murder?"

"A student was killed a month ago, like the professor; a single shot to the back of the head. Berkeley PD called me."

"Why were you involved with a murder in Berkeley?"

"They suspected the kid of selling drugs on campus. His supplier is a dealer in San Francisco I've dealt with. Berkeley wanted to know if I thought there was a connection."

"Is there?"

"I don't think so. Both victims were killed with 9mm bullets, but that's the only connection. There's nothing to indicate that Professor Chen was using or selling drugs. You never answered my question."

"It's possible."

"You think it's possible that this security clearance you're reviewing is connected to the professor's murder? How?"

Drake drummed his fingers of his left hand on the table and

considered how much he wanted to tell Detective Cabrillo. The last thing he wanted was a Detective from San Francisco investigating the murder of Grace Liu, Wayne Berryman's intern at SkySage.

If Cabrillo turned up something, however, that might get him closer to finding Michael Bridge's killer, he needed to know about it.

"Before I answer that, tell me how you're officially involved with the murder of Professor Chen."

"I'm not, unless there's some evidence that she was killed by my drug dealer."

"If I tell you that it might be connected to a murder of a person who was employed by the defense contractor that's a client of Puget Sound Security, the company I work for, and that murder is already under investigation in another jurisdiction, would you feel obligated to share that information with Berkeley PD?"

"If I thought it would benefit my friends on Berkeley PD, yes."

"Would you be willing to let me decide if I thought it would benefit Berkeley's investigation, before you shared the information with them. I was a senior prosecutor in the Portland DA's office for five years. I've made decisions like this before, when it involved overlapping investigations."

Cabrillo looked at Drake for a long minute before answering. "You played straight with me when you were working on that matter for Energy Integrated Solutions, Inc. a couple of years ago. I might be willing to let you make that decision, if you tell me everything."

Drake reached across the table and shook hands with Detective Cabrillo.

"The student of Professor's Chen I mentioned was murdered last weekend. Her murder and one other triggered the security clearance of our client, the defense contractor. I came here to ask Professor Chen about her student and if she knew anything that might indicate that she was spying for China."

Cabrillo lowered his voice. "You're saying this possibly involves espionage and China? Are you working with the FBI on this?"

"Not yet."

"Why not?"

"Two reasons. I don't have any evidence that China is involved.

Telling the FBI what I think is going on would put the spotlight on some very important people. The other reason is that the president has asked me not to."

"The president, or the president of this defense contractor?"

"The president."

Cabrillo shook his head and said, "Man oh man, if all this is true, you're involved in something way above my pay grade."

Drake took out his phone and pulled up his contacts. He held his phone up to Cabrillo, offering to show him the private number for the president of the United States.

Cabrillo's eyes opened wide.

"I'll call him if you want. I need you to trust me on this."

Cabrillo waved off the the phone Drake was holding up. "How can I help?"

"I'd like to pay my respects to Professor Chen's husband, maybe he knows something that can help me. Would you like to come along?"

Chapter Forty-Seven

ON THE DRIVE west from Berkeley, Detective Cabrillo called his station and got the address for Professor Chen's home.

He was impressed. "Fourteenth Avenue in the Sunset District. That's expensive real estate up there."

"What does Mr. Chen do for a living?" Drake asked.

"Her husband is one Francis Zhang. She used her maiden name. He owns a travel agency in China Town. I looked him up when Berkeley PD asked for my help."

"Do you know anything about him?"

"He was waiting to have dinner with he after her lecture, at a restaurant near the campus when she was shot. Berkeley PD confirmed his alibi, so I didn't get anything more than that."

Drake a mental note to learn more about Francis Zhang. Another China connection.

Professor Chen's home was near the top of a hilltop with views to the city to the east and the ocean to the west. It was a square box of a house, two-stories tall with a red tiled roof, sand-colored stucco exterior with white-trimmed windows and door.

Cabrillo parked on the expanse of red brick stamped concrete in front of the house and turned off the engine.

"Do you want me to introduce you and tell him why we're here?" Cabrillo asked.

"Thanks, that might make him a little more willing to talk to me," Drake agreed.

They got out and walked to the front door, with the detective leading the way and ringing the doorbell.

Drake was ready to leave after waiting for several minutes, when the door was opened by a middle-aged Chinese woman wearing a white housekeeping uniform.

"May I help you," she asked.

"We're sorry to intrude at a time like this, but is Mr. Zhang home?" Detective Cabrillo asked, holding out his police ID.

"No, sorry, he is not here."

"Do you know where we might find him? It is important."

"I do not know," she said. "He was gone when I arrive. Might try at office."

"His travel agency?" Cabrillo asked.

"Yes."

"Thank you." Cabrillo gave her his business card. "Would you give this to him and asked him to call me, when it's convenient?"

The housekeeper took the business card, bowed and closed the door.

When they were back in Cabrillo's car, Drake asked, "Did you get a good look inside? Ultra-modern interior design, million-dollar view from the deck of the city below, not a trace of Asian décor. It wasn't what I expected."

Cabrillo laughed. "You don't get out much, do you?"

"I guess not," Drake said.

"I've got time, if you want to see if he's at his travel agency?"

"It's worth a try, although I can't imagine he's working the day after his wife was murdered."

Cabrillo shook his head. "You'd be amazed at the way people react when someone they love is murdered."

Drake remembered how he reacted when he learned that his mother had been killed by a drunk driver. He was a freshman at the University of Oregon, when he'd been called out of class by the assistant head football coach. He'd listened, without hearing, how his mother had been in an accident, that she had volunteered to work a late shift for a friend at the hospital and was on her way home when it happened.

He missed school for a week. When he went back to class and football practice he'd felt empty and numb, but he'd kept his emotions hidden. A year later, on the anniversary of her death, was when he cried for the first time.

"I saw a little of it when I was a prosecutor in Portland," Drake said. "I'm glad I don't see it as often as you do."

"It never gets easier."

Neither man spoke again, as Cabrillo navigated his way through the streets of San Francisco. When they reached the intersection of Clay Street and Stockton Street in China Town, Cabrillo turned right and parked at the curb in the middle of the block.

"That's Zhang's travel agency," Cabrillo said and pointed across the street.

Premier Travel and Tours appeared to be open for business. Squeezed in between a Chinese market and a tea house on the ground level, it was a small ordinary store front. A large red awning with gold Chinese characters running from end to end across it announced its business.

After dodging traffic and crossing the street, a faint smell of incense greeted them as Cabrillo held the door open for Drake to enter the travel agency.

Posters of travel attractions in China lined one wall, above racks of tour brochures and a collection of paperback books about China. On the opposite wall were posters advertising tours to famous tourist attractions on the west coast of America.

In the middle of the room were three desks, with young Chinese women sitting at each, wearing telephone headsets and talking to clients.

Drake and Cabrillo stood in front of the first desk and waited for the travel agent to finish talking and look up.

"May I help you?" she asked.

"I'm Detective Cabrillo and this is Mr. Drake," Cabrillo said. "We'd like to speak with Mr. Zhang, if he's here."

The woman frowned and said, "This isn't a good time. Can you come back?"

"I appreciate that it isn't a good time," Cabrillo said, "But I do need to speak with him. I'll only need a few minutes."

"Is this about his wife?"

"Yes."

"I'll go see if he's available," she said and walked to the back of the agency and knocked on the door. Windows on each side of the door had their shades drawn and the room appeared to be dark inside.

The young woman opened the door and spoke to someone before returning to them.

"Mr. Zhang has to leave in a few minutes but will meet with you until then. Follow me, please."

Chapter Forty-Eight

FRANCIS ZHANG REMAINED seated when Drake and Cabrillo walked in. He was sitting behind a dark wood desk with a brass banker's lamp on it.

Incense was burning in a ceramic bowl, surrounded by burning red candles on a lamp stand to his left.

The flickering flame of the candles provided the only light in the room and reflected off the lenses of his oval wire-rimmed glasses. Drake couldn't see behind the lenses to know which of the two of them Zhang was looking at:

"Mr. Zhang, my name is John Cabrillo. I'm a Detective from the San Francisco Police Department. This is Mr. Drake. We're sorry for your loss, sir."

Zhang held out his hand. "May I see your badge, Mr. Cabrillo?"

Cabrillo opened badge holder and handed it to him. When it was handed back, Zhang asked, "Mr. Drake, are you also with the police?"

"No, I'm here on another matter. Detective Cabrillo let me come with him so we wouldn't have to bother you on two occasions with questions."

"I assume Detective Cabrillo is here to ask me questions about my wife's murder. What questions do you have, if you're not with the police?"

"I work for a company that's reviewing the security clearance for a client of ours," Drake explained. "One of its employees was murdered. I'm trying to find out if her death had anything to do with the work she was doing.

"She was one of your wife's students. I'm told that your wife helped her get her position with our client. I flew down from Seattle this morning to ask your wife what she could tell me about her student and what role she played in her being hired."

"I'm sure my wife helped many of her students find employment" Zhang said. "Why is that important to you?"

"It may not be important," Drake admitted. "Did your wife know a person by the name of Wayne Berryman? She introduced her student to him, and he hired her to work as an intern for my client."

"I don't know Wayne Berryman, Mr. Drake and I'm afraid I need to leave now."

Zhang stood and handed Cabrillo his business card. "If there's anything you think I might know that I haven't already told the officers from the Berkeley police department, please call me."

Cabrillo said that he would and thanked him for talking with them, as Zhang walked around to open the door and usher them out.

When he passed between them, Drake could feel the hostility radiating from the man.

When they were out on the sidewalk, Drake said to Cabrillo, "I think he knows Wayne Berryman."

"Why?"

"Because he would know his father, Walter Berryman. He didn't ask if I meant your former governor, Walter Berryman. He denied knowing Wayne Berryman too quickly."

"That's reading a lot into his saying he didn't know him."

"Maybe, but there's an easy way to find out if he's lying. Do we have time to find Wayne Berryman's firm and ask him if he knows Francis Zhang?"

"Let me find where his office is located and I'll tell you," Cabrillo said and took his phone out. "Yeah, we have time. It's on the twenty-fourth floor of the Transamerica Pyramid building, a couple of blocks east of here."

Fifteen minutes later, they were in an elevator on its way up to Berryman Private Equity, LLC.

The first thing Drake noticed as they approached the receptionist sitting behind a curved black marble reception desk, was how she was dressed. She was beautiful and obviously proud of voluptuous body, judging by the way she was displaying it.

Before they stopped in front of her desk, another similarly dressed attractive woman walked into the reception area with a flower display and placed it on the reception desk.

If Wayne Berryman was the person doing the hiring, it was apparent that he had an eye for beautiful women.

"May I help you, gentlemen," the receptionist asked.

"We'd like to speak to Mr. Berryman," Drake said.

"Do you have an appointment?"

"No, we don't," Cabrillo said and held out an opened black leather badge holder for her to see.

"I'll see if he's available," she said and pushed a button on her console. "There are two gentlemen her to see Mr. Berryman. One of them is a police detective. Does he have time to speak to them?"

She listened for a moment and said, "He's on a long-distance call. Do you have time to wait?"

"How long are we talking about?" Cabrillo asked. "If it's more convenient, he could come down to the station to talk to me."

"I'm sure that won't be necessary. It shouldn't be long. Would you like coffee while you wait?"

Cabrillo and Drake said yes.

Their coffees arrived before they had time to be seated. Drake walked with his to the floor-to-ceiling windows that looked down at the waterfront and the bay. The view was as good as the coffee.

"I think I could work here," Cabrillo said when he joined Drake at the windows.

"Because of the pay or the benefits?" Drake asked.

Cabrillo laughed. "The pay, of course. I'm married."

"Of course."

After being offered another cup of coffee and rifling through copies of the *Wall Street Journal*, *Barron's* and *The Economist* for half an hour, they were told Mr. Berryman apologized for keeping them waiting but had to leave. A wildfire was threatening his vineyard and his vineyard manager wanted him there.

"That's BS," Drake told Cabrillo in the elevator. "I have a vineyard. As often as they have wildfires in Napa, his vineyard manager would know what needed to be done. He skipped out to avoid talking with us."

"Are you going to stick around and try to talk with him?" Cabrillo asked.

"Not tonight. I have a private investigator who's finding out everything he can about Francis Zhang before I come back. I think the answers I'm looking for are here in San Francisco."

Chapter Forty-Nine

AFTER DETECTIVE CABRILLO dropped Drake off in front of Terminal Two at San Francisco's International Airport, Drake took the elevator to the Alaska Airlines' Lounge on the fourth floor with an hour to kill before departure.

His visit to San Francisco wasn't a complete bust, but he still didn't know who helped Grace Liu become an intern at SkySage. It could have been Jennifer Chen, her art history professor, but he didn't get a chance to find out before she was murdered.

The professor's husband, Francis Zhang, had denied knowing Wayne Berryman, but Drake didn't believe him. He also didn't believe Berryman had to suddenly leave his office because a wildfire was threatening his vineyard in Napa.

When he was back in his office, the first thing he was going to do was find out who and what Francis Zhang was. There was more to the man than his being the owner of a travel agency, who just happened to conduct tours to China. Drake was sure of it.

He showed his membership card to the receptionist and went straight to the bar to order a glass of Knob Creek Bourbon. The fireplace room in the Lounge offered the highest view of the bay and the runways of any of the lounges at SFO and he was going to enjoy the bourbon and the view and think about where to go from here.

He didn't know who killed Congressman Bridge's son, although he had an idea.

He didn't know who came after him on Bainbridge Island and stabbed his dog, but he had an idea it was the kung fu instructor, Tony Lee.

And he didn't know who killed the intern, Grace Liu, and made it look like a suicide, or killed her art history professor, but he didn't think it was a coincidence they died less than a week apart.

Drake watched a United Airlines Boeing 737-900 accelerate down the runway and wondered about its destination. The last time he'd flown United Airlines, before switching to Alaska Airlines, had been a nonstop flight to Dulles International Airport in Washington, D.C. to visit Senator Hazelton and his mother-in-law.

Seeing the United Airline's flight take off, reminded him that he hadn't had time to call the senator to find out what he'd learned about Secretary Berryman. Now was as good a time as any to find out.

"Good evening, senator," he said when his father-in-law answered. "Do you have time to talk?"

"I'm in my study with the door closed, listening to a recording of another committee's hearing yesterday. A break from the arguing I'm listening to will lower my blood pressure. What's on your mind?"

"I'm in San Francisco, following up on a lead I thought might answer a few questions about security at SkySage. The person I wanted to talk with was murdered before I had a chance to meet with her. She was Chinese American, married to a foreign-born Chinese travel agent. China keeps turning up everywhere. What have you been able to find out about Secretary Berryman and China?"

"A couple of interesting things. When he was running for governor in two of his campaigns in California, he received a healthy campaign donation each time from a nonprofit organization that advocated for more H-1B visas. Nothing surprising about that, with high-tech firms crying every year for more H-1B visas for high-skilled workers, especially coming from China. But when he was vetted for his cabinet position, it was discovered the nonprofit get its money from Hong Kong private equity firm with links to a Chinese bank run by the CCP."

"That private equity firm wouldn't happen to be HK Capital, LLC, by some chance?"

"Yes, the same private equity firm that provided the startup money for his son's firm."

"Why wasn't there a CFIUS review of the foreign investor when his son's firm was investing in SkySage?"

"Care to venture a guess?"

Drake thought for a moment. "The CFIUS committee is run out of the Treasury Department. Did the Secretary block the review?"

"He didn't directly. His staff determined that the foreign investment was a passive minority investment allowed by the "safe harbor" exception to CFIUS jurisdiction."

"Sure, CFIUS only has jurisdiction to review transactions that could result in control of U.S. business by a foreign person that could impact U.S. national security. But what about a U.S. citizen with links to a foreign power that acquires an equity investment with control in a U.S. business that has access to top secret information?"

"It's legal because it's an investment by one U.S. firm in another U.S. firm."

"That needs to be changed," Drake said. "Doesn't the president have the authority to review Berryman Private Equity, LLC's investment in SkySage?"

"He does, but not without evidence of foreign control of a person engaged in interstate commerce in the U.S."

"Like Wayne Berryman?"

"Like Wayne Berryman."

"Can you get someone to look into this?"

"We have, you," Senator Hazelton said. "The president won't authorize anything until we have evidence of a threat to national security. At this point, we have a couple of murders that may or may not be connected to anything having to do with China."

"There connected, I just haven't been able to prove it. Did I mention that I'm being audited by the IRS, a full field audit?"

"When did this happen?"

"Two days after I questioned Wayne Berryman at his villa in Napa."

"Do you have reason to think his father had anything to do with it?"

"It's too much of a coincidence," Drake said.

"I'll see what I can find out. What are you doing next? Anything I can help you with?"

"Not at the moment, thanks."

"Be careful, Adam," Senator Hazelton cautioned. "If China's involved and responsible for these murders, it's an escalation of their efforts to steal our intellectual property."

"Understood, Sir. Tell Mom I'm going to come see you both, as soon as I can. There's something I need to talk with you about."

"Can you give me a hint? You know she's not going to rest until she knows what it's about."

"Just tell her it's something I hope will make her happy."

Chapter Fifty

AFTER PETER CHENG called Wayne Berryman and told him to get out of his office and not to talk with Adam Drake, he called Francis Zhang back.

"That was close," he told Zhang. "They were waiting to see him when you called me"

"He doesn't know me," Zhang said. "You had to be the one to warn him."

"We have two problems, then. You're not sure we can trust him, and I agree. And we need to replace our source at SkySage. They do not want to lose the opportunity to get JEDI."

"We don't have time to get another intern in at SkySage."

"Then we need someone else. What about Berryman?" Cheng asked.

"I thought you said he was worried he was being used to spy for us?" Will he agree to do that now?"

"Not by choice."

"How then?"

"By not giving him a choice."

"What are they thinking?"

"I instructed him to go to his villa," Cheng said. "When he goes there, he always takes that young secretary with him. If something were to happen to her while she's there, we'll make think he's responsible. When we help him cover it up, he will do what we tell him to do."

"That might work on television I'm not sure he'll fall for it," Zhang worried.

"We'll make sure there's evidence that's convincing. Berryman isn't the kind of man that's willing to risk going to jail."

"We'll have to move quickly, before this attorney gets back to him and he screws it up again.".

"He's on his way to his villa now. How quickly can you get someone there?"

"By tonight," Zhang said.

"If his mistress is there, do it. I'll fly over and be the one to tell him what we want from him tomorrow morning."

"If he doesn't agree, what then?"

"Tell your man to hang around. They police might find two dead bodies, not just one."

ZHANG DIDN'T WASTE time making the necessary arrangements.

He called Tony Lee. "Where are you?"

"Here."

"Where's here?"

"A Gentlemen's Club, why?"

Music was pumping in the background. "Come to my office. I have something that needs to be done tonight."

Zhang turned on his desk lamp and took a small black notebook out of the desk's drawer. It contained a list of sources the MSS considered reliable for supplies he might need for covert operations in America.

He thumbed through the notebook for the page listing pharmaceutical supplies and found the private phone number of a pharmacist in China Town he'd used in the past.

"I'd like to place an order for delivery," he said.

"What is it you need?"
"Enough Ketamine for two people."
"On your account or cash on delivery?"
"Cash on delivery. How soon may I expect it?"
"Is thirty minutes soon enough?"
"That will be fine, thank you."
"Happy to be of service."

The pharmaceutical ketamine would be delivered in liquid form that Tony Lee could mix with alcohol for Berryman and his mistress. The challenge would be to get the drug mixed and served to Berryman.

Zhang went to a closed bookcase behind his desk and got out his laptop. On it was the MSS file on Berryman, complete with his drinking and sexual habits. Listed on his preference for alcohol was his favorite, a bottle of Macallan 18 Year Sherry Oak Scotch Whiskey.

As a gift from his Hong Kong investor, Peter Cheng, and to be delivered and served by Tony Lee, Berryman would be salivating by the time it was mixed with a healthy dose of ketamine and given to him and his guest to drink.

Zhang looked at his watch and saw that he had enough time to go home and change his clothes before meeting Tony Lee.

He was invited to attend a reception at the Chinese consulate for China's ambassador who was stopping in San Francisco on his way to Washington, D.C., to meet with the president.

The invitation, he knew, was in recognition of the work he was doing for his country. His wife had received the invitation, to protect his cover, but he knew who it was meant for.

Someone traveling with the ambassador would seek him out for a report on Project Yoda and, of course, he would reassure them that everything was proceeding as planned.

If everything went as planned tonight, it would be. It if didn't, he would find another way to make sure their mission didn't fail.

The problem was that they were running out of time. If the security review at SkySage denied the company its facility clearance for the work it was doing for Microsoft, it was over.

Which meant they only had one choice; make sure the facility clearance wasn't denied.

He knew one person who could work to make sure the facility clearance wasn't denied. And he was confident he knew what it would cost to buy the SkySage FSO's cooperation.

When SkySage, Inc. had initially been identified as a research company working on artificial intelligence for U.S. space programs, intelligence agents working as "spotters" started looking for potential targets for recruitment. The targets were examined for ways they might be encouraged to spy for China. The usual motives were considered; money, ideology, coercion and ego. They had been particularly successful in recruiting Westerners with cash.

The FSO at SkySage didn't have a financial problem that could be exploited, but he did have a taste for expensive things. They found a "Some Day" list on the laptop he kept in his apartment that included a twenty-nine-foot Defiance tuna fishing boat, a GMC Sierra 2500 diesel pickup, an Airstream International travel trailer and a long-list of expensive hunting rifles.

The total cost of items on his dream list would require the next ten years of his entire salary at SkySage to purchase. Unless he could find a source that would pay him a healthy consulting fee for his advice on defense contractor security, for example.

Chapter Fifty-One

TONY LEE TURNED off the Silverado Trail and drove slowly through the vineyard to Berryman's villa. He was wearing a pair of black slacks, a white shirt and black tie to look like a runner making a delivery from the city.

He parked in front of the Mediterranean-style villa and walked under a massive stone portico to the front door. When he rang the doorbell, he stepped back and stood with a gold-wrapped box held out in both hands.

He remained motionless for five minutes before he saw through the etched panes in the door a man coming to answer the doorbell. Wayne Berryman was wearing a swimming suit and had a white towel wrapped around his neck.

When he opened the door, Lee introduced himself. "Mr. Berryman, Mr. Peter Cheng wants you to have this bottle of your favorite Scotch, as an invitation to meet him tomorrow for lunch. He apologizes for not letting you know that he is coming to San Francisco, but that it is important that you meet with him."

Berryman frowned and asked, "Did he say where he wants to meet for lunch?"

"He said he would let you choose the place and time."

"I don't have his mobile number. How can I reach him?"

"He said as soon as he knows that you're available to meet, he will call you."

"How's he supposed to know that I'm available? I just said I don't know his number."

"I'm sorry, I must apologize. Mr. Berryman asked me to pour you a glass of your favorite Scotch and send him a picture of you toasting him with it. That will let him know that his last-minute invitation hasn't offended you."

Berryman stared at him, and then shook his head and waved him. "Cheng is a strange man. This isn't necessary, but if that's what he wants, let's see if he remembers what my favorite Scotch is."

Lee followed Berryman through the house out to the pool area. At the far end of the long rectangular pool was a covered eating area and bar. In the pool was a beautiful young woman swimming laps in the nude.

As they walked past where she was swimming, Berryman dropped his towel at the pool's edge and continued walking to the outdoor bar.

When they got there, Berryman sat on one of the bar stools at the counter and said, "Let's see what you've brought me. Tumblers are under the bar."

Lee walked behind the bar and slipped one the ketamine vials out of his pocket as he bent down to get a tumbler. In his peripheral vision, he saw that Berryman wasn't paying any attention to him as he unwrapped his gift.

"Son of a gun!" Berryman exclaimed. "He did remember. A bottle of Macallan Eighteen Year Sherry Oak."

"Allow me to pour for you, sir," Lee said. "Would the lady like a taste of your Scotch?"

When Berryman swiveled on his bar stool and called to ask his mistress if she wanted a taste of the best Scotch in the world, as she was coming up the steps toward them drying her hair with his towel, Lee emptied the vial in Berryman's tumbler and then quickly filled it with the Scotch.

"I don't like Scotch, but I would have another glass of wine," she said and smiled at their new bartender, who was having a hard time reminding himself that she was off limits later that night.

Berryman raised his tumbler to admire the dark amber color of the Scotch and then held the tumbler and inhaled deeply. Satisfied, he took a sip and waited before swallowing. He took another sip and smiled.

"That's a treat," he said.

Lee took out his phone and said, "If you'd like Mr. Cheng to know you're available for lunch, raise your glass and I'll send him your picture."

"Come here, honey," he told his mistress and pulled her close. "Let's show him I really enjoyed his gift."

Lee took the picture of Berryman raising his glass in toast in his left hand, with his right arm wrapped around his topless mistress. "I'll get that off to Mr. Cheng right away. What wine would the lady like me to pour for her?"

"The chardonnay in the wine cooler is fine," she said and waited for him to pour it for her. Lee selected a wine glass from the ceiling rack and leaned down to take a bottle of chardonnay out of the wine refrigerator under the bar. Before he stood and handed it to her, he emptied her dose of ketamine in the glass.

She took a sip, nodded approvingly and turned to walked away. Both men were given a tantalizing look at her swaying hips on her way to the pool-side lounge for her coverup.

"Beautiful, isn't she?" Berryman asked, then finished off his Scotch and held out his tumbler for a refill.

"Yes, sir, she surely is."

Lee took his time refilling the tumbler. A heavy dose of ketamine can take as long as thirty minutes to take effect, or as little as five minutes. The dose each of them had in their drinks was supposed to take effect in less than ten minutes, according to Zhang.

To stay around until it did, Lee asked Berryman what made the Scotch he was drinking so special.

"For me, it's smooth and easy to drink. I could try and impress you with a spiel about its nose, how it tastes of dried figs and apricots dipped in chocolate and such, but the truth is, it's a status symbol that I've acquired a taste for."

"It's expensive then?"

"I really don't … I expect… it."

Berryman had a confused look on his face and shook his head, blinking as he tried to focus his eyes. He looked at Lee and tried to speak, slurring his words.

Lee smiled and shrugged his shoulders, "Sorry, I didn't understand that."

Berryman grabbed across the bar to keep from falling, knocking his tumbler to the tiled floor and slid off his bar stool.

"Miss," he yelled. "I think he's had a heart attack."

"Oh God," she screamed and stumbled towards them, weaving from side to side until she dropped to her knees, holding her wine glass out to keep from dropping it.

Lee ignored her when she crumbled to her side and came around the bar to kneel beside Berryman. "Mr. Cheng's going to be disappointed when he learns tomorrow that you've been a bad boy, won't he?" he whispered.

Chapter Fifty-Two

THE NEXT MORNING Peter Cheng rang the doorbell chimes at Wayne Berryman's villa in Napa. When no one came to the door, he let himself end and called out, "Wayne, it's me, Peter Cheng."

He didn't wait for an answer and went searching for Berryman. He found him sitting on the floor at the foot of his bed in the master bedroom. His chin was resting on his chest and there was a bottle of whiskey upright between his legs.

His mistress was lying on a blood-stained silk sheet, her naked body splotched with a dozen stab wounds across her breasts and abdomen. Her eyes were open, staring at the mirrored ceiling over the bed. A chef's knife with blood on the blade was laying in the middle of the bed.

Cheng wondered if Berryman had a camera installed somewhere that recorded his conquests. He would have the cleanup men search the villa for one before they left with the woman's body.

"What have you done?" Cheng said softly and got on his knees in front of Berryman. "Wayne, what happened?"

Berryman didn't answer and didn't look up.

"Wayne, can you hear me?"

Berryman said something indecipherable.

"Wayne, was anyone else here? Were you alone with her?"

Berryman nodded his head up and down and looked up at Cheng. "Help me," he mumbled.

"Can you stand up? Let's get you in the shower. We need to get you cleaned up."

Cheng helped Berryman to his feet and walked him to the ensuite master bathroom.

He kept a hand on Berryman's arm and stepped into the doorless open shower to turn on the water. When it began falling from the rainfall shower head, Cheng told Berryman to take his swimming suit off, splattered with blood, and get in.

"I need to make a call," Cheng said backing away, "Not to the police, to someone who can help you with this."

Berryman stood dumbly in the shower, looking at the floor with water washing over him.

"Send the men in," he ordered. "Look for hidden cameras and a recorder somewhere in the villa. Keep everyone quiet, I want the only voice he hears to be mine."

He returned and stood just outside the open shower. "You're in shock, Wayne. Anybody would be. Can you remember what happened?"

"I can't remember anything."

"Do you know who she is?"

"She works for me."

"Do you think anyone knows she was here with you?"

"I don't know."

"Does she live alone, or does she live with someone?"

"I bought her a condo."

"Did she come here with you or did she drive herself?"

"Car's in the garage."

"Okay, that helps. Wash yourself well and then get dressed. I'll make coffee and we'll go outside and talk."

"What am I going to do, Peter?"

"We'll talk about that," Cheng said and left to find a coffee maker in the kitchen.

Berryman made it easy for him. There was a Keurig coffee

maker in the kitchen with a drawer full of Sumatra K-cups beneath it. He was searching the cupboards for coffee cups when the doorbell chimed.

Four men with face masks, wearing white hooded disposable hazmat suits and blue latex booties over their shoes, were outside when he opened the door. An unmarked white van was parked out front.

"The master bedroom is through there," Cheng pointed. He stepped aside to let the men pass by.

He was in the kitchen waiting for the second cup of coffee to brew when Berryman came in wearing a gray tennis warmup.

"Who are those men, Peter? Why are they here?"

Cheng handed him a cup of coffee and waited for his cup to finish brewing.

"Come outside and I'll explain."

"Did you call them?"

Cheng picked up his cup of coffee and crossed the kitchen without answering. He opened the door out onto a graveled path, leading to a bench beside a pond and cascading water feature.

"Outside," he said.

Berryman followed him down the path and sat beside him on the bench.

"What are you doing, Peter?"

Cheng turned to face him. "I'm trying to keep you from going to prison, Wayne! I'm trying to save your company and my investment, Wayne! I will do whatever is required to accomplish that, Wayne. You just killed a woman in your bed, in your villa. What do you think I'm doing?"

"I'm not sure."

"Let me explain it for you, then. When these men leave, there won't be a trace of evidence she was ever here. Her body will never be found. We'll return her car to her condo, so it looks like she took off somewhere from there. You will tell the police when they question you, and they will eventually question you, that she was here last night and left this morning. You don't know where she is now and you're sorry that you can't be more help.

"That's what I'm doing, Wayne."

"Why did you come here this morning, Peter? How did you even know where I was?"

Cheng turned away and watched the water cascading down a descending row of copper kettles in the middle of the pond.

"You really don't remember, do you? I called you yesterday and said leave your office, that attorney you told me about might be coming to see you. I invited you to lunch today to discuss SkySage and you didn't get back to me. I was worried and came here to see if you were okay."

"Did I really kill her? I don't remember anything."

"It looks that way. You were sitting on the floor with a bottle of Scotch between your legs when I got here. You must have been drinking heavily, maybe blacked out. I don't know. It doesn't matter now. No one is going to find out what happened. I'm making sure of that."

"Thank you, Peter."

"Just do what I tell you and you'll be fine."

Chapter 53

Drake woke up early Thursday morning in the Portland Marriott Downtown Waterfront in an upper floor room with a view of Mount Hood painted a soft pink at sunrise.

The towering snow-capped mountain was a friendly landmark, passing by outside his window as it had the night before when he landed in Portland, telling him he was home.

He didn't feel the same when he saw Mount Rainier before landing at the Seattle-Tacoma International Airport, and never expect to. Oregon would always be the state he loved, even though he'd abandoned her for another.

He got out of bed, stretched and worked through a morning routine of squats, push-ups, planking, jumping jacks and reverse lunges. It was eighteen minutes invested in one of the oldest exercise routines he knew of, but it worked for him when he traveled and kept him fit, along with his running.

Fit and hungry each morning. He scanned the room service

menu and ordered the hotel's Farmer's Omelet and coffee, before sitting on the edge of the bed and calling Liz in Seattle.

"Were you awake?" he asked.

"Once the sun's up, I start to. How was San Francisco?"

"Not productive, I'm afraid."

"What now?"

"I'm going to meet with Paul after breakfast and ask him to dig deep about the professor's husband. We'll see where we go from there."

"Are you coming back today?"

"I'll be on the first flight I can get after I meet Paul. I have an appointment with my tax attorney about the IRS audit, but that shouldn't take long. Lancer okay?"

"He's on the mend. He'll ask you to take him for a walk as soon as you get here."

"Tell him I'm on the way. Would you like to go out for dinner tonight?"

"Let's order something and stay home. How about Chinese?"

Drake laughed. "Goodbye, I'll see you tonight."

He was still chuckling to himself when room service arrived.

After breakfast and a shower and shave, he called Paul Benning and asked to meet him.

"Good morning Paul. Can I buy you breakfast or a cup of coffee this morning?"

"Both," Benning said. "Margo's visiting her sister and I'm on my own. Where are you?"

"At the Marriott."

"I'll meet you in fifteen minutes."

Drake turned on the news and watched the morning parade of soundbites about morning traffic snarls, last night's peaceful protests led by Rose City Antifa and news out of Washington about a news anchor's fall from grace.

Five minutes was all he could take and left his room early to meet Benning in the hotel's restaurant.

Benning had a spring in his step and a smile on his face as he walked to Drake's table.

"Thanks for giving me a reason for not having to eat a bowl of oatmeal this morning," Benning said as he sat down.

"When the wife's away..." Drake said.

"I shouldn't complain. I'm feeling good and Margo's happy."

"You look good. Keeping busy?"

"I am, thanks for asking. Margo's great at drumming up business and your retainer has been keeping me busy. Do you have something new for me?"

Drake saw the waiter approaching and said, "I do. Go ahead and order breakfast and we'll talk. I had the Farmer's Omelet in my room. I'd recommend it."

Benning took his advice and ordered the omelet and coffee with cream.

"I was in San Francisco yesterday," Drake said. "I went there to talk with the art history professor who introduced our dead intern, Grace Liu, to Wayne Berryman. She was murdered on campus the night before I got there."

"Is that what you want me to look into?"

"No, it's something else. Do you remember Detective Cabrillo in San Francisco?"

"I met him when Mike Casey was poisoned by that lady assassin."

"I met him on the Berkeley campus investigating the professor's murder. He's assisting the Berkeley PD and will call me if he learns anything that might help us. What I need is for you to find out everything you can about the professor's husband."

"How is he involved in Michael Bridge's murder and the intern's?"

"I don't know yet, but I think he is. He might have been the one to introduce Grace Liu to Wayne Berryman, not his wife. He said he doesn't know Berryman, but I don't believe him. He and his wife were well known in San Francisco's art world. He would have known Berryman."

"Am I trying to prove the husband knew Berryman?" Benning asked.

"That and more. I want to know everything about the husband.

His name is Peter Zhang. He owns the Premier Travel and Tour agency in China Town. It provides tours to China and tours of the U.S. for Chinese students. Who is he, where does he come from, where does he make his money? Everything you can find. Use Kevin at PSS if he can help."

"Do you want me to go to San Francisco?"

"If you need to. I'm going back to talk to Wayne Berryman again, as soon as I know more about Zhang."

"How soon do you need this?"

"As soon as you can dig it up."

"Give me a day of two."

"Have you heard anything more about Michael Bridge's homicide investigation?"

"Nothing new," Benning said. "The sheriff doesn't have a lot to go on, but he's working it."

"All right. Let me know if you need an advance for any of this."

Benning saw the waiter bringing his breakfast and said, "Breakfast will do, for now, but Margo's away for a couple of days. I might have to come here again to keep up my energy, though."

"Whatever it takes Paul," Drake smiled. "Whatever it takes."

Chapter Fifty-Three

THE JIGSAW PUZZLE Drake was working on started to take shape Thursday afternoon in Seattle when Detective Cabrillo called him at PSS Headquarters.

"We got a break," Cabrillo said. "A groundskeeper on the Berkeley campus found a shell casing at Sather Gate, where Professor Chen was murdered. He was stripping the burlap off the bottom of a newly planted tree when he found the casing. Someone must have kicked it there when they were walking across the plaza. We recovered a print from the casing and know who it belongs to. You'll never guess who."

"You're going to make me ask? Who does it belong to?"

"A tour guide who works for Premier Travel and Tours, Francis Zhangs' agency. His name is Tony Lee."

Drake raised a clenched fist in the air. "Yes!" Does it match the bullet you recovered from Jennifer Chen?"

"Exact match."

"How did you match the fingerprint to Lee?"

"He has a commercial driver's license to drive a tour bus for Zhang."

"Have you talked to Zhang about Lee?"

"He said he fired Lee over a year ago. A Chinese student made a complaint that Lee was sexually harassing her on a tour bus."

"Did Zhang have any idea why Lee would want to kill his wife?"

"The only thing he could think of was that Lee wanted to get back at him. He said Lee was a very angry young man."

"Angry and dangerous," Drake added. "He came after me and stabbed my German Shepherd. I tried to find him here in Seattle, but he'd left town."

"Is there more to this story that I need to know?"

"There is," Drake admitted. "Give me a little time to sort it out and I'll share what I know or think I know. If you find Lee, will you call me?"

"If you'll call me with anything you learn that will help me find him. I'm getting the feeling you're way ahead of me on this."

"I will."

Drake tried to make sense of what he'd just learned and decided to get some help. He left his office and stopped at Liz's open door.

"I need your help with something," he said when she looked up. "Give me a couple minutes and meet me in the conference room."

"Okay."

He continued down the hall and knocked on Mike Casey's door.

"Come on in," he heard Casey say.

"Mike, I need your help. Do you have time to join me in the conference room with Liz?"

"I have a conference call in twenty minutes. If that's not enough time, can we meet later?"

"It should be. I'll take what I can get for now," Drake said.

When Drake was joined in the conference room by his two advisors, he got right to the point. "I need to know if you put the pieces of this puzzle together the same way I do."

"Fire away," Casey said.

"Mike, you remember Detective Cabrillo in San Francisco?"

"Not a found memory, all together, but sure."

"He just called and told me they've identified the person who killed the art history professor I went to San Francisco to meet,"

Drake said. "He's Tony Lee, the Kung fu instructor here in Seattle. The man who I believe stabbed Lancer."

"The man you went to meet the other night when the Antifa mob showed up," Casey said matter-of-factly. "Why is he in San Francisco killing this professor?"

"You heard about the other night." Drake said.

"Our GPS microchips monitor recorded a number of our employees together the other night on the same street as his Kung fu studio. I asked why and was told."

"Mike, I should have told you about that."

"It would have been nice," Casey said, "But it wasn't necessary. It was a Special Project matter and you're the head of Special Projects. Does Detective Cabrillo have any idea why Tony Lee would want to kill this professor?"

"He talked to the woman's husband, who said he'd fired Lee a year ago and might have wanted to get back at him."

"What's the connection between Lee and the husband?" Liz asked.

"The husband owns a travel agency in China Town that conducts tours of U.S. for Chinese students who are thinking of coming here to earn advance degrees on H-1B visas," Drake explained. "Lee was one of the husband's tour guides."

"What is the husband's involvement in all of this?" Casey asked.

"His wife, a Chinese American art history professor at the University of California…"

Liz interrupted and said, "Was the person who introduced Grace Liu, the intern at SkySage, to Wayne Berryman."

Drake nodded. "I met the husband, Francis Zhang, with Detective Cabrillo, and asked him if he knew Wayne Berryman. He said he didn't, but I don't believe him."

"Okay, how does all of this relate to our security concerns at SkySage?" Casey asked.

"That's why I wanted to see if you can see the pieces of the puzzle fitting together the way I do," Drake said.

"First, I think Tony Lee came after me on Bainbridge Island

because he killed Michael Bridge and knew I had his tablet. He was in Hood River when I got it out of Bridge's car at the impound lot.

"Second, we found on the tablet that Michael Bridge was looking into the initial funding documents between Berryman Private Equity, LLC, that related to the intern program at SkySage. The same day that Liz met with Grace Liu at SkySage, she committed suicide that night. Paul Benning looked at the suicide report and doesn't think it was suicide. The FSO at SkySage agrees.

"Third, when I went to talk with Professor Chen, she was murdered the night before I got there by Tony Lee; the same man I think killed Michael Bridge, and may have killed Grace Liu. Now he's killed Professor Chen who introduced Grace Liu to Wayne Berryman."

"Okay," Casey said, "Assuming all of this is true, who's pulling the strings and had Tony Lee kill three people, Wayne Berryman?"

"I don't think it's one person. I think this is industrial espionage aimed at stealing what SkySage is developing for the Pentagon's JEDI project. I think it's China."

Chapter Fifty-Four

DRAKE WATCHED his fiancé and his best friend consider his hypothesis and its implications.

Casey crossed his arms over his chest, leaned back in his chair and stared at the ceiling.

Liz had a concerned look on her face and he thought he knew what she was going to say.

"If China is behind this, and I agree that it looks like they might be, we need to get the FBI involved."

He was right. "That's the president's call Liz. But if we did, what would we tell them? Two of the three murders are already being investigated as homicides, in Oregon and California. The FBI doesn't have jurisdiction to investigate either of them. The only thing we can offer them regarding China is that Grace Liu and Professor Chen were both Chinese Americans. We have nothing that proves China is involved."

"You're right, we don't," Casey said. "But we do have a client handling top secret information that we're concerned about. Aren't we obligated to notify SkySage and Microsoft that we may have a security problem, before we have evidence to prove it?"

"We told the FSO at SkySage that we're reviewing its facility clearance," Drake reminded him. "I'd like to wait until that's completed before we jeopardize the company's contract with Microsoft."

"If we don't get the FBI involved, where do we go from here?" Liz asked. "Tony Lee seems to be the key but no one knows where he is."

"Detective Cabrillo is looking for him, but so were we and we didn't find him," Drake pointed out. "I think Professor Chen's husband, Francis Zhang, is who we target next. I asked Paul Benning to take a deep dive into his past and any relationship he can find between Zhang and Wayne Berryman. I told Paul to use Kevin as a resource, if he needs his special talents."

"Have you gotten anything from Benning?" Casey asked.

"I just asked him to investigate Zhang yesterday," Drake said. "I thought I might ask Kevin to go ahead and have a look at Zhang and his travel agency, in a way that Paul can't. Zhang said he fired Tony Lee a year ago. I'd like to know if that's true and if there's anything that suggests he's been in touch with Lee since then."

"Do we all agree that we proceed with this, as a review of our client's facility clearance, without the need to get the FBI involved just yet?" Casey asked.

"I agree, for now," Liz said.

"Agreed," Drake said.

Casey clapped his hands and stood. "All right, then. Let's get working on the SkySage facility clearance review."

Drake walked Liz back to her office, before going to talk with Kevin in IT.

"I told you we should have told Mike about taking the guys with us, when we went to Lee's Kung fu studio," Liz said softly.

"You're right. I'd feel better right now if he was angry about it, instead of letting me know he knew about it the way he did."

"Buy him a bottle of that expensive Bourbon he likes and say you're sorry. He might forget about it someday."

"Thanks," Drake said and walked towards the stairs to go see Kevin McRoberts.

He was surprised to see Kevin's desk was clear of energy drink cans and his office neat and clean. It usually looked like the darkened cave of black hat hacker, hiding away and surviving on sugar and Cheetos, which is what Kevin had once been.

The IT director's office had windows looking his IT staff with blinds that were usually closed. Today, the blinds were opened and the lights were on in his office.

Kevin was leaning forward, resting his forearms on the edge of his desk, staring at the large monitor in front of his face when Drake got his attention by knocking on the window next to his door.

"Hi Kevin," Drake said when he opened the door.

"Hey, Mr. Drake, come on in."

"I like what you've done with the place."

"It wasn't me. My girlfriend cleaned it up, told me I needed to look like the head of an IT division of a company and not some gamer pulling an all-nighter."

"Girlfriend, huh? Bring her by my office sometime, I'd like to meet her."

"I will, Mr. Drake. What can I do for you today?"

"Has Paul Benning called you?"

"No, I haven't heard from him in a while, why?"

"I told him to call you, if he needed help. I asked him to do something for us. It involves investigating a man named Francis Zhang. Zhang owns a travel and tour agency in San Francisco, called Premier Travel and Tours. I asked Paul to find out everything he can about the man. I also want you to see if you can find anything that indicates Zhang's been in contact with Tony Lee, the man you identified for me on the Bainbridge ferry."

"Does that include paying Zhang a visit, t the way I usually do when you ask me to look into something?" Kevin asked.

"It does, with the usual admonition to be careful. It's possible that Zhang might be involved in industrial espionage for China."

"Like a spy for China?"

"Like a spy for China. And if he is, I don't want Chinese hackers finding out we've been nosing around and following it back to us."

"They'll never know I was there, Mr. Drake."
"Make sure they don't Kevin. There's a lot at stake on this one."

Chapter Fifty-Five

IN SAN FRANCISCO, Wayne Berryman was closing the door of his office at Berryman Private Equity, LLC, to leave for a lunch meeting when his phone purred in his pocket. When he saw that Peter Cheng was calling, he stepped back inside and closed the door.

"Have your secretary call and tell the client you're meeting for lunch that you've come down with something and can't make it. Be at your pied-a-terre in thirty minutes and wait for my call."

"How do you know about that?"

"Wayne, we know everything about you and where you go when you want to be with your mistress in the city. No one will to think to look for you there."

"Who's looking for me?"

"I'll explain when I call you. Thirty minutes, don't be late."

Berryman froze, staring at the phone in his hand, and couldn't seem to make his feet move. Had the police found out about the nightmare that had happened at his villa? Cheng had promised him he would take care of everything.

He hit the number on his speed dial and called the building's valet parking service to have his car brought up from underground parking, told his secretary he wasn't feeling well and left his office.

His pied-a-terre, as Cheng called it, was a luxury condo on Russian Hill that he'd paid a fortune for that technically was owned by the firm, as an asset in its retirement account. Arguably, it was something clients could use when they visited San Francisco, but so far, he had been the only one that had the pleasure of staying there.

Thinking about his use of the condo brought a momentary sense of sadness and shame. He would never again enjoy the sexual gratification his nubile young mistress had given him. And when the fleeting image of her lying in his bloody bed flashed across his mind, he wondered if he could ever enjoy sex again without remembering that night.

Driving across the city to his condo, cocooned in the safety he felt inside his Mercedes 450S, he tried to imagine what life would be like if Cheng hadn't been able to take care of things, as he'd promised. Would he lose everything? Would he go to prison? Would he be perp-walked through a crowd of reporters when they arrested him?

He wanted to pound the steering wheel and scream at the pedestrians on the sidewalks. It wasn't fair! He wasn't a bad man! He didn't deserve to be made to feel like he was feeling!

When he drove down the ramp to underground parking and the reserved parking space he paid extra for, he stayed in his car until the panic he was feeling subsided.

He jumped when there was a knock on his window.

"We need to hurry," an Asian man in his late twenties said. "You don't want to be late for your call."

"Who are you?"

"That's not important. Mr. Cheng sent me."

"Why?"

"To make sure you're safe."

Berryman felt his chest tightening at the mention of his safety. The man looked vaguely familiar and knew that Cheng would be calling, but there was a coldness in the man's eyes that alarmed him.

"Get out of the car, Berryman. I'm here to protect you, not hurt you."

He hesitated and then unlocked the car door. He really didn't have a choice, if he wanted to find out what was going on.

Berryman got out and walked to the elevator two parking spaces away.

"Have we met?" he asked the man.

"We all look alike, don't we?"

"You look familiar, that's all," Berryman said.

The elevator doors pulled back. "Let's go. You're going to miss your call."

Berryman punched number twelve, the top floor, the doors closed, and the elevator accelerated upwards.

When the elevator stopped and they waited for the doors to open, the man said, "Let me make sure there's no one waiting for the elevator. If it's clear, walk quickly to your place and get inside. It's better if no one knows you're here."

"What about my car?"

"It will be moved after you've talked with Mr. Cheng."

When the doors opened and Tony Lee looked to make sure no one was outside, he waved Berryman out and followed him down the white marble hallway. Unit eight was the last condo on the south end of the floor.

Inside, Lee locked the door and held out his hand. "Give me your phone."

"Why, I'm waiting for Cheng to call."

"We don't want his number on your phone. We'll use my phone."

When Lee had Berryman's phone in his pocket, he took out his phone and called Cheng.

"We're here," Lee told Cheng. "I'll put him on."

"Why don't you sit down somewhere, Wayne," said. "We have things to discuss."

Berryman took the phone he was handed and sat down on the leather couch, in front of the wall mounted electric fireplace. "Why am I here, Peter?" he asked.

"We believe the attorney from Seattle, who came to your villa, will be looking for you. We don't want him to find you."

"This isn't about the police, then?"

"I told you I'd take care of that. No one knows she's missing and won't be coming back."

"Why am I hiding from this attorney? I don't understand. I don't have anything to hide?"

"Of course, you do, Wayne. Surely you understand by now why we're helping you."

"Who is 'we', Peter? I asked you before and you didn't answer me."

"We are foreign investors who want you to help us obtain the artificial intelligence SkySage is developing for the Pentagon."

"You want me to help you do what? Help you with industrial espionage? I never agreed to that."

"Not directly, but you must have suspected that was the quid pro quo. Why did you think we insisted that you have an intern program when we funded your startup? Why do you think we encouraged you to put Grace Liu at SkySage?"

"To spy for you? I would never have agreed to do that, if I had known. That's a one-way ticket to prison."

"So is murder, Wayne. Do what we're asking, and you won't spend the rest of your life in an eight-by-ten jail cell."

"You set me up, Peter. The attorney asked me if I found HK Capital, LLC, or if you found me. You wanted me to help you plant someone at SkySage from the very beginning, didn't you? How's that working out for you, Peter, now that your spy is dead?"

"She's no longer necessary, Wayne. We have you."

Chapter Fifty-Six

DRAKE WAS PULLING TOGETHER records for his IRS audit at PSS Headquarters his desk Friday morning when Paul Benning called from San Francisco.

"Thought I'd call with what I have before I leave here," Benning said.

"Are you in California?"

"Yes, waiting for my flight at the airport. Sorry I don't have more to report, but I haven't been able to dig up much on Francis Zhang. He's a naturalized citizen, owns a travel agency and goes the opera. I did learn that he plays tai chi every morning in a park and seems to live well."

"How did you find out about the tai chi?"

"I staked out his house and watched him in the park."

"You said he's a naturalized citizen. How long has he been in the U.S.?"

"He entered the country from China on an H-1B visa in 2009 and became a citizen in 2014."

"H-IB's are temporary visas for people in special occupations. What was his?"

"That's a little peculiar, from what I can find out," Benning said. "He was sponsored by the Center for Chinese Studies at the University of California, Berkeley campus, as a consultant travel agent to assist with student's travel to and from China."

"Since when did being a travel agent become classified as a special occupation?"

"Probably when both the university and the Chinese consulate in San Francisco sponsored his visa."

"Interesting, considering all the other Chinese connections we're discovering," Drake mused. "When you get back, see if you can identify the names of his visa sponsors. I'd like to know if they show up on anyone's watch list."

"If I can, I'll include them in my report."

"Thanks Paul."

So, Francis Zhang had connections. He wondered who they were in the Chinese consulate in San Francisco. The number of stories reported in the news in the last couple of years involving Chinese spies operating out of Chinese consulates in the U.S.

Drake called Kevin McRoberts in IT on the second floor to learn if there was anything else that might connect Zhang with his growing concern about Chinese espionage.

"Kevin, have you been able to look into that matter I asked you about?"

"Yes, but I didn't find much. There's nothing that indicates Zhang has been in touch with Lee recently. Lee was an employee who was terminated, officially, but he's still being paid by the travel agency."

"I don't understand."

"In the agency's system, it says he was terminated a year ago. I couldn't tell when the record of his termination was entered. I didn't want to dig any further, with the constraints on my assignment, but I remembered I'd looked at Lee's account at his credit union. When I checked his account again, he's still receiving money every month from Premier Travel and Tours."

"As severance pay, or can you tell?"

"There was nothing in the travel agency's IT system that I could find about it being severance pay."

"Is Lee still using his credit union account?"

"The last time he used his debit card was three days ago."

"Where?"

"On a United flight from Seattle to San Francisco."

The day before Zhang's wife was killed.

"And it hasn't been used since then?"

"Correct."

"He's using cash or someone's paying his bills," Drake said. "Kevin, go back and look for any unusual expenditure Zhang may have made from his agency account; car rentals, hotel rooms, the kind of expense you might make if you were paying the bills for someone from out of town."

"Like Tony Lee. I'm on it, Mr. Drake."

His phone buzzed and he saw he had a text from Mike Casey.

Bring Liz and join me in my office.

Drake stopped outside Liz's open door and leaned in. "Mike wants to see us."

"Did he say why?"

"He did not."

"I've never been summoned to his office before."

"Neither have I," Drake said as he waited at her door.

When they arrived at the office at the other end of the hallway, CEO Casey was sitting at his desk with a worried look on his face.

Drake waited for Liz to enter and sit down before he closed the door and asked, "What's up, Mike?"

"Microsoft called," Casey said. "They heard about our review of the facility security clearance for SkySage and they're concerned. They want a guaranty from us that their lead AI subcontractor hasn't been compromised."

"We're not there yet," Drake said. "Are they willing to wait until we complete our review?"

"They want an answer by Monday."

"What if we can't complete our review by then?" Liz asked.

"They feel obligated to notify the Pentagon that they may have to cancel their contract with SkySage, incur unexpected costs and need more time to complete the JEDI project."

"Since the government isn't responsible for a defense contractor's cost overruns, Microsoft would have to eat the additional cost of bringing in another subcontractor to finish the project," Drake said. "Which means, they'll look to us to cover their loss, because we told them SkySage could be trusted to handle top secret information."

"That's the way I read it," Casey said. "They're giving us until Monday to tell them SkySage can continue working on JEDI or get ready to be sued. Any ideas, counselor, about how we keep that from happening?"

Drake stared at a spot on the wall behind Casey's head while he formulated a plan.

"Wayne Berryman is the key," he said. "I can't prove it, but I think China tried to penetrate SkySage by arranging for Berryman to get a spy inside the company, an intern like Grace Liu. Think this through with me.

"When Michael Bridge started asking questions about the intern arrangement with Berryman and was looking for the original funding documents between Berryman Private Equity, LLC, and SkySage, they killed him.

"When Liz met with Grace Liu, the intern, they panicked and had her killed.

"When I went to San Francisco to talk with the art history professor who introduced Liu to Wayne Berryman, she was murdered.

"The only reason I can think of that explains why those three murders happened, is they're protecting Wayne Berryman. As far as we know, he's the only one now who has access to top secret information at SkySage and has a connection to China."

"How do we prove that Berryman's working with China by Monday?" Casey asked.

"We find Berryman and ask him," Liz said. "We have the leverage to get him to tell us everything he knows."

Drake nodded his agreement and looked across the desk to

Casey. "Can we pry you away from your family for the weekend and get you to fly us to San Francisco?"

"With what's at stake, you bet. Go pack a bag. We're flying to San Francisco."

Chapter Fifty-Seven

THE PSS GULFSTREAM G-650 was in the air two hours later, with Mike Casey at the controls. Steve Carson, the company's pilot, was along for the flight as Casey's co-pilot.

Drake and Liz were alone in the passenger compartment, making plans for the night. Casey's assistant had made reservations before they left Seattle at the Four Seasons.

Liz was on the phone lining up ground transportation and Drake was talking with Detective Cabrillo in San Francisco.

"...we had BOLO's out for Tony Lee, as soon as we identified his print on the shell casing, but no luck so far," Cabrillo reported.

"He used a debit card on a United Airlines flight from Seattle to San Francisco the day before Zhang's was killed, but he hasn't used it again," Drake said.

"Do I want to know how you found that out?"

"Probably not. He's also continuing to receive money from Zhang's travel agency. We couldn't determine if it's his severance pay, or he's still employed by Zhang and Zhang lied to us. You might ask Zhang about it."

"I went back to ask Zhang if I could see Lee's personnel file, but he's taking some time off. His agency didn't know where he was and said he hasn't been in touch with them."

"Let me see if I can find out where Mr. Zhang is," Drake said.

"I forgot to ask why you're coming to San Francisco," Cabrillo said, "Care to tell me?"

"For the same reason I told you last time. If I find anything that will help your homicide investigation, I'll let you know. If you find Tony Lee or discover where Zhang is, I'd like to think you'll reciprocate and let me know."

"I said I would, don't worry."

"We're staying at the Four Seasons. Let's find time to meet and compare notes sometime this weekend."

"Why do you think I'll be working this weekend?"

"Because I think you're that kind of guy. You want to solve your case just as badly as I want to solve mine."

Cabrillo laughed and said, "You sound like you've been talking to my wife."

"Stay in touch, Detective."

"You do the same."

Drake turned and saw that Liz was watching him.

"What did Detective Cabrillo have to say?" she asked.

"He has no idea where Tony Lee or Francis Zhang are. It looks like Wayne Berryman's our only shot at finding out what he may or may not be doing for China."

"Lee might be in the wind, but can't we find out where Zhang is?"

"Cabrillo said he'd tried to talk to him again and couldn't find him. I didn't ask how hard he looked."

"Kevin might be able to help us find him. Want me to text him and ask him to get us a list of places where Zhang could be? You know his home and travel agency addresses, maybe he has a vacation place somewhere?"

"Good idea," Drake said, as he released his seatbelt and stood up. "Care for an inflight beverage before we land?"

"White wine, if there is some. Thanks."

Drake walked to the cabin and asked Casey and Carson if they wanted anything.

"Nothing for me," Casey said.

"I'll have a Pepsi, if you're headed that way," Carson said. "I didn't have time to resupply the plane but there should be some in the back."

"I heard you calling someone," Casey said. "Anything new?"

"Detective Cabrillo says there's a BOLO out for Tony Lee, but he's in the wind. He tried to talk with Francis Zhang again, but he's taking some time off. His travel agency says they don't know where he is."

"Is Wayne Berryman in town or should we turn around and go home?" Casey asked.

"We'll find Berryman, wherever he is. We don't have a choice."

Drake went to the galley and returned with a glass of white wine for Liz, a Pepsi for Steve Carson and a glass of Jim Beam for himself.

"Did you call Kevin yet?" he asked.

"His line was busy, why?"

"Ask him to find all the addresses where we might find Wayne Berryman. We'll have to make the most of the time we have, if we're going to satisfy Microsoft by Monday."

"Can we do that, even if we find Berryman?" Liz asked. "We know about three murders, but we can we say there's no security risk at SkySage until we prove there isn't?"

Drake swirled the light amber whiskey in his glass and took a sip before saying, "I agree. I believe the three deaths are related and that there was an attempt to plant a Chinese spy at SkySage. If we can prove the attempt failed and no security risk exists now, SkySage will be okay. If we can't, we'll have to get the FBI involved and let them sort it out."

"We'll have a lot of explaining to do, if we get the FBI involved."

"I've gone to the FBI before and they've ignored me. They would this time too. If they try to fault what we've done, I'll have to play my trump card."

"The president?"

"The president."

"They will be a lot of blowback on him for letting us pursue this on our own."

"He can handle it. Besides, what could the FBI have down as quickly as we have? You know how they slow walk an investigation, when someone like the Secretary of the Treasury Department might be involved."

"A few instances do come to mind," Liz said.

"Ten minutes to touch down," Casey called out from the cockpit. "Thank you for choosing PSS Airlines for your flight to San Francisco. We hope you have a successful visit and will allow us to serve your transportation needs again."

Drake laughed. "Count on it, captain!"

Chapter Fifty-Eight

THE PSS CREW met for breakfast Saturday morning in the MKT Restaurant at the Four Seasons Hotel on Market to coordinate their search for Wayne Berryman.

Liz had a list of the properties Kevin McRoberts had called her about late the night before.

"There are three properties Wayne Berryman owns or has owned," Liz said. "His ex-wife got the house in Presidio Heights. There's the villa in Napa and his current residence, at One Steuart Lane at the Embarcadero, where he lives with his second wife."

Drake set his coffee cup down and wrinkled his brow. "You mean he doesn't live with that young woman in the bikini we saw at his villa?"

Liz smiled and said, "Kevin found another property, owned by his firm, that might tell us where she does live. There's a pied-á-terre on Russian Hill. We might look for him there."

"Liz rented two Tahoes," Casey said. "Why don't Steve and I check out his firm, since you've already been there. They might give us something. You and Liz go to his place at the Embarcadero to talk to his wife. If we don't get anything at either place, we could try that trysting pad he has on Russian Hill.?"

"That works," Drake said. "I'll check with Detective Cabrillo on the way and find out if he's got anything on Tony Lee or Francis Zhang."

While Liz finished her granola and berries, Drake told Casey that he should be the one to go to the FBI.

"If they won't give us a little more time to finish our security assessment review, we won't have a choice," Casey agreed. "They will want to hear everything we know, and it'll be better it we volunteer giving it to them."

"I feel badly for SkySage," Liz said. "Berryman's the culprit here. If this is all related to Berryman's intern program, whether he's doing something on behalf of China or not, the only thing SkySage did wrong was take his money."

"That's what 'due diligence' is all about," Casey said, "But I agree. It would have been hard to see this coming."

Liz finished her cup of coffee and set her napkin down. "Let's go find out what Berryman has to say."

"Lead the way, Ms. Strobel," Drake said, as the men stood and followed her out of the restaurant.

Mike Casey and Steve Carson left the hotel on foot to see if Berryman was in his office in the Transamerica Pyramid building nearby. Drake and Liz waited at the parking valet stand for their rented SUV Liz to be brought up from the parking garage.

Drake decided to call Detective Cabrillo. "Good morning, Detective. We're leaving the hotel to look for Wayne Berryman. Is there anything new on Lee or Zhang?"

"Nothing on Lee," Cabrillo said. "I came in early this morning and thought I'd see if there was anything on the internet that would help me find Zhang. He's mentioned a couple of times attending cultural events at the Chinese consulate, but there's no reason to think he's staying there.

"There is one thing that might be a possibility. I found a retreat center in Humboldt County that hosts Kung fu exhibits and classes for martial art students from around the world. Zhang is on a list of the retreat's former instructors, but he's not mentioned as one of the instructors for the exhibition this weekend."

"Interesting," Drake said, "Zhang and Tony Lee are both Kung fu instructors. Maybe that's where we'll find them."

"Want to go and watch some Kung fu?" Cabrillo asked.

"When does the exhibition start?"

"Noon today."

"Let me think about it. If we can't find Berryman today, I might ride along. I have a score to settle with Mr. Lee."

"Just remember it's my BOLO and he's my murder suspect."

"Don't worry, I won't get in your way if we find him."

"Let me know if you find Berryman."

"I will."

Liz waited until they were driving away from the valet stand to ask, "What did Cabrillo have to say?"

"No sign of Lee," Drake said, as he waited to pull out into traffic to drive south to One Steaurt Lane at the Embarcadero. "But he was on the internet looking for Francis Zhang and found something interesting. Zhang's a Kung fu instructor, like Tony Lee."

"What a coincidence."

"Cabrillo found that Zhang has been an instructor at a martial arts retreat center in Humboldt County. It's having an exhibition this weekend. Cabrillo asked if I wanted to go with him and see if Zhang might be there."

"If we can't find Berryman, that may be the last shot we have to get some answers."

"We'll find Berryman," Drake said. "His wife will know something."

One Steaurt Lane turned out to be a Rubik's cube-looking luxury condo development on the waterfront just north of the San Francisco-Oakland Bay Bridge.

When Wayne Berryman's second wife agreed to take their call from the building's front desk, she didn't know anything, More specifically, she said she didn't know where her husband was and, frankly, didn't care if he was dead or alive."

Chapter Fifty-Nine

MIKE CASEY and Steve Carson had returned to the hotel and were waiting out front when Drake stopped to pick them up.

Berryman's receptionist had been polite, Casey said, but had curtly told them his whereabouts were none of their business. If they wanted to speak with him, they needed to make an appointment like everyone else.

"Looks like were off to see if Berryman's hiding out in his pied-a-terre," Drake said and entered the address on a note Liz handed him in the SUV's GPS navigation system.

"This will be interesting," Casey said when he heard what Mrs. Berryman had said about her husband. "Odds are, he's not alone."

Berryman's pied-a-terre was on Green street in the Russian Hill neighborhood northwest of their hotel. When Drake turned onto Columbus Avenue for the short drive there, he asked if anyone knew why it was called Russian Hill.

Steve Carson did. "Back in the Gold Russ days, a minister found seven graves on the top of the hill. The graves were inscribed in Cyrillic and it was assumed the dead were Russian sailors or fur trappers. The small cemetery was eventually moved to another location, but the name Russian Hill remained."

"Are you a history buff?" Liz asked.

"Not really, I lived here for several years after I left the Air Force and flew for United Airlines. I was curious about the names given to the seven hills in the city and looked it up."

When Drake turned left and drove up Green Street, he saw that Russian Hill was an upscale residential community with some pricey real estate located there. Among them was Berryman's luxury condo tower.

"Berryman is Unit 36 on the twelfth floor," Drake said when he pulled to the curb in front of the building and parked. "With the view this place must have, he's paying a pretty penny for his privacy."

"Can't wait to see it," Casey said. "I'm liking this guy less and less and I haven't even met him."

"Meeting him isn't likely to change your mind," Drake said and opened his door to get out.

They huddled for a minute on the sidewalk before entering the building's lobby.

"If we take the elevator and he comes down the stairs, why don't Mike and Steve keep an eye on the stairs," Drake said. "If he lets us in, we'll call you to join us. If we think he's here but doesn't let us in, I'll call Detective Cabrillo to get him to open his door."

"Sounds like we have a plan, Stan," Casey said, remembering a lyric from Simon and Garfunkel's *50 Ways to Leave Your Lover*.

Drake led the way into the building and crossed the lobby to stand in front of the elevator door with Liz. Casey and Carson peeled off and positioned themselves by the door to the stairs.

Before he had a chance to step forward and push the elevator's up button, the door chimed and started to open.

Tony Lee stood in the middle of the elevator looking straight ahead. His eyes opened wide when he saw Drake.

Drake reacted first. He sprang forward onto his left foot, slammed a palm strike on the top of Lee's head, knocking it back, and shot a fist punch to Lee's throat. Lee fell back, hit his head on the rear wall and fell to the floor.

Drake jumped into the elevator to make sure he didn't get up.

Lee was unconscious.

"Let's go up and see if Berryman's alive," Drake said.

Liz stepped in and pushed the button for the twelfth floor. Casey and Carson had run over and joined them before the door closed.

Drake kneeled and checked Lee for weapons. He found a compact 9mm pistol in the right pocket of Lee's leather jacket and a M&P spring assisted knife in the pocket of his jeans.

He handed both weapons to Casey. "Cabrillo will be interested to see if this is the gun that killed Zhang's wife."

Carson stood in the corner of the elevator, staring at Drake. "I've never seen anyone move that quickly. You put him down in less than a second."

"Fastest reaction time in the Unit," Casey said. "That's one reason I was glad he was my partner."

"Mike and Steve, why don't you stand in front of the door, in case it opens and someone's standing there," Drake said. "If we can get him to Berryman's room without anyone seeing him, the easier it will be to keep our names out of this."

"Twelfth floor coming up," Liz said.

Drake pulled Lee's body to the back of the elevator and moved back to stand between Casey and Carson at the door before it opened.

The hallway was empty, and Liz stepped out to check the numbers of the first two units to the right of the elevator.

"Unit 36 is that way," she said and pointed down the hallway to her left.

Casey handed the pistol and knife back to Drake and leaned down to lift Lee up by his shoulders. "Steve and I will bring him, go check on Berryman."

Drake jogged down the hallway to the door with a gold number 36 above the electronic door lock. He pressed the button next to the door lock and heard a chime play inside.

When Carson and Casey got there and no one had come to open the door, Drake asked Liz to search Lee's pockets. "He might have had a key card or fob to open the door."

She found a key fob in the left pocket of Lee's leather jacket and handed it to Drake.

When he placed it against the door lock, a green light went on and the lock clicked open.

Drake opened the door slowly and called out, "Berryman?"

Berryman didn't answer. Drake waited and called out again.

"Bring Lee in and we'll search the place," he said.

The condo was decorated chic modern, with white walls, white marble floors and stainless-steel fixtures. Beyond the mirror-walled entry, the hallway led to a large room with a floor-to-ceiling window and a spectacular view of Alcatraz and the bay.

Wayne Berryman was sitting in the middle of the room with duct tape across his mouth and duct taped to a straight-backed wooden chair.

Chapter Sixty

DRAKE WALKED across the room to pick up a roll of duct tape on the floor and tossed it to Casey.

"Secure Lee and have a look around," Drake said to the others.

Wayne Berryman grunted loudly and shook his head from side to side.

Drake came around and stood in from of Berryman. "What's going on, Wayne? Why is this man in your condo?"

Berryman glared at Drake and grunted louder.

"Sorry, I guess if I want answers, you need to be able to talk," Drake said. "On the other hand, I know you've been lying to me and probably will again. I might just leave you this way until the police get here."

Berryman started grunting again, so Drake reached over and ripped the duct tape off.

"Get me out of this chair!" Berryman demanded.

"When you tell me why you're tied up and how you know the man in the other room."

"I don't know the man!'

"I think you do, Wayne. He's a killer. Is that why he's here, to torture and kill you to keep us from finding out that you're helping China spy on SkySage."

Berryman blinked twice, before saying, "I'm doing no such thing and you know it."

"No, I don't know it, Wayne. I think you knew what you were signing up for when HK Capital, LLC, came calling and wanted to help you get your company started."

"I won't say it again, get me out of this chair, dammit," Berryman shouted.

Casey walked in and said, "He's conscious. Do you want to talk with him before we call Detective Cabrillo?"

Drake nodded yes and asked, "Did you find anything?"

"Nothing in the condo. Lee has a cell phone, but it's locked."

"Call Kevin and see if he can get anything off it."

"There's a closet full of a woman's clothes, but nothing I could find in any of them," Liz said.

Drake turned back to Berryman and asked, "Where is your mistress, Wayne? I thought we might find her here with you."

Berryman's eyes squinted slightly at the mention of his mistress.

Drake noticed it and asked, "Something happen with you and your mistress, Wayne? If she's left you, good luck going home to the missus, from what I hear."

"What do you want, Drake?" Berryman asked.

"I want to know everything, Wayne. I want to know why Michael Bridge was killed. I want to know why Grace Liu was killed. I want to know why the art professor I think you knew was killed. I want to know what role you played in all or any of it, Wayne."

Berryman stared hard at Drake. "If I tell you what I know, can you guarantee that I'll be protected?"

Drake crossed his arms across his chest, looked to Liz and Casey with a puzzled look on his face, and looked back to Berryman. "Why do you think you need protection?"

"Because you were right when you asked if the guy in the other room was here to keep me from talking to you. I swear that I don't know why the other people were killed, but they killed my mistress to blackmail me. I don't think they'll think twice about killing me to keep me quiet."

Drake noticed that Liz had her phone out to record Berryman.

"Tell me about you mistress," Drake said. "How do you know they killed her?"

"Because I found her lying beside me in my bloody bed, that's how. I woke up and figured I must have done it. I'd been drinking and didn't remember anything about the night. They told me I killed her, but don't worry they said, they'd take care of it."

"Did you kill her?" Drake asked.

"I thought I had, until the guy in the other room showed up today. I thought he looked familiar. When he was taping me in this chair, I remembered where I'd seen him. He was at my villa they day she was killed. He delivered a bottle of my favorite Scotch from the man who showed up the next morning, saying he'd take care of everything."

"Who was that?"

"Peter Cheng, the manager of HK Capital, LLC."

"Is Cheng here in San Francisco?"

"I don't know. Would you please get me out of this chair, I've told you everything I know?"

"One more question, Wayne," Drake said. "Does Tony Lee work for Cheng?"

"Not directly, I think. He was on the phone and it sounded like he was taking orders from someone, but I don't think it was Cheng. I heard him say "Yes, Major". Cheng's not military, as far as I know."

"We're going to cut the duct tape off, Wayne. Don't do anything foolish, if you want us to protect you. I'm going in the other room and see if Lee will confirm any of what you've told us."

Drake left the room and motioned for Liz to come with him.

"Get Lee's phone from Mike and see if you can find out who Lee's taking orders from," Drake said when she joined him in the hallway. "I'll use my phone to record what Lee has to say."

"If he can say anything at all, after the throat punch you gave him," Liz said and returned to get Lee's phone from Casey.

Drake found Tony Lee was hog-tied and lying face down on the marble floor in the kitchen. His hands were duct taped behind his back and his ankles were taped together and pulled back toward his hands with his belt.

His head was turned to the side and his eyes were open.

Drake squatted down and ripped the duct tape from Lee's mouth.

"I said we'd meet sometime," Drake told him. "Although I would have preferred having more time alone with you before the police get here. So, let's make the most of it, Tony. Who told you to kill Michael Bridge when he was windsurfing on the Columbia River? Was he the man Berryman heard you call Major?"

Lee closed his eyes and was silent.

"As sloppy as you've been, Major must be his name, because there's no way you're a soldier. You tried to get me and stabbed my dog instead, for God's sake. You're probably nothing more than a Chinese spy who's also not very good at what you do."

Lee's eyes snapped open. "Untie me and find out," he hissed.

Chapter Sixty-One

DRAKE RETURNED to find Wayne Berryman sitting on the sofa, staring into an empty crystal tumbler. Casey and Carson were standing behind the sofa, with Liz next to them on her phone.

"Is he okay?" Drake asked when he joined them.

"He just finished his second Scotch, but hasn't said a word since you left," Casey reported.

"Did you get anything from Lee?" Carson asked.

"No, and I don't think Detective Cabrillo will get anything from him either," Drake said. "He's too calm, coming around and finding himself hog-tied on the floor. He's had training."

"Do we keep Berryman, or will Cabrillo want to take both of them in for questioning?" Casey asked Drake.

"He'll take Lee, not sure about Berryman."

Berryman jumped up on the other side of the sofa. "You said you'd protect me, Drake! I can't go with the police."

"I never said I'd protect you, Wayne. Detective Cabrillo will protect you, if you're honest with him and tell him why we found you taped to a chair in your condo."

"I can't do that."

"You don't have a choice, Wayne. You're involved in foreign

espionage and murder. Get a lawyer and figure out what you're going to tell the FBI. when Detective Cabrillo ultimately hands you over to them."

Liz finished her call and motioned with her head for the others to follow her.

She stopped on the other side of the room and waited for them to crowd around her.

"I used the software Kevin loaded on my iPad to unlock Lee's burner phone," she said, patting her cross-carry shoulder bag concealing her Glock 19 and her iPad. "Kevin was able to access the carrier's database and traced the call Lee made to this Major. The GPS coordinates show the call terminated north of here in Humboldt County. He says Google Earth shows the place to be some sort of a retreat on top of a mountain."

"Could Kevin identify the person Lee called," Drake asked.

"That's where it gets interesting," she said. "Using the carrier's call detail records and the GPS location logs, Kevin was able to find that Lee's had several calls from two places you visited; from Francis Zhang's residence and his travel agency in China Town."

"That can't be right," Casey said. "Why would Lee kill Zhang's wife if they're working together?"

"To keep me from talking with her," Drake answered. "They were afraid of what she might tell me."

"Then all of this has been a coverup, to keep anyone from finding out China had a spy at SkySage," Liz said.

"Then why kill Grace Liu, if she was their spy?" Casey asked.

"Because they didn't need her any longer, if they had me," Berryman said from the other side of the room.

He was standing at the mini bar fixing another drink.

"That's why they killed my mistress, to blackmail me and get me to spy for them at SkySage. Peter Cheng admitted that to me when he called this morning and told me to come here."

Drake crossed the room and stood in front of Berryman.

"You must have suspected that's what Cheng wanted all along. You're a smart guy, Berryman. How far were you willing to let this go, Wayne?" Drake demanded.

Berryman returned to the sofa and sat back, looking up at the ceiling. "I'm not as smart as you think, but I am smart enough to stop talking and hire a lawyer. It's clear that I've been set up."

Drake spun around and walked away from the privileged princeling of America's ruling class.

No lawyer's going to get you out of this one, Berryman, Drake thought. *Not if I have anything to say about it!*

"I'll call Cabrillo to get these two off our hands," he told Casey. "Let's keep what we know about Zhang's location to ourselves, for now. We need to figure out where we go from here."

"Are you thinking about going after Zhang and Cheng ourselves?" Casey asked.

"We may be the only ones who can act quickly enough to keep them from skipping out and making it back to China," Drake said.

"While you call Detective Cabrillo, I'll call Kevin and get him started pulling up everything he can find about this mountain top retreat," Casey said.

"Steve," Drake said, "Find out how long it will take us to get to this retreat in Humboldt County. We have until Monday to tell Microsoft we're not concerned about SkySage. If it will take us too long to drive there, we'll need transportation that will get us there quicker."

"Can we do this by ourselves?" Liz asked. "Kevin said the place covers a lot of acres, has a main house, cabins and several large buildings. Do we need to call in some of the team from Special Projects?"

"What do you think, Mike?" Drake asked.

"You're the head of Special Projects," Casey said. "It's your call."

"All right, we'll finish here and regroup back at the hotel. We'll know more about this retreat by then."

Chapter Sixty-Two

AFTER DETECTIVE CABRILLO pulled Drake aside and heard what happened when they got to Berryman's pied-a-terre, Cabrillo arrested Lee for the murder of Jennifer Chen and had him taken to his station downtown for processing.

Berryman had called his lawyer before he was taken downtown for questioning about his claim that his mistress had been murdered.

Drake did not tell the detective anything about the calls Tony Lee had received from Francis Zhang or the mountain top retreat in Humboldt County. If they were going after Zhang, they didn't need the San Francisco Police Department or the FBI getting in the way.

The MKT Restaurant and Bar at the Four Seasons Hotel had just opened the bar when Drake, Liz, Casey and Carson were escorted to a round leather-backed booth at the far end of the restaurant.

There was a scattering of customers seated near the windows with a fifth-floor view of Market Street and downtown San Francisco, but they were far enough away from them that privacy was not an issue.

When their waiter left after taking their orders for a late lunch,

Drake asked Steve Carson how long it was going to take them to get to the retreat.

"The GPS coordinates Kevin gave me puts our destination two hundred and seventeen miles north of here. Driving there on US-101 will take four hours, plus or minus, depending on traffic.

"The closest airport is the Arcata-Eureka airport. From there, Miranda, California is the closest town to the retreat. It's fifty-eight miles south southeast of Eureka, approximately a one-hour drive.

"The Arcata-Eureka Helicopter Charter Services has a fleet of helicopters we could use to fly there in a quarter of an hour," Carson reported.

"Mike, did Kevin get us more intel on this retreat?" Drake asked.

"When it sold several years ago, it was purchased by a nonprofit foundation dedicated to the study of Shaolin Kung Fu, as practiced by warrior monks for six hundred years. The foundation receives donations from people from all over the world, but most of them come from China.

"The retreat has a main house, fifteen guest cabins, a larger structure that's called an exhibition and training hall. The place is self-sufficient with solar power, and water.

"What caught my attention was the mention of running trails and an obstacle course. It's on a smaller scale, but it reminds me of some of the places we trained at in remote locations when we were in the Unit," Casey observed.

"Are there people there now?" Liz asked.

"There are, but we don't know how many,' Casey said. "The retreat is hosting an exhibition of the discipline of Shaolin Long Fist Kung Fu."

"This could be exciting," Liz said. "Martial artists from all over the world, studying the Kung fu discipline Bruce Lee made famous, on a mountain top retreat with someone we think is a Chinese spy."

"That's also good news, Liz," Drake said. "If the retreat is open to the public, what's to stop us from going in and looking around?"

"Is there any way to find out if it is open to the public?" Carson asked.

"Let's call and find out," Casey said. "Kevin sent me a picture of the main page on the retreat's website."

He opened his phone, studied the image in the text from Kevin and dialed the number.

After listening to his call ringing for half a minute, someone finally answered it.

"Yes?"

"Is this the Redwood Shaolin Retreat Center?"

"Yes."

"Is the Shaolin Long Fist exhibition open to the public?"

"No."

"Why is that? Aren't there kung fu students from around the world attending the exhibition? Surely some publicity would benefit the retreat."

"Only members can attend by invitation to exhibitions."

"Is membership open to the public? Could I become a member and attend?"

"Membership is by invitation also. Thank you for your interest in the exhibition," the man said and hung up.

Casey lowered his phone and shook his head. "The exhibition isn't open to the public. Members only and membership is by invitation."

"No wonder Zhang's there," Liz said.

"We don't need an invitation to just visit the place," Drake said.

"It didn't sound like we'll be greeted warmly, judging by the conversation I just had."

"What if we took a look around without them knowing it?" Drake asked and grinned. "We've used the Black Hornet nano drone before."

Casey considered Drake's suggestion and turned to Steve Carson, the PSS pilot.

"Can you fly to Seattle and get back here with Morales and a few others by sunrise?"

"Sure, no problem," Carson said. "How many others?"

"How many passengers can one of the helicopters you said were available to charter at that airport hold?"

"They list a Eurocopter AS 365 Dauphin in their fleet. I think it can carry eight passengers. We'll need to make sure it's available this weekend, before I bring four guys back with me."

"Who are you thinking about, Mike?" Drake asked.

"Bringing Morales for recon with the Black Hornet, as well as Dan Norris and two members of the hostage rescue unit. We might as well have the manpower, if we need it."

"Before we do something like that," Liz said, "Shouldn't we let the president know what we're thinking of doing. We've stayed within the plausible limits of a SkySage facility security assessment review. But dragging someone we think is a Chinese spy off private property, that's owned by a Chinese-funded nonprofit, will have blowback. I'd like to know the president has our backs if we do this."

"Liz is right," Casey agreed.

"I'll call him right now, if we agree this is something we're going to do," Drake said.

He saw three thumbs go up around the booth and left to call the president.

Chapter Sixty-Three

PRESIDENT BENJAMIN BALLARD was in the Executive Residence of the White House when he took Drake's call.

"Good evening, Adam."

"Mr. President, I need your advice. Before I explain on what, I need to know that I'm not compromising you or your administration in any way."

"Does this involve Congressman Bridge and what I asked you to look into for me?"

"Yes sir, it does."

"Then I'm already compromised for asking you to do it, aren't I? What have you learned?"

"I believe the man who killed Congressman Bridge's son did it to cover up Chinese espionage at SkySage, where Michael Bridge worked."

"What evidence do we have that China's involved in his death?"

Drake explained the path he followed to reach that conclusion; the punctured wetsuit Michael Bridge was wearing when he was killed, the disputed suicide of Wayne Berryman's intern at SkySage and the murder of the art professor by the man now in custody in San Francisco for her death, one Tony Lee.

"Lee worked for a Chinses/American named Francis Zhang, as a tour guide. Zhang's travel agency in San Francisco's China Town specializes in taking Chinese student on tours here and taking Americans on tours in China.

"Lee killed Zhang's wife on the Cal Berkeley campus, I believe, to keep her from talking to me. He was holding Wayne Berryman hostage in Berryman's condo in San Francisco today when we rescued Berryman.

"Berryman claims he was being blackmailed to spy for China. He says a man by the name of Peter Cheng convinced him that he had murdered his mistress. Berryman woke up one morning and found the woman in his bloody bed, stabbed to death. Cheng said he would keep anyone from finding out if Berryman agreed to replace China's spy at SkySage.

"Cheng's firm, HK Capital, LLC, in Hong Kong, was the source of startup funding for Wayne Berryman's private equity firm. Berryman then invested heavily in SkySage and now sits on its board of directors.

"We don't know where Peter Cheng is, but the man Tony Lee was taking calls from, Francis Zhang, is presently at a martial arts retreat in northern California. We want to go in and bring Zhang out before he slips away to China."

The president silently considered the implications of what he'd just heard and what he was being asked to authorize.

"When you say 'we', I suppose that means you and your friends at Puget Sound Security."

"Yes sir."

"What do plan on doing with this Zhang, if you find him?"

"What would you like us to do?"

"That is the problem, isn't it?"

"He could be held for questioning about his wife's murder," Drake suggested. "If that developed any information about espionage, the FBI could take over and handle it from there."

"Can we make sure that information about espionage is discovered?"

"There's a police detective here in San Francisco I trust. I can make sure that he investigates Zhang's relationship with Tony Lee and the calls Zhang made to Lee's burner phone while Berryman was being held in his condo. When Berryman is questioned about being tied up in his condo by Lee and his story that he was being blackmailed to spy for China, the FBI would have to be called in."

"Can we prove that Berryman was being blackmailed?"

"When he told us about it, we recorded it on a cell phone."

"Is there any evidence that my Secretary of the Treasury, Walter Berryman, is involved in any of this," the president asked.

"Not directly, but I wouldn't be surprised if you discover he has campaign contributions that will trace back to China."

"No, I wouldn't be surprised either. We'll cross that bridge when we come to it. When are you planning on going to this retreat to find Zhang?"

"This weekend."

"Have you shared any of this with Congressman Bridge?"

"I thought you might want to be the one to do that, when the time is right."

"Yes, I guess it should be me. Let me know if I can help with anything this weekend."

"Thank you, sir."

"Good luck Adam. Call me when you find Zhang."

"Yes sir."

Drake returned to the Four Season's restaurant and bar and walked to their booth through the tables of the other early diners.

"It's a go. He wished us good luck," he said as he sat down.

"Did he say anything about getting the FBI involved?" Liz asked.

"We're going to let Detective Cabrillo do that, after he questions Wayne Berryman about being blackmailed to spy for China."

"What does he want us to do with Zhang when we find him?" Casey asked.

"Let Cabrillo take him in for questioning about the murder of his wife. When Cabrillo has evidence of espionage involving Berryman, Lee and Zhang, he can turn it all over to the FBI and let them take it from there."

"Cabrillo should go with us to the retreat and take Zhang into custody," Liz asked. "Then we wouldn't be responsible for getting him back to San Francisco."

"Good idea," Drake said. "I'll ask him to come with us."

"If we're going through with this, we should be on our way," Steve Carson said.

"I'll call headquarters and have them waiting for us when we land," Casey said. "Any requests for breakfast, Steve, when we get there?"

"Coffee and maybe steak and eggs, since you're buying," Carson said.

"Better have some pastries too, for the flight back," Casey smiled. "Wouldn't want to be short on energy tomorrow."

"Go ahead, have your foodie fun," Drake said. "Liz and I will stay here, maybe hit the gym and then order room service."

"With a "Do Not Disturb" sign left on the door?" Casey grinned.

Chapter Sixty-Four

FRANCIS ZHANG SWORE and sat back in his black leather office chair. He had waited an extra thirty minutes for a call from his agent, Tony Lee.

He knew what protocol required when an agent failed to report in two times, in succession. Lee had failed to call the night before and hadn't called this morning, nine hours later. Zhang's orders were to report the failure to MSS and wait for instructions.

Peter Cheng was in Washington, D.C., arranging meetings with influential Americans the Ministry of State Security had identified for cultivation. Which meant his orders from MSS agents operating out of the embassy would be relayed swiftly to Cheng.

His last communication with Tony Lee had been yesterday when he told Lee to get Wayne Berryman to his condo. When Lee hadn't called to report that he had Berryman there, he'd assumed Lee was having trouble tracking down Berryman and needed more time. That didn't excuse Lee for failing to report in, but with everything else that had gone wrong in Operation Yoda, he hadn't been willing to admit complete failure.

He knew what it would mean if Berryman was alive and said enough to expose a Chinese espionage operation. Espionage that involved the murder of the son of a U.S. Congressman, involvement of the son of the current Secretary of the Treasury and attempted infiltration of the Pentagon's top-secret JEDI project.

America would respond aggressively, and war was possible.

And Francis Zhang and Peter Cheng would be taken back to China and executed, along with their families and friends.

Zhang wasn't willing to accept that.

He was the only one who knew that Lee had failed to report in. Calling Cheng, before he knew for certain why Lee had missed calling him, was premature. He needed time to think of a way to stay alive.

After taking time to make sure he wanted to do what he was about to do, Zhang called the owner of a cleaning company he knew that was loyal to the CCP.

"Huang, this is Francis Zhang. I have a job for you."

"How may I assist you?"

"A friend of ours has a condo on Russian Hill that needs cleaning. Please go to the address I'll text you. The owner, Mr. Berryman, wants to make sure it's spotless. Go there today and let me know what you think."

"Will the owner be there to meet me?" Huang asked.

"He should be, he's staying there."

"I'll leave for this condo as soon as I have the address."

"It's on its way. Thank you, Huang."

"We must all do what we can."

Zhang knew that Huang could be trusted. He'd sent him to Berryman's villa in Napa to make sure there was no evidence that Berryman's mistress had been killed there.

His second call was to a contact in Chinatown. Johnny Jiang was a Triad, the Chinese crime syndicate that began as a secret society in ancient China. He was also a fentanyl distributor with ties to the new Los Zheng Chinese cartel now operating out of Ensenada, Baja California, Mexico.

"Johnny, this is Z."

"Let me call you back."

Zhang waited for Jiang to call. He knew the younger man was

just being careful, but his unnecessary caution was an insult, one he would have to overlook this time. He needed Jiang's help.

"Sorry, I could not speak freely."

"I need two favors. There's a man that I need to find. If he's where I think he might be, I need you to service him."

"In what way?"

"You will know when you locate him. I will text you his name and where I think he might be. Same arrangement as before."

"The other favor?"

"I may need to visit your family in Ensenada. Can you arrange for me to travel there?"

"How long will you be staying?"

"Not long."

"How soon do you need me to make the travel arrangements?"

"Possibly today."

"Call me when you need to leave."

Zhang hoped that it wouldn't be today, but that depended on what Peter Cheng said when he called him.

Cheng had to realize that if they abandoned their plan, their fate was sealed. If he could convince Cheng they still had a chance to get what they needed from SkySage without Berryman, they still might survive.

His research on the personnel of SkySage had discovered one person, with a top-secret clearance that would give him access to JEDI. It would take time to compromise him, of course, but it was doable.

If he couldn't convince Cheng to try again to penetrate SkySage, he wasn't going back to China to be executed. MSS would come after him, but he had enough money in an offshore account, to make the hunt difficult for them. And until they found him, he intended to live well.

Before he had time to leave his office, the owner of the cleaning company called him.

"I couldn't get in the condo. It's a crime scene. I asked a neighbor down the hall what happened. She said she saw two men, the owner of the condo and a Chinese man, led away by the police," Huang reported.

Zhang took a deep breath. "It's what I was afraid of. Did the woman know where the men were taken?"

"No, the detective she talked with didn't say anything about that."

"Did she happen to get the detective's name?"

"Yes, Detective Cabrillo. She remembered his name, she said, because her last name is Castillo."

Chapter Sixty-Five

DRAKE AND LIZ watched the PSS Gulfstream G-650 taxi to the loading area at the Signature Flight Support terminal at the San Francisco International Airport Sunday morning. As soon as it rolled to a stop, they walked out pulling their luggage and boarded for the short flight to the Arcata-Eureka airport.

Detective Cabrillo was with them. He'd agreed to ride along, incase he was needed to lawfully detain Francis Zhang for questioning about Tony Lee, arrested for the murder of Zhang's wife.

Mike Casey was piloting the G-650, with Steve Carson as his co-pilot. Onboard with them were Dan Norris, two members of the PSS Hostage Rescue unit and Marco Morales.

Norris briefed Drake and Liz about what they'd learned about the retreat before flying to San Francisco, while Casey got the G-650 in line for taking off.

"The valley below the mountain top where the retreat is located has been socked in by fog for most of last week," he said. "It is again this morning. The fog usually burns off late-morning or early-afternoon, but we can't count on it to do that.

"Two Suburbans are waiting for us when we land, along with a Eurocopter Dauphin we're leasing for the day. Steve will follow us down in the Eurocopter, flying above the fog, to be there if we need him or if Zhang makes a run for it.

"I used near real-time satellite imagery from Zoom Earth on the flight down. There doesn't appear to be much going on. I don't anticipate that we'll have any trouble getting up to the retreat center," Norris said.

Drake looked to Detective Cabrillo and asked, "If we do, how do you want to handle it?"

"By the book. I know you have an interest in Zhang that might be different than mine. But if he's involved in any of the murders you told me about, I want a clean case to present to the District Attorney."

"Buckle up, boys and girls, we're about to take off," Casey called out from the cockpit.

Drake felt the increasing G-forces push him back into his seat, as the G-650 raced down the runway. When they were airborne, and the rate of acceleration decreased, he felt a momentary sensation of being weightless, as the plane began its climb. It was the point at which he always relaxed and settled in for the flight ahead.

"Has Wayne Berryman said anything beyond what he told us at his condo?" Drake asked Cabrillo in the seat across from him.

"No, his lawyer won't let him say anything about anything."

"Have you identified his mistress?"

"She works at his firm, but we can't find her."

"What about Peter Cheng, the man Berryman said told him he would take care of his dead mistress?"

"Cheng flew to Washington, D.C. The Metro police are looking for him."

When Drake felt the G-650 level off, he unbuckled his seat belt and went forward to talk with Casey in the cockpit.

He squatted down between the two pilots' seats and put his hand on Casey's right shoulder. "Have you given any thought to what we're going to do, if we can't guarantee Microsoft that SkySage deserves its facility security clearance?"

"That's all I've been thinking about. So far, I haven't come up with anything. There's too much at stake for the country, if we're not sure the JEDI work SkySage is doing hasn't been compromised, to chance it and give them a pass. If we don't come up with something this weekend, PSS isn't likely to weather the storm if Microsoft comes after us for any cost overruns they incur.

"I have Kevin going over everything on their IT system to see if it's been breached. He hasn't found anything, but that doesn't mean Berryman's intern didn't get her hands on something before she was killed," Casey said.

"If she did, she had to pass it on to someone. I don't think Berryman was that someone. That leaves Zhang and Peter Cheng, of the people we know about. If they did, it would already be in China. They wouldn't have needed to kill Michael Bridge of Grace Liu, or Zhang's wife and give us a reason to think something was going on."

"Maybe they were just trying to cover their tracks, so we'd never find out that SkySage had been compromised," Casey suggested.

"Then there was no reason to kill Grace Liu. They could stop Michael Bridge from snooping around and leave Liu in place to keep passing along information. Mike, I don't think they got what they were after."

"How can we be sure?"

"I don't know. We'll find a way.

Drake returned to the main cabin and sat down next to Liz.

"We're running out of time to wrap this up before Monday," he said. "I got us into this and wish I hadn't."

"You did the right thing. You had no way of knowing what was involved, when you agreed to go to that autopsy with the congressman."

"Yeah, but I could have let it go when they opened the homicide investigation. I could have let the sheriff in Hood River handle it."

"You could have, but that's not you," Liz said. "We have today and tomorrow. Let's find Zhang and have him explain his relationship with Tony Lee and Peter Cheng. That may give us what we need to put this puzzle together and tell Microsoft what they need to hear."

Drake felt the G-650 reduce speed and start its descent to the

Arcata-Eureka airport. Looking down out his window at the redwood coast of northern California, he saw the small valleys inland from the coastline were filled with fog.

"We're five minutes from landing," Casey called out. "Seats and seatbelts, everyone."

We're coming for you Zhang, Drake thought. *Get ready to answer some questions.*

Chapter Sixty-Six

THE TWO GRAY Chevrolet Suburbans pulled over onto the shoulder of the road across from a cattle guard on the mountaintop retreat's western boundary. A gravel driveway ran due east from the cattle guard straight through an open field sloping up to the tree line a hundred yards away.

A black four-rail vinyl fence line extended north and south along the road for at least two hundred yards until it disappeared in dense fog. On the fence post to the left of the cattle guard was a red and white no trespassing sign, warning of guard dogs on the property.

Drake was driving the lead SUV with Detective Cabrillo riding shotgun. Liz was in the seat behind Cabrillo and Casey was sitting behind Drake.

Dan Norris was behind the wheel of the second SUV, with Marco Morales next to him. The two members of the HRT unit sat behind them.

Drake picked up his pair of Steiner tactical binoculars and glassed the edge of the tree line for any sign of guard dogs or their handlers.

"Once we across the field, the trees are ten feet away on either side of the driveway," he said. "I don't like it."

"That's because you won't see the dogs until the last second when they attack," Casey teased his friend, who wasn't fond of guard dogs. "Just keep your window up and you'll be fine."

"Thanks, Mike. That helps."

"How far is it to the retreat center through the trees?" Liz asked.

"From the road to the retreat center, it's seventh tenths of a mile according to the satellite surveillance imagery," Casey told her. "This isn't a very tall mountain."

Drake reached forward and touched the Phone icon on the Suburban's MyLink home screen and called Dan Norris in the second SUV.

"We're going in," he said. "Any questions?"

"We'll follow your lead if we run into trouble." Norris reply

"Just defend yourselves, if we do. We're just here to talk to Francis Zhang, nothing more."

"Roger that, just a normal "knock and talk" approach to a martial arts retreat, where a suspected felon and spy might be hiding, and there's a no trespassing sign warning of guard dogs. What could go wrong?"

Drake checked his mirrors and pulled back onto the road. Norris was right behind him when he signaled to turn left and then drove across the cattle guard.

The fog was beginning to lift a little, but the road through the tree line sill looked like a dark tunnel they were about to enter.

Unlike the straight path that cut across the middle of the field, the driveway on the other side of the field curved to the south fifty yards into the tunnel and began to climb up the mountain. A hundred yards later, it doubled back on itself, climbing again through the dense stand of Douglas fir trees.

Drake broke the silence in the SUV by saying how the driveway reminded him of a trip he took with his parents when his Dad was home on leave from the army.

"At the top of the Cascades, the old McKenzie Highway has much tighter switchbacks than this. It's so steep and twisty, they close it during the winter when it snows. If you ever get the chance, take the scenic drive on your way over the Cascades to Central Oregon."

He slowed to drive around the next switchback. Halfway to the next switchback, Liz yelled as a wolf jumped out from the trees and leaped up against her door's window.

Drake slammed on the brakes, as three more wolves ran out onto the driveway, howling and jumping up at the windows on both sides of the SUV.

"Those aren't guard dogs," Cabrillo said excitedly. "They're wolves!"

A voice coming from the MyLink speaker corrected the detective over the open line from the second SUV.

"Actually, they're Chinese wolfdogs, a cross between a German Shepherd and a wolf," Morales said. "China bred them in Kunming, China, for their police and army. These look like they're closer to a wolf than a German Shepherd, which means they're illegal in California."

"What do you want to do?" Casey asked Drake.

"We drive on to the retreat center. Detective Cabrillo is here to talk to Zhang. A pack of wolfdogs frothing at the mouth won't stop him, right Detective?"

"Right you are, amigo. Drive on."

Drake slowly drove forward, past the wolfdogs snarling and jumping on both sides of the SUV, and then increased his speed. It wasn't enough to leave the wolfdogs behind, as he had to slow down for the next switchback, but it kept them from jumping up at the windows.

The two SUVs drove around two more switchbacks, with the wolfdogs running and barking alongside the lead SUV, until the driveway turned uphill and ran straight for fifty of sixty yards to an open area at the top of the mountain.

Twelve men wearing traditional black kung fu uniforms stood in a line at the entrance to the open area. Parked behind them were three dark red four-seat ATVs. Each man had a short wooden stick thirty inches of so long hanging loosely from his right hand.

Drake drove ahead slowly and stopped ten yards in front of the welcoming party. The pack of wolfdogs continued barking and snarling around the two SUVs, but they were no longer lunging at the windows.

Detective Cabrillo took his clip-on badge holder off his belt and rolled down his window far enough to hold it out. "Call off your dogs. I'm here on official business."

"Unless you have a warrant, turn around and leave," the man in the middle of the line called out.

"I just want to talk," Cabrillo said. "I don't need a warrant for that."

"Get out of that car without a warrant and those dogs will tear you to pieces," the man warned.

"Big mistake, saying that. You can shoot a dog in self defense and you just threatened me with one of them." Cabrillo pulled his SIG Sauer P226 from his shoulder holster and lowered his window.

"This is BS, man!" the man shouted. "You can't come here and shoot guard dogs. You were warned."

"One of these wolfdogs your favorite?" Cabrillo asked, pointing his pistol at one and then the other wolfdog outside his window.

After a short conversation between the leader and the man on his right, the second man raised a silent dog whistle to his lips.

The four wolfdogs took off like greyhounds chasing a mechanical rabbit and ran past the line of men toward a structure behind them.

"While Cabrillo goes forward to tell them why he's here, let's all calmly get out and stand beside our vehicles," Drake told everyone. "If this goes south, defend yourself."

Chapter Sixty-Seven

DETECTIVE CABRILLO HOLSTERED his pistol and got out of the lead SUV. The others followed his lead and stood beside their SUVs.

"I'm Detective Cabrillo, from the San Francisco Police Department," he announced as he approached the line of men. "I'd like to speak to Francis Zhang."

"There's no one here by that name," the lead man said.

Late twenties, five feet ten, medium length straight black hair down over his ears. It was hard to guess his weight, with the loose-fitting black kung fu uniform he was wearing.

But Drake had no problem judging the man for what he was. He was a soldier, or at least had been at one time. He recognized the look of a man seemingly relaxed, but ready to strike like a cobra. The end of his fighting stick was circling ever so slightly.

"This is about his wife's murder," Cabrillo said. "I'm sure he'll want to hear what we've learned about the man who killed her."

"Like I said, he's not here."

"But he was here, wasn't he?"

The man didn't answer, as he looked from Cabrillo back to Drake and then to the others around the SUVs.

Casey heard the whine of a helicopter turbine as it began to spool up for takeoff. "There's a helicopter getting ready to take off back there," he said softly from behind Drake. "That's gotta be Zhang."

Drake looked behind Casey to Norris standing beside the second SUV. "Dan, stop that helicopter from taking off."

"Let's move," Norris told his men.

When the men guarding the retreat center noticed the movement, their sticks were raised in unison and they assumed a fighting stance. Their round wooden sticks were held up in front of their bodies at a forty-five-degree angle, ready to strike.

Norris and the two men from the HRT unit started to jog toward the sound of the helicopter spooling up, when half of the black-clad line of men moved to block their path.

The man closest to Norris rushed toward him with his fighting stick raised above his head when Detective Cabrillo fired a warning shot in the air and stopped him.

"Let them pass," he said, in the stillness that followed the shot.

Norris had drawn his pistol and circled the man cautiously before jogging on with his team flanking him.

As the six men who broke rank to stop Norris and his men moved back in line, the leader took out his silent dog whistle and raised it to his lips. When he lowered it, he smirked and raised a hand to his ear to hear the wolfdogs when they attacked.

"Hope their good shots," he said over the sound of barking dogs and the rising pitch of a helicopter's turbine approaching maximum revolutions.

Four shots rang out, muffled by the snarl of a small engine of a helicopter taking off.

A small black one-seat helicopter rose from behind the main building, piloted by a man Drake recognized as Francis Zhang.

Casey watched with Drake as Zhang escaped. "It's an ultralight private helicopter called a Mosquito XET. Top speed of a hundred miles an hour, his range is about a hundred miles with the twelve gallons of fuel it carries. Didn't figure on him having one of those."

"How can he fly in this fog?" Drake asked.

"Unless he's practiced flying an escape route, he won't get far. This mountain is surrounded by several taller mountains."

"Can Steve track him?"

"Only if he has a visual, which he doesn't unless Zhang flies above the fog. "I'll call Steve and ask what the ceiling is right now. We might get lucky"

Norris and his men jogged back and joined them beside the lead SUV.

"The wolfdogs slowed us down enough for him to get away," Norris said. "Sorry."

Drake nodded toward the twelve men blocking their entrance to the retreat center. "What do you want to do with them?" he asked Cabrillo.

"I'd like to know who they are, but I'm not going to arrest them for obstructing justice, especially here in Humboldt County. I don't know the District Attorney well enough to ask him to prosecute them for me."

Liz stood next to Drake and slipped her new iPhone out of her pocket. "Turn your back to them," she told Drake. "I'll take their picture over your shoulder. Maybe Kevin can ID them for us."

Drake turned around and said to Cabrillo standing next to her, "If you can get them to back up a little so we can turn around, we may as well get out here. I'm not going to drive backwards down all those switchbacks."

"Consider it done," Cabrillo said and walked toward the line of men.

While they kept an eye on Cabrillo to make sure he returned unharmed, Casey's phone buzzed in his pocket.

"Go ahead Steve, we're about finished down here," he said.

Casey reached out and put a hand on Drake's shoulder. "Can we get there from here, or do we need you to get us close?"

Casey listened and then said, "When we get down to the road, give us directions and we'll see how close we can get in these SUVs."

"What did Steve say?" Drake asked.

"He thinks Zhang may have crashed. He saw a burst of red light through the fog from an explosion or something five or six miles from here."

Drake turned around and saw Cabrillo flash him a thumbs up and said, "Load 'em up. If that's Zhang and he survived, we still might get what we came for."

Chapter Sixty-Eight

RACING down the mountain and taking the switchbacks as fast as he dared, Drake slid the lead SUV to a stop at the cattle guard. "Which way, Steve, right or left," he asked.

"Turn left at the road," Carson answered from the Eurocopter AS365 hovering over them above the fog. "My map shows the road running straight down the valley and then veering west around another mountain taller than the one you're leaving. The top of that mountain is above the fog and the red burst was maybe a hundred yards from the top."

"Roger that," Drake said and fishtailed out onto the road after spinning the wheels crossing the cattle guard.

"I'll bet Zhang's escape route was to follow the road to a landing site nearby, but he didn't count on the fog hiding the mountain," Casey said from the seat behind Drake. "Flying low at a hundred miles an hour, he wouldn't have time to pull up if he saw the road turning west."

"Could he survive a crash in that little helicopter?" Liz asked, sitting next to Casey.

"Doubtful, if he flew into the side of the mountain," Casey said.

"Possible, if he clipped a tree or something and it slowed him down."

"We're about a mile away," Drake said, calculating his speed and the time he'd been driving since crossing the cattleguard. "We'll park the SUVs and take off for the crash site. But someone should stay back and direct the EMTs, if we need to call an ambulance. Any volunteers?"

No one offered to stay back.

"Detective, would you mind? If he's alive and we learn something that's beyond the scope of your murder investigation, you might not want to get involved."

Cabrillo snorted. "It's too late for that. Remember, I'm providing the official reason for trying to find him at the retreat. I can't turn it all over to you at this point."

"We'll draw straws and someone from HRT will stay," Norris's voice boomed out from the MyLink speaker on the dash. "We'll be the first to find the crash site anyway, and you don't need three guys up there with our qualifications. Two of us can handle it."

Loud boisterous laughing from the passengers in the lead SUV answered the challenge.

When Drake slowed down and pulled over to the shoulder of the road, he reminded them that while this wasn't a race, they needed to be careful when they reached the site.

Then he threw open his door, ran across the road, jumped over a shallow ditch and disappeared into the Douglas Fir trees that bordered the road.

Ten yards into the gloom beneath the tall trees, darkened by the fog, Drake waited for the others to join him. The steep slope and the closeness of second growth trees to one another made running impossible and foolish.

"Marco, why don't you take point," Drake said. "You're good at finding your way through stuff like this."

Marco Morales, former Army Long Reconnaissance Patrol (LRRP) Ranger, nodded and moved in front of Drake to lead the way up the mountain.

The fragrance of the fir trees and the soft cushion of the needles on the ground beneath his feet brought a rush of memories of hiking in to fish the high lakes of the Cascades with Drake's father. Whenever he was home on leave from the army during fishing season, the two of them would spend a week together, camping and fishing and hiking.

These were the most sacred memories he had of his father, because there was so few of them. His father had been killed in some foreign country the army wouldn't name, on a mission there was no record of, when Drake was still in grade school. His father had been a special forces operator, like Drake had become when it was his time to serve.

They followed Morales straight up the steep slope for fifteen or twenty minutes until he found a deer trail that made it easier to walk through the trees. Another ten minutes and the smell of smoke signaled they were getting close to a possible crash site.

Morales held up his fist and stopped their progress. "If he survived, he could be armed and waiting for us. Let me scout ahead and make sure he's not, before you follow."

Drake waited until Morales was out of sight and then headed up the trail, with the others walking single file behind him. After a hundred yards, the wreckage of the ultralight helicopter came into view through the trees. Morales was motioning them forward.

When they reached the wreckage, Morales was searching the ground around the crumpled frame of the ultralight and the scorched plexiglass bubble of the cockpit.

"There's no sign of Zhang but he's hurt," Morales said, pointing to some red drops of blood on blackened fir needles.

Casey walked closer to the wreckage and examined the front of one of the landing skids. It was bent at angle outward from what was left of the helicopter's small frame.

He looked up through the trees above and pointed. "It looks like he snagged the top of a tree with his landing skid. He couldn't gain altitude fast enough and came crashing down."

"We have to find him," Drake said. "Let's stay together and

search the area. There'll be something that shows us which way he went."

Liz found it at the base of a fir tree uphill. "Up here!" she shouted."

Chapter Sixty-Nine

DRAKE BENT DOWN TO get a closer look at the small pool of clear vomit Liz was pointing at. "Clear vomit's a sign of a head injury or concussion."

"If he's disoriented, who knows where's he's headed," Casey said. "He could be going in circles."

"This way," Morales said, moving laterally to the right, away from the others. "There's vomit and some blood over here."

Drake looked in the direction where Morales stood. "Let's spread out and walk in a line due west from here. He has a head start, but he won't be moving that fast. Finding him alive is the best chance we have to wrap this up for SkySage."

With an arm's length distance between them, six men and one woman carefully searched the ground ahead of them, as they moved though the steep forested slope of the mountain.

Casey was to the right of Morales on the end of the line and found the next sign of Zhang. "It's not much, but there's a spot of blood on the ground here. I can see down through the trees in a straight line for fifty yards or so. He might have gone that way."

"We'll wait while you check it out, Mike," Drake said.

Casey veered right thirty degrees and moved slowly down through the opening in the trees. When he was twenty yards away, he stopped and turned back. Holding his right arm out horizontally in front of his body, he raised his forearm back vertically and gave the signal to join him.

He then turned away, extended his right arm parallel to the ground and then raised his forearm up until it was perpendicular, signaling contact made to the right. Casey had spotted Zhang.

Drake silently led the others down through the trees and stood next to Casey.

Zhang was slumped back against the foot of a large fir tree thirty feet away.

"Is he alive?" Drake asked.

"I can't tell," Casey said. "He's facing away, but he hasn't moved."

Drake pulled his Kimber Ultra Carry II out from his new small of the back (SOB) leather belt holster and kept it aimed at Zhang, as he moved cautiously forward.

Zhang had what looked like a SIG Sauer P228 in his right hand resting on top of his leg.

Drake stepped behind a small fir tree to his right and looked around it to see if Zhang was alive. Zhang's head was facing downhill and he couldn't see his eyes.

"Zhang, toss your pistol away. We just want to talk."

Ten seconds later, he asked, "Zhang, do you hear me?"

Drake stepped around the tree with his pistol aimed at Zhang's head, then lowered it. Zhang's eyes were closed and his chin was resting on his left shoulder.

He moved between the trees to Zhang and knelt to check for a pulse. "He's dead," he called out and stood.

The left side of the man's head was covered in blood from a deep gash that extended from his temple back to a spot above his ear.

Drake took the pistol laying on Zhang's right leg and saw that it was a Norinco Type 34, the Chinese clone of the SIG Sauer P228.

While he waited for the others to join him, he searched Zhang. In the right pocket of his brown leather bomber jacket was a burner phone Drake was familiar with, a Plum Ram 7 military-grade burner phone. In the inside breast pocket of the jacket, was a blue United States passport book.

Drake laid the phone and passport on the ground next to the Type 34 pistol.

"Looks like he was planning a trip," Detective Cabrillo said pointing at the passport.

"Like a trip out of the country?" Morales asked and picked up the pistol. "China maybe?"

"Does he have anything else on him?" Liz asked. "Did you check his pants pockets?"

"Let me take a picture of him before he's moved," Cabrillo said and took a picture of Zhang with his phone.

Drake took a hold of Zhang's shoulders and tipped him to one side for Liz to search his rear pants pockets.

Liz held up a black leather wallet so Cabrillo could take a picture of it before she opened it.

She took out five one hundred-dollar bills from the wallet, along with a driver's license, assorted credit cards and two membership cards. One was for the Society for Asian Art and the other was for the National Association for China's Peaceful Unification.

"Nothing helpful," she said.

"Not directly, maybe," Detective Cabrillo said. "The National Association for China's Peaceful Unification has been associated with China's United Front activities. I'm familiar with it in San Francisco. It aims to influence politicians in foreign countries and neutralize sources of opposition to the policies and goals of the Chinese Communist Party. His membership does tell us something about his politics."

"But it doesn't prove that an espionage operation at SkySage failed," Drake said. "We still don't have what we came here for, evidence that China didn't get its hands on SkySage's AI development for JEDI."

"Unless there's something on Zhang's phone that helps us find what we need," Liz said. "Lee's phone led us to Zhang. Maybe Zhang's phone will tell us who he reports to."

Casey picked up Zhang's phone. "Kevin can find out."

Chapter Seventy

DETECTIVE CABRILLO WAITED with Drake and Liz for the Humboldt County Sheriff's deputies to arrive and take control of the crash site. Casey and the other three men returned to the airport to wait for them in the comfort of the PSS Gulfstream G-650.

No one seemed to know if the FAA or the NTSB investigated ultralite helicopter crashes, but if they did, the fewer of them who were involved the better. Explaining why they visited the Kung Fu retreat with a former FBI HRT commander, a former Ranger LRRP and two former Navy SEALs would require them to tell more of what they knew than they were prepared to.

After introducing themselves to the Humboldt County deputies and leaving Detective Cabrillo to answer their questions, Drake and Liz waited in the remaining SUV for Cabrillo to join them.

"I'd like to take another shot at Wayne Berryman," Drake told Liz. "When his attorney tells him what he's facing, he'll be begging for a deal."

"If he isn't, we're in trouble. I don't think Tony Lee is going to tell us anything."

"No, I agree. He isn't going to talk unless he's waterboarded, and we know that's not going to happen. Even if it did, his training would get him through even that."

Detective Cabrillo shook hands with the two deputy sheriffs and started walking toward their SUV. Halfway to them, he stopped and took his cellphone out from the black leather case on his belt.

With it held up to his ear and his head bowed, he nodded twice and then looked at Drake and shook his head.

"I don't think we're going to like what Cabrillo's about to tell us," he said to Liz.

Detective Cabrillo opened the rear door of the SUV and got in behind Liz. "Good news and bad news," he said.

Drake turned around to face Cabrillo. ""Do we want to hear the bad news first?"

"Probably not. The good news is we're free to leave for the airport. The bad news is they just found Wayne Berryman dead in his cell."

"How could that have happened?" Liz exclaimed.

"They think he was poisoned. He'd just met with his lawyer. He had a cup of coffee that one of the civilian staff brought him, and then collapsed in his holding cell not long after his lawyer left."

"Do they suspect his lawyer?" Drake asked.

"No reason to, at this point," Cabrillo said. "The employee who took Berryman his coffee is Chinese/American and can't be located."

Drake turned the SUV around and drove north to the airport in Eureka. They were running out of time and individuals to question who might have been involved in an espionage plot at SkySage, Inc.

If they couldn't prove that the plot had failed, their client would lose its biggest contract and probably any future contracts that involved handling and protecting top secret information.

And Puget Sound Security would take a financial hit it might not be able to survive.

The only sounds in the SUV were from the humming tires on the blacktop and, the muffled exhaust from its engine and the rushing wind outside. They were all thinking about the questions they hadn't been able to answer.

Drake and Liz reached the same conclusion at the same time.

"We have to find…" Liz said.

"Berryman's investor from Hong Kong," Drake finished for her.

"But we don't know where he is. If he made it back to Hong Kong, they're not going to let us get to him."

"Maybe he stuck around to make sure Berryman didn't talk," Cabrillo offered.

"Can you check and see if Peter Cheng, the manager of HK Capital, LLC, is still in San Francisco?" Drake asked Cabrillo. "Find out if he's planning to fly home, if he already hasn't? We might get lucky."

Cabrillo got his phone out and called his station. "I'll get someone on it," he said, as he waited for his assistant to answer.

Drake used his MyLink Bluetooth connection and called Casey. "Mike, we're headed your way. Are we ready to fly back to San Francisco?"

"Just waiting for you three. Everything all right with the locals?"

"Detective Cabrillo handled it but Berryman's dead."

"What?"

"They think he was poisoned. They found him in his holding cell. One of the civilian employees brought him coffee and now they can't find the employee."

"That's it then. Zhang's dead, Berryman's dead and Tony Lee's not going to help us."

"Maybe not. We still have the guy who told Berryman he'd take care of his dead mistress. Cabrillo's trying to find out if he's still in San Francisco or buying a ticket to fly home to Hong Kong. He wouldn't leave until he knew Berryman had been silenced."

"Pray that Cabrillo finds him. I have to make a call Monday that I'm dreading if we don't get some answers."

"We'll find him, Mike. Has Kevin been able to find out who Zhang was calling?"

"I haven't checked since we got back to the airport. I'll call Kevin."

"Any chance you have something to eat when we get there?"

Drake asked. "Climbing that mountain to find Zhang made me hungry?"

"You know me well enough to know the answer to that. Of course, there's food… while it lasts."

Chapter Seventy-One

WHEN THEY BOARDED the PSS jet, Drake was relieved to find that Casey had ordered enough pub food from a nearby grill to satisfy everyone, including a nice Chef salad for Liz.

Casey was eating one of the largest burritos he'd ever seen.

Drake sat down across from Casey and asked, "Was Kevin able to get anything from Zhang's phone?"

Casey put his burrito down onto the paper plate on his lap and nodded. "Zhang made a number of calls to the Grand Hyatt at Union Square in San Francisco. The last call Zhang received was from the same number he'd been calling, but it originated from the Hay-Adams in Washington, D.C. He got it just before we arrived at the retreat."

"Zhang could have been talking to anyone," Drake shrugged. "That doesn't help much."

"If that was from Cheng's phone, we'd at least know where to look for him."

Detective Cabrillo was standing in the aisle next to the galley, talking on the phone when they heard him say "Yes" loudly and walk toward them.

"Peter Cheng checked out of the Grand Hyatt Friday afternoon and flew to D.C.," he said proudly. "I have a green light to detain and question him about Berryman's claim that Cheng was involved in the murder of his mistress. We've learned that she was a secretary at Berryman's firm and that she's missing."

"Do you know where Cheng is in D.C.?" Drake asked.

"He's in D.C., that's all I know."

Drake looked to Casey before saying, "We may know where he is."

Cabrillo grimaced before asking, "Like you knew where Zhang was?"

"Perhaps," Drake smiled.

"And if you tell me, you'll want me to go with you to D.C. and arrest him, I suppose?"

"I suppose."

"Will you have room for another passenger, if I say yes?"

"Mike...?"

Casey checked the time on his watch. "It's twelve thirty, Pacific Time. If we leave right now, we can be in D.C. by seven o'clock tonight. Will that work for you, Detective?"

"Absolutely."

"Dan, does the HRT team need to get back to Seattle?" Casey asked.

"No, HRT's good to go if you want us to tag along."

"Okay, we'll be wheels up as soon as we file our flight plan."

Drake got up and moved across the aisle from Liz. "I think I'll call Senator Hazelton and let him know we're coming. He might be able to reach out to the committee and locate Cheng for us. I also told him that I had a surprise for he and Mom."

"And would that be this?" she asked, lifting her left hand to admire the ring on her finger.

"That's the only surprise I can think of."

"I doubt they'll be surprised."

"We'll see." Drake got up and kissed the top of her head. "You want something from the galley?"

"I'm fine, thanks."

Drake walked back to the aft galley and sat down in the seat across from it to call his father-in-law. It was three thirty on Saturday afternoon and he guessed the senator was either playing golf or helping his wife, Meredith, take care of her prized roses on the back deck of their Georgetown rowhouse.

He guessed wrong. Senator Hazelton was just saying goodbye to members of the "committee", small "c", after grilling lunch for them on the back deck.

"Adam, give me a minute to get the guys back here," Senator Hazelton said. "If you're calling about what you ask us to look into, they'll want to hear what you've learned as well."

"Sure, call them back. That is why I'm calling."

The four current members of the informal group that came together to deal with the Antifa and anarchist violence the summer, before consisted of the former Director of National Intelligence, Michael Montgomery, the former head of the counterterrorism division of the NYPD, the former chairman of the Senate Select Committee on Intelligence, Senator Martin Montez and Senator Hazelton, the current chairman of the Senate Select Committee on Intelligence.

While Senator Hazelton left to reconvene the committee on the back deck, Drake's mother-in-law came online.

"Hello Adam. When are you going to come visit us?"

"Actually, we'll be there tonight. We're just getting ready to takeoff from California."

"Is Liz coming with you?"

"She is."

"Then you must come for dinner."

"We might not be able to make it tonight, but I promise we'll come see you before we leave."

"You'd better," she said. "Here's your father-in-law."

"Adam, we're all here and you're on speaker phone," Senator Hazelton said. "Why don't you go first and tell us why you're calling."

"Hello everyone. I have a lot to tell you, but I'd better do that in person. The reason I called is to ask for your help finding someone I believe is in your city. The man's name is Peter Cheng, the manager of Hong Kong Capital, LLC. My information is that he's staying at the Hay-Adams or has made calls from there as late as this morning."

"Is this about the matter we discussed involving Congressman Bridge and his son?" Senator Hazelton asked. "I shared our conversation about that with the committee."

"Yes, it does," Drake said.

"I think I may know where Mr. Cheng is," Senator Montez said. "His name was on a list of prominent Chinese businessmen here to lobby Congress about the U.S. and China trade agreement. They were invited by the Secretary of the Treasury, Walter Berryman, to play a round of golf at the Congressional Country Club this afternoon."

"Is there any way to confirm that and keep an eye on Cheng?" Drake asked.

"I think I can arrange for someone to do that," Mark Holland said.

"I'm about to take off from California, ETA Ronald Reagan National at seven o'clock tonight," Drake said. "A detective from the San Francisco Police Department will be with me. He's coming to detain Mr. Cheng for questioning, before he has a chance to escape to China."

"Is this a matter the FBI should be involved in?" Senator Hazelton asked.

"It depends on what Mr. Cheng has to say about his recent activities."

"Do you need anything else?" Mark Holland asked.

"Not at this point. I'm coming with some of the men who helped me in the recent past. It will be the president's call on how this is handled after Cheng is questioned by Detective Cabrillo."

"Enjoy the flight, son," Senator Hazelton said. "I'll relay the information about Cheng's location when you get here."

"Thanks for your help, gentlemen. I'll tell you the rest of the story later."

Chapter Seventy-Two

WITH A STRONG TAILWIND boosting their speed, the PSS Gulfstream G-650 landed at Ronald Reagan National Airport at six fifteen Sunday evening. As it taxied to the Signature Flight Support terminal, Drake called Senator Hazelton to let him know they had landed.

"Mark Holland is waiting for you at the Hay-Adams Hotel," Senator Hazelton said. "After spending the afternoon playing golf, the Chinese businessmen are scheduled to have dinner in the Hay-Adams Private Dining room at seven o'clock tonight. Mark Holland says the dining room was booked by Secretary Berryman for three hours. Holland will meet you in the lobby when you get there."

"Do we know if he's met with Secretary Berryman, by any chance?" Drake asked.

"Unknown, but the Secretary is on the dinner's program as a guest speaker."

"Thank you, senator. We're staying at the Hyatt Place tonight. Tomorrow, if everything goes as planned, Liz and I would like to come over tomorrow and say hello, if you're available."

"Of course, we're available for you two whenever you're in town. Let me know how it goes tonight."

"I will."

Drake stood to tell the others seated behind him what he'd learned. "Cheng is having dinner at the Hay-Adams tonight at seven o'clock with a group of Chinese businessmen. Secretary Berryman is their host and their guest speaker. This shouldn't take long."

"What's the plan after we find Cheng?" Dan Norris asked. "Is he going back to San Francisco?"

"I'm still working on that," Drake said. "The plan was to make sure he didn't escape to China. Detective Cabrillo could have arrested him in San Francisco, but we didn't find him there. We rushed here because by the time we convinced the FBI to do something, he'd be back in China.

"When we have Cheng, my "plan" is to call the president and let him tell us what to do with Cheng. If Cheng is acting on behalf of China and responsible for the death of a U.S. citizen, especially the son of a U.S. Congressman, it's an act of war.

"And if a member of the president's cabinet is involved in some way, how he handles it will decide the fate of his administration and his presidency. That's my plan, Dan, to hand the ball off to the president and let him run with it."

The Gulfstream rolled to a stop outside the Signature terminal and Casey announced from the cockpit that ground transportation was waiting for them curbside and they would be leaving in ten minutes.

After making brief pit stops where necessary and loading their luggage in two silver Lincoln Navigators, the seven members of the PSS team and Detective Cabrillo left Arlington, Virginia, to make the fifteen-minute drive to the Hay-Adams Hotel on H Street Northwest.

As they crossed the Potomac on I-395 at dusk, with the lights coming on in the city, Drake felt a of ambivalent about his country's capital. The nation's founders had been concerned that people in the city would have too much influence on Congress and decided that people living there should not be represented in the House of Representatives or the Senate. And now the people living inside the

The SkySage Affair

Beltway bubble seemed to be the only ones who had any influence at all in the way the country was governed.

And yet it was a majestic place, with a rich history.

Like the hotel they were approaching across the street from Lafayette Square, one of the city's most famous landmarks.

Leaving their two Lincoln Navigators with the hotel's parking valet attendants, Drake entered the hotel with Liz on his arm. They were dressed a little to casually for the Hay-Adams, judging by the more formal attire people in the lobby were wearing, but they hadn't planned on being in Washington.

Drake and the other men wore sport coats and slacks, leaving it to Liz to dress up the group's appearance. She wore a below the knee simple black dress, to conceal the Sig P365 in a garter holster on her left thigh, and heels.

The man walking across the lobby to meet them was dressed even more casually than they were. Mark Holland was wearing a black windbreaker over a light blue polo, tan khakis and brown Sperry Top-Sider deck shoes.

Holland shook hands with Drake and said softly, "You may have some trouble getting to Cheng. There are sixteen men in the group for the dinner Secretary Berryman is hosting. Six of them are security, from the looks of them. China's keeping a close watch on these guys."

"Where's Cheng?"

"They're all downstairs in the hotel's bar, having a drink before dinner."

"Can we separate Cheng from his security?" Drake asked.

Holland shook his head. "I don't see how, without putting a lot of people at risk."

"What if we get him to shake his security and come to us" Liz asked.

Drake looked puzzled. "How?"

"We have Zhang's phone. We could send him a message telling him he's about to be arrested, that he can't trust his security and get out of the hotel. We intercept him when he makes a run for it."

"It might work," Holland said. "You have time to set it up, but you'll need help to pull it off. You don't want to create an international incident that involves China."

"What kind of help are you thinking about?" Drake asked, although he had an idea what Holland had in mind.

Holland nodded in the direction of the White House across Lafayette Square.

Chapter Seventy-Three

DRAKE LISTENED as Mark Holland explained what he had in mind.

"I had a friend inside the Hay-Adams send me a list of its current guests. There's a delegation of Chinese Christian pastors here for a private meeting with the president next week. They're asking him to speak out on China's persecution of Christianity," Holland said. "I also checked out the security guards minding the businessmen's group Cheng's with. They're from a Chinese private security company the CCP employs to protect China's interests abroad."

"Okay, how does that help us?"

"This particular company has a history of letting its employees disregard gun laws when they operate abroad. To make sure the Christian pastors are safe and won't be intimidated by these CCP thugs, you could ask the president to have the Secret Service come over and make sure they're not breaking our D.C. gun laws. When they're being searched, we send the text to Cheng. If he doesn't make a run for it, we go in and escort him out."

"I like it. The president has a reason for disarming the security guards, the guests of the Hay-Adams are protected, and Peter Cheng is arrested quietly. Do you have someone keeping an eye on Cheng?" Drake asked.

"One man in Off The Record and another near the private dining room," Holland said. "I've been covering the lobby."

"Mike, Liz, what do you think?"

"We'll need to make sure Cheng doesn't try to hide somewhere inside and wait us out," Casey said. "We have to keep him boxed in."

"Liz?"

"We also have to make sure he can't make a run for it if he manages to leave the hotel."

"All right, you guys figure that out and I'll call the president."

Drake left the lobby and walked outside under the portico and stood next to a column, looking south toward the White House.

Lafayette Square was closed to the public, with a thirteen-foot-tall black fence across H Street and additional fencing and concrete barricades blocking all the entrances. Pennsylvania Avenue was also closed to traffic and had been since the bombing of the Federal Office Building in Oklahoma City in 1995.

The capital was a fortress now. He felt sorry for the president, cooped up day after day in a White House that had once been open to anyone who walked through its door and wanted to talk with their elected leader.

"Mr. President, Adam Drake. I'm here in Washington and need your help."

"What's happened, Adam?"

"The man we tried to talk to at the mountain retreat fled in an ultralight helicopter. He died when it crashed in the fog on the side of a mountain. The Chinese businessman I told you about is in the Hay-Adams tonight, having a dinner being hosted by the Secretary of the Treasury. Cheng's group includes private security guards from a Chinese private security company owned by the CCP. We need to neutralize the security guards to arrest Cheng without creating an international incident."

"How do we do that?"

"You have a private meeting with a group of Chinese Christian pastors next week. Treat them as visiting dignitaries, who the Secret Service has a duty to protect. Send in the Secret Service to make sure they're safe, by making sure the CCP's security guards aren't armed. They have a reputation for ignoring guns laws when they operate abroad. When the Secret Service introduces itself to the CCP guards, we warn Cheng he's about to be arrested. When he tries to make a run for it, we arrest him."

"Who arrests him and for what?"

"There's a San Francisco detective with me pursuing Cheng on a murder charge. He can make the arrest, unless you want the FBI to do it."

"If he's working with you, let him do it. How soon do you need the Secret Service there?"

"As soon as they can get here. I'll wait for them in the lobby."

"Give me fifteen minutes to get it organized," President Ballard said. "Good luck."

"Thank you, Mr. President."

Drake dashed back into the hotel and motioned for his team to huddle up.

When they gathered around, he said, "President Ballard is sending the Secret Service here. When they disarm Cheng's security guards, Liz sends Cheng a message that he's about to be arrested. When he makes a run for it, Cabrillo arrests him."

"And then what?" Dan Norris asked. "What are we going to do with Cheng after we arrest him?"

"Do you have a suggestion?" Drake asked.

"Why not let the FBI sit in on Cheng's initial questioning here in D.C.? They might let us use their field office."

"Do you have a particular FBI agent in mind for that?" Drake asked with a wink.

"She's worked with us before," Norris said.

"Is that okay with you, detective, if the SIAC that heads the Counterintelligence Division here in D.C., sits in when you question Cheng?" Drake asked.

"If it will help us make sure this guy gets what he deserves, invite her."

"Dan, go ahead and call Kate," Drake said. "Let's split up and partner with Mark Holland's guys to make sure Cheng doesn't slip through our fingers. Detective Cabrillo, Liz and I will keep a lookout here in the lobby and wait for the FBI."

Chapter Seventy-Four

DRAKE SPOTTED the lead Secret Service agent as soon as he entered the hotel lobby with a dozen agents following him. A stocky man in his forties, five ten or eleven with a shaved head and eyes quickly sweeping the lobby looking for him, the agent crossed the room and held out his hand.

"Agent Wilson," he said. "The president said you could use our help."

Drake shook hands and introduced Detective Cabrillo standing beside him. "We're in pursuit of a Chinese national that Detective Cabrillo is here to arrest on a felony murder charge. He's in the private dining room with a group of Chinese businessmen and six Chinese private security guards. We'd like to make sure our suspect can be extracted safely."

"Was it your idea for us to say we're here to make sure these guards aren't armed, in violation of our gun laws?"

"It was."

"How did you get the president to go along with that?"

A steely gaze preceded Drake's answer. "Does it matter?"

"It does, if there's something else involved that could make this go sideways and get someone hurt."

"One of these Chinese businessmen might also be involved in espionage on behalf of China," Drake said.

"Isn't that something the FBI should handle?"

Drake started to explain that there hadn't been time to involve the FBI when FBI Special Agent In Charge Kate Perkins walked up behind Agent Wilson and said, "That's why I'm here, Agent Wilson."

Wilson turned and said, "I wasn't told that you were involved."

"There wasn't time, Carl."

"Thanks for coming, Kate," Drake said. "If you're ready, Agent Wilson, take your men to the private dining room and make sure the Chinese security guards aren't carrying."

When the other Secret Service men were quickly briefed and left to distract the private security guards, Liz joined Drake and Kate Perkins with Francis Zhang's burner phone in her hand.

"Ready when you are," she said.

"Send the text," Drake told Liz and turned to Kate Perkins.

"The phone Liz has belonged to a Chinese cohort in San Francisco Cheng was communicating with just before that man died. She's sending him a message that he's about to be arrested, make a run for it. With any luck, he'll separate himself from the guards so we can arrest him."

"Dan didn't give me a lot of information, just that I should trust you and that the president was involved," she said. "Care to elaborate?"

"There's not enough time to tell you everything right now, Kate. If you'll cooperate with us when Peter Cheng is arrested on a homicide charge and then participate in Cheng's questioning, I think you'll be interested."

"Why involve me in this?"

"Because I trust you and the president likes you," Drake said and smiled. "Besides, it's time for a woman to run the FBI."

"That'll be the day," she huffed.

Drake's phone vibrated in his pocket. "He's headed your way," he heard an agent say.

"Cheng's headed our way," he said.

The SkySage Affair

Detective Cabrillo recognized him first, from San Francisco International Airport's surveillance videos he'd watched.

"He's coming toward us, gray suit, receding hairline," Cabrillo said.

Cheng was starting across the lobby when his head snapped suddenly to the left, looking directly at them. He spun around and sprinted toward a boisterous group of people getting on an elevator.

Drake ran after him, reaching the elevator just as it closed.

SIAC Perkins rushed up behind him "That's the private security elevator for the *Top of the Hay*. We'll have to take a different one."

With the other elevators having hotel guests waiting to use them, Perkins held open her black blazer to expose her FBI badge in a belt clip and commandeered the closest one.

"Liz, make sure some of the Secret Service guys stay here to watch the elevators, then join us," Drake said before joining Agent Perkins and Detective Cabrillo in the elevator.

"On it," she said and backed away when the elevator door started to close.

"The *Top of the Hay* has five contiguous meeting spaces," Perkins said. "If this function is using all of them, it will hold two or three hundred people. If they're using all of them, we'll have to split up and search each one."

When they reached the rooftop, the elevator door opened onto a reception area.

Agent Perkins looked around and said, "It looks like the three rooms that look down on Sixteenth Street from the balcony are opened onto each other. The two rooms that look down on H Street probably are as well. That leaves the restrooms and the kitchen and service areas to search. If he followed the crowd, he'll be somewhere in one of these five rooms. I'll start at the other end in the *Lincoln room* and work back to you."

"Which is the biggest room?" Drake asked. "I'll start there."

"It's the *George Washington room* around the corner," Perkins said.

Hundreds of people were at the *Top of the Hay*, attending a wedding reception. Drake followed Perkins's directions and entered the large room.

A hundred or more people were laughing and talking, standing around small round tables decorated with arrangements of pink roses.

Servers wearing black vests over white shirts and black bowties were circulating under crystal chandeliers with trays of champagne flutes.

A string quartet was playing music from Vivaldi's *Four Seasons*, seated near white-trimmed glass-paned French doors that opened onto a balcony.

No one seemed to pay any attention to Drake as he started through the room searching for Peter Cheng.

Chapter Seventy-Five

DRAKE WALKED through the center of the room sweeping his eyes from side to side through each vector, looking for his Chinese prey in a gray suit. His six-foot two-inch height allowed him to see over the heads of most of the guests, but he didn't see Cheng.

When he reached the French doors, he stepped out onto the balcony and looked to his right. The bride and groom were posing for pictures at the far end, surrounded by two older couples standing behind the photographer. There were others standing at the railing, admiring the view across Lafayette Square and the White House in the distance. Cheng was not one of them.

Drake pivoted to his left and saw a man wearing a gray suit moving out of sight around the corner at the other end of the balcony.

Jogging behind a group of people at the railing taking pictures, Drake reached the corner in time to see Cheng walk quickly through the doors of the second of three meeting rooms on that side of the rooftop addition to the Hay-Adams.

Drake ran after him and burst though the French doors of the *Thomas Jefferson* room in time to see Cheng running through the crowded room.

An alert guest pulled the woman beside him out of the way to keep Cheng from colliding with her and shouted, "WATCH IT, YOU FOOL!"

Heads turned to see what had caused the commotion. When they saw someone chasing the man, they cleared a path through the room.

When Drake reached the hallway and the reception area, he saw Detective Cabrillo running toward him and pointing.

"He ran down there," Cabrillo shouted.

Drake sprinted ahead to the hallway between the restrooms, when he heard Agent Perkins shouting, "Not the restrooms, the kitchen."

"Is there a way out of there?" Drake asked when Perkins got closer.

"There are only three ways up here," she said. "The two old elevators that were extended when they added the rooftop rooms and the new express elevator."

"You stay and guard the elevators. We'll go find him," Drake told her.

"Detective Cabrillo takes the elevators, we go," Perkins said. "He doesn't have jurisdiction here, I do."

Cabrillo started to argue, then nodded. "She's right, go."

Drake held the door open and followed Agent Perkins into the kitchen and service area.

Across an expanse of tiled floor, two white-coated chefs leaned over dishes of appetizers, checking the plating for the wedding reception guests. Two more chefs were at stations behind them, working with their backs turned to Drake and Perkins.

A line of servers stood against the far wall, waiting for a call to action.

Agent Perkins held open her blazer to display the FBI badge on the waistband of her pants and asked the nearest server, "Where's the man who just ran in here?"

The young server raised his arm and pointed a finger to the back of the kitchen.

Beyond the two chefs at their workstations, a bank of ovens

spanned two thirds of the width of the kitchen area, leaving a narrow walkway on both sides to the back of the kitchen.

Drake moved to the right and pulled his Kimber from its holster before starting toward the back of the kitchen area.

Agent Perkins took her pistol out, nodded to Drake and moved forward on the opposite side of the kitchen.

A stainless steel walk-in cooler behind the bank of ovens occupied the space between the two walkways. Drake thought of searching it but kept moving.

He stopped and darted his head around a corner to look down a row of floor-to-ceiling storage racks. Cheng wasn't hiding there.

Ahead was an open area with a dishwashing station with racks for china, glassware, and bins for flatware.

Peter Cheng was leaning back against the far counter holding a phone to his ear, waiting for them.

Drake holstered his pistol and approached Cheng with his hand held out. "Give me the phone, Cheng."

"Are you arresting me?"

Drake moved closer and took the phone from Cheng. "Who did you call?"

"My embassy. I am a Chinese citizen and I demand that you take me there."

Agent Perkins stepped around the corner opposite Drake and said, "Mr. Cheng, I'm FBI Special Agent Perkins. Do you have a gun or a knife on you?"

"I'm a businessman. Why would I need a weapon?"

Agent Perkins took flex cuffs from the pocket of her blazer and handed them to Drake.

"Put your hands on your head and turn around," she said. "Mr. Drake is going to search and then restrain you. We're taking you to my FBI Field Office where you'll be detained and questioned."

Cheng was staring at Drake.

"I see that you recognize my name," Drake said. "Did Francis Zhang tell you about me?"

Cheng continued staring.

"Or, did Wayne Berryman?"

When Cheng didn't respond, Drake searched him quickly, pulling his hands down behind his back and slipping the flex cuffs over his wrists.

"Time to go, Mr. Cheng," Agent Perkins said and led them back past a line of silent kitchen staff, to the hallway where Detective Cabrillo was waiting.

Cabrillo fell in beside Drake and said, "Liz has the Navigators idling out front. Where are we taking him?"

"We're taking him to FBI Field Office."

"Did you arrest him?"

"He's being detained for questioning. You can have the pleasure after he's been thoroughly interrogated."

Agent Perkins led the procession to the express elevator with Cheng in the grips of Drake and Cabrillo on each side. Her FBI badge bought them a quick and private ride in the express elevator to the lobby below.

Chapter Seventy-Six

DRAKE AND DETECTIVE CABRILLO rode with Special Agent in Charge Perkins in the backseat of her white Ford Explorer with Peter Cheng sitting between them, as they drove to the Washington Field Office of the FBI.

The rest of the PSS team left the Hay-Adams in search of someplace to have dinner.

Kate Perkins, as Special Agent in Charge of the FBI's Counterintelligence Division, wasn't asked to explain why she needed to use an interview room that night, accompanied by a detective from San Francisco and an attorney from a west coast security company.

After Peter Cheng's flex cuffs were removed and he'd declined an offer of coffee or water, SIAC Perkins advised him that she was allowing Detective Cabrillo to interview him first, as a courtesy, regarding an investigation in California. She would decide after Detective Cabrillo finished, if there was anything the FBI needed to investigate.

"I am a Chinese citizen and demand that I be allowed to call the Chinese Embassy," Cheng said calmly.

"Mr. Cheng, I am Detective Cabrillo from the San Francisco Police Department."

Cabrillo paused and took a deep breath and looked down at notes he'd written on a small black leather notebook, before continuing.

"I'm investigating the murder of a professor at the University of California, Mrs. Zhang. I'm hoping you can help me out."

"I don't see how I can assist you with that," Cheng said and shrugged his shoulders. "I don't know this person."

"But you do know her husband. What can you tell me about him?"

"Zhang is the third most common surname in China. I know many people with that name."

"How about the Zhang you've spoken with over the phone?"

Cheng's expression changed ever so slightly, a calm look of understanding replacing his look of feigned indignation.

"What is this really about?" he asked.

"Why don't you tell us about your relationship with Francis Zhang?"

Cabrillo suggested.

"I've never met Francis Zhang."

"But you have talked with him."

"Yes, I have talked with him."

"Did you talk with him about your investment in Wayne Berryman's private equity firm?"

"Why would I do that?" Cheng asked.

"Didn't Francis Zhang supply the Chinese intern Wayne Berryman placed at SkySage, LLC?" Cabrillo asked.

"He might have. How would I know?"

"Isn't that what you had in mind when you approached Wayne Berryman and offered to fund his equity firm's start up?"

"Why would I care about his interns?"

"Because that's how China and the CCP steal intellectual property, using Chinese Americans students to spy for it?"

"I'm not a spy!" Cheng insisted.

"What are you, then?"

"I am a Chinese businessman."

Drake was standing behind Detective Cabrillo, leaning against the wall, and stepped forward to ask, "Isn't it true that China's National Intelligence Law requires every Chinese citizen, wherever they live, to participate in intelligence work?"

"YES."

"Isn't that what you were doing when you and your joint venture partner, with money from the Bank of China, helped Wayne Berryman start his company?"

"That's not a crime, is it?" Cheng asked.

"Killing Americans on U.S. soil to aid an intelligence operation is, Mr. Cheng."

"I didn't kill anyone."

"Perhaps not directly, but Francis Zhang and his employee, Tony Lee, did, didn't they?"

"I don't have any idea what those men did," Cheng said.

"Wayne Berryman says you murdered his mistress and tried to convince him that he had killed her," Drake continued. "That you were blackmailing him to force him to steal Top Secret information from SkySage, LLC."

"Berryman's lying," Cheng hissed. "Why would I have his mistress killed? Besides, Berryman told me he didn't have access to the JEDI project."

"Why in the world would he have told you that?" SIAC Perkins smiled, as she intervened.

Cheng looked slowly from Agent Perkins to Drake. "I want a lawyer."

"Let me explain your current situation, Mr. Cheng," Agent Perkins said. "If what I'm hearing is true, you have been involved in espionage that directly concerns a major weapon system of the United States. That is a federal crime and a death-eligible capital federal offense. If it's also true that your involvement has caused the deaths of U.S. citizens, you may be facing capital murder charges in one or more state jurisdictions."

"I had nothing to do with that."

"And, if an American citizen was killed on American soil

because of this espionage, some would consider that an act of war committed by your country against ours. I think China might not welcome you home with a parade down Tiananmen Square, if you are ever allowed to return home."

"If you cooperate with me, I'll do what I can to keep you from being executed as a Chinese spy," Agent Perkins promised.

"The people you arrest for espionage aren't executed," Cheng said. "Why would I?"

Drake leaned down to put his hands on the back of Cabrillo's chair and stared at Chen. "None of them were involved in killing the son of a United States member of Congress, who happens to be a close friend of the president. You might get lucky and escape the needle, but I wouldn't count on it."

"I think you're bluffing," Cheng said.

"Please stand up, Peter Cheng," Agent Perkins said. "I've heard enough. I'm arresting you under 18 U.S. Code Section 794 for espionage committed against the United States of America."

Detective Cabrillo stood and announced that he was also arresting Cheng.

"Peter Cheng, you are also under arrest for murder in the state of California. If, and when, the government is finished with your espionage prosecution, you will be extradited to stand trial in California."

Chapter Seventy-Seven

DRAKE STAYED BEHIND in the interview room, when Agent Perkins and Detective Cabrillo left with Peter Cheng, and called the president.

"The Secret Service tells me that you have your man in custody," President Ballard said.

"Yes, sir. The FBI have him in the D.C. field office. He's been arrested and charged with espionage and murder."

"Does that mean that Agent Perkins made the arrest?"

"She did. Detective Cabrillo from San Francisco made the homicide arrest."

"Are you satisfied China didn't get their hands on anything at SkySage?"

"We are. JEDI is a Special Access Program. That allowed us to verify that no one involved with Peter Cheng, Francis Zhang or Wayne Berryman gained access to any Top-Secret information.

"It was an elaborate plan, though, that could have been successful. If Michael Bridge hadn't been killed when he started asking questions and you hadn't asked me to help with his father, they might have found a way to get what they wanted. Cheng and HK

Capital, LLC, should never have made it past a CFIUS review. You might want to ask Treasury how it did."

"Do you think Secretary Berryman was complicit?"

"I don't have enough information to answer that, Mr. President. China's been buying influence by making the children and families of powerful decision makers wealthy around the world. It could have started back when China saw that Governor Berryman had a national political future and decided to bankroll his son. It doesn't mean that Secretary Berryman is any more complicit than other politicians of ours with financial ties to China and the CCP."

"No, but it doesn't excuse any role he may have played either. I don't see how I can keep him in the cabinet with what we know. Did you discover who killed Congressman Bridge's son?"

"Not yet. The person I think did kill him is being held in San Francisco for murder. He may be willing to tell us his role in all of this when he comes begging for a plea deal."

Drake heard the president drumming his fingers on some hard surface, pausing before he continued.

"I need to bring Director Walker and the AG in on this, before I ruffle too many feathers. When Agent Perkins gets Cheng squared away, bring her to the White House with you, Adam. I'll have you explain everything you've uncovered, since I asked you to meet with Congressman Bridge in Portland."

"What would you like me to say when I'm asked why I didn't go to the FBI with any of this?"

"I'll give you some cover on that," the president said. "Your clients, Microsoft and SkySage, were involved and you needed to move fast. I agreed."

"Sir, you don't need to do that," Drake said.

"Yes, I do. Let me know when you're headed my way."

"I will."

Drake left the interview room and found Detective Cabrillo standing by himself in the hallway.

"Agent Perkins told me to wait here, said she'd be right back," Cabrillo said.

"President Ballard wants me to go to the White House with

Perkins to brief Director Walker and the Attorney General about Peter Cheng. What are your plans?"

"Dinner and a hot shower," Cabrillo said.

"Let me call and find out where the others are. Someone can come and get you."

"Thanks, but I think I'll walk the National Mall first and say hello to President Lincoln. I'll call Casey to find out where we're staying and call a cab."

Drake saw Agent Perkins walk out of an office and come their way.

She wore a tight-lipped smile and said, "News travels fast. I'm told the Director wants an explanation ASAP about why I arrested a Chinese national for espionage and he didn't know anything about it."

"You're in luck," Drake grinned. "President Ballard wants us at the White House to brief the Director and the Attorney General on Cheng and China. He'll let me explain why I didn't involve the FBI."

"This will be interesting. China's embassy has already called, demanding to know why Citizen Cheng was arrested."

"Has Cheng said anything more?" Drake asked.

"Citizen Cheng is deep in thought, trying to think of a way out of this."

"Good luck with that," Cabrillo huffed. "Cheng's doing time."

"If he survives," Drake said. "It didn't take them long to find a Chinese American to slip in and silence Wayne Berryman."

"He'll be well-protected," Perkins promised. "Am I driving us to the White House?"

"Unless you want to ask the Director to ride over with him?"

"Very funny, Drake. If this doesn't go well, I prefer to have my own wheels when it's time to leave."

Detective Cabrillo left to walk over to the National Mall and Agent Perkins returned to her office for the keys to her SUV, leaving Drake to think about the meeting at the White House.

He knew the president would have his back, but his past experiences with the FBI had been unpleasant when he'd taken matters into his own hands. But the need to keep someone in the FBI from telling Secretary Berryman his son was being investigated had been necessary. For all he knew, Berryman the elder may have been more involved than his son.

He was willing to take the heat for keeping the government out of his efforts to find who killed Congressman Bridge's son.

Chapter Seventy-Eight

PRESIDENT BENJAMIN BALLARD was sitting behind the Resolute Desk when Special Agent Perkins and Drake were ushered into the Oval Office, the most famous room in the world.

The president got up to greet them and shook their hands. "Thank you for coming. Attorney General Radcliff and Director Walker are on their way. Would you care for something to drink before they get here?"

Perkins declined but Drake agreed to have some of the bourbon he saw in a bottle on a side tray, if the president was joining him.

While the president poured their drinks from a crystal decanter into matching crystal glasses. Drake looked around the room he'd seen so often on television but never in person.

The Resolute Desk and the photos of the president's family on a table behind the desk. The three large windows with gold drapes behind the desk, a bust of Abraham Lincoln to the right side of the windows and the Remington bronze statue, *The Bronco Buster* so many presidents like to display, to the left side.

Across the dark blue carpet with the president's seal to the southwest were two white sofas, with a bouquet of peach roses sitting on a small table between them. The fireplace on the north end of the oval room with the portrait of President George Washington hanging above it.

President Ballard touched Drake on his arm to get his attention and handed him his drink. "I'm still reacting the same way every time I walk in here. More history's been made here than any place in the world, since 1934 when President Roosevelt had the Oval Office built."

"It's an honor to be here," Drake said.

"Come, let's sit down before the others arrive," the president said and motioned to the white sofas.

President Ballard waited until Perkins and Drake were sitting on one sofa and then sat down next to Special Agent Perkins and said, "The Director may have heard something about tonight, but I don't think the Attorney General has. When I ask you to tell them what led to tonight's arrest of Peter Cheng, tell them everything.

"The Director might want a more detail than you give him, but I'll try to keep this as short as possible. I'll ask the Director to allow Special Agent Perkins to take your statement later, Drake. The FBI will takeover on Cheng's case, but I need advice tonight on how I should deal with Secretary Berryman and his son's involvement."

"How would you like me to explain my involvement, Mr. President?" Kate Perkins asked.

"I gave the go ahead when he called and trusted him to catch Cheng before he made a run for China's Embassy. Having you and the Secret Service assist him was my call. It won't be a problem."

A Secret Service agent knocked on the northwest door of the Oval Office and entered the room. "Mr. President, the Attorney General and the Director of the FBI."

The president nodded and stood. "Would either of you like a drink before we get started? Help yourself."

The Attorney General saw that the president and Drake had drinks in their hands and smiled. "Certainly, Mr. President. Thank you."

The Director stayed where he was, looking at Special Agent Perkins. "I didn't know you were going to be here, Kate. Is this about what took place at the Hay-Adams tonight?"

"It will all be explained in a minute, Bill," President Ballard said. "Have you met Adam Drake?"

"We haven't met, but I know about what he did out in Nevada. Nice to meet you, Drake."

Attorney General Radcliff returned with a glass of bourbon and took a seat on the sofa across from the president, Special Agent Perkins and Drake.

The president continued standing and waited for the Director to sit before beginning. "When Matthew Bridge's son was killed in Oregon, I asked Adam Drake to meet him in Portland, where Drake has an office. I asked him to help Congressman Bridge in any way he could. Matt's a friend, as you know, and had told me he was certain his son did not have a heart attack and may have met with foul play.

"Michael Bridge was working at SkySage, Inc., one of Microsoft's subcontractors on the JEDI project. I didn't want the project to get in the news, if Matt was overreacting and grasping for ways to explain his healthy young son's death due to an unlikely heart attack. I asked Drake to quietly look into it for me. He did and that has led to his identifying a Chinese national and an espionage plot. The Chinese national is here in Washington and Drake asked me for help tonight to prevent this person from escaping to China.

"I understand that you will have questions about why I allowed Drake to act alone. He will explain the circumstances that led me to authorize that, but tonight I need your advice on something else. It's possible that a member my cabinet may have been involved, directly or indirectly, in a Chinese attempt to steal top secret information from the JEDI project."

The Director of the FBI stared at the president. "Is that why you didn't get me involved, Mr. President? Because you were protecting someone in your cabinet?"

"If I had come to you, Bill, you would have opened an investigation and my cabinet member would have heard about it before the end of the day. We wouldn't know any of this, if that had happened."

"Who's the cabinet member?" Attorney General Radcliff asked.

"Secretary Berryman," the president said.

"Why do you think Berryman may have been involved?" the Director asked.

"His son Wayne Berryman's private equity firm provided the startup funding for SkySage, Inc., with money from a Hong Kong firm that has ties to the Bank of China."

"How did this pass CFIUS review?" the Attorney General asked.

"There was no review," the president said, "By the CFIUS committee chaired by the Treasury Department and Secretary Berryman."

"What about Berryman's son?" the Director asked. "What does he say about this?"

"Wayne Berryman was killed yesterday while in custody in a San Francisco jail," the president said. "Why don't I let Adam Drake take us through this from the beginning. Then I'd like your thoughts on how we proceed."

Chapter Seventy-Nine

MONDAY MORNING DRAKE and Liz took a cab from the Hyatt Place National Mall to Georgetown for brunch with Senator and Mrs. Hazelton.

Mike Casey, the PSS pilot Steve Carson, Dan Norris and his two HRT team members had left the hotel early to drive to the airport and return to Seattle. They had finished the night at the hotel's Rooftop Bar hearing about Peter Cheng's arrest and Drake's meeting in the Oval Office with President Ballard, the Attorney General and the Director of the FBI.

Detective Cabrillo was staying another day in the capital to finish dealing with his end of Peter Cheng's arrest. He'd agreed to meet Drake at the FBI Field Office that afternoon to complete his statement about pursuing Cheng from San Francisco. Today, he'd said he was spending as much of the day as possible exploring the city.

Before their cab had time to let them out and drive off in front of the Hazelton's stately white rowhouse, Meredith Hazelton was waving at them from an open front door.

Drake took Liz's hand and started up the steps. "Here we go."

"Nervous? Liz asked.

"A little."

"Liz, you look lovely," Meredith said, wearing a sleeveless flowing maxi dress in pale yellow.

"And you look elegant," Liz replied, wearing a white jacket with black vertical stripes over a black silk blouse and white pants.

Meredith kissed Liz on the cheek and turned to hug Drake.

"Hi Mom," he said, feeling underdressed in his black polo and khakis.

"It's been too long," she said and punched his arm before throwing her arms around him.

"I know," he said.

She turned back and put her arm around Liz's waist and led her inside. "Come on," she said over her shoulder to Drake, "He's taking the morning off and fixing Mimosas on the patio."

He followed behind the two smiling women and wondered how long it would be before his mother-in-law noticed the engagement ring Liz was wearing.

As it turned out, it was Senator Hazelton who noticed it first when he handed Liz her Mimosa and she accepted it with her left hand.

The senator smiled when he saw it and stepped in closer to hug her. "It took him long enough."

Meredith saw the ring, as Liz held her hand out for her Mimosa and said, "Finally! Welcome to the family, Liz."

"Not even a little bit surprised?" Drake asked.

"Not even a little," the senator said. "Our bet was which month you would tell us. I guessed Christmas. Meredith guessed June and now I owe her an Italian dinner at Filomena's."

"Have you set a date for the wedding?" Meredith asked.

"No Mom, we haven't. I'm thinking we'll elope and save the fuss."

Liz was shaking her head and smiling. "He's teasing you. We haven't had time to discuss it since he proposed."

"I know you've been busy," the senator said. "Let's eat and you can tell us everything."

When they walked back inside to the dining room, Drake saw that his mother-in-law had gone all out for their brunch. On the sideboard was a buffet warming tray with a quiche, a pile of pancakes and an asparagus salad. Next to the warming tray was a delicious-looking apple breakfast cobbler.

"Is that the caramel apple cobbler you've made before?" Drake asked.

"I remembered that you liked it," Meredith smiled.

After they served themselves and sat down to eat, Drake gave a brief synopsis of events that led up to last night's visit to the White House and the meeting with the president, the Attorney General and the Director of the FBI.

"The president asked me to stay after the others left," he said. "He's going to have the Treasury Department reimburse SkySage, Inc. for the fee he wants us to charge them for our facility security clearance review. He feels the whole thing can be traced back to the Treasury Department not reviewing his son's involvement with China and the investment Wayne Berryman made in SkySage, Inc."

"Is he getting rid of Secretary Berryman?" Senator Hazelton asked.

"Soon, after the FBI has a chance to evaluate his role in setting up his son with Peter Cheng and HK Capital, LLC."

"How does he plan on responding to Chinese espionage that included the murder of Congressman Bridge's son?"

"Harshly," Drake said. "He's wanted to know what I thought about calling for a summit of the Quad, the members of the Quadrilateral Security Dialogue, Australia, Japan, India and the U.S. He wants to propose adding a duty to defend one another and formalize the alliance to establish a balance of military power in the region.

"He wants to punish violators caught stealing intellectual property and cyber-espionage with tariffs and making it harder for those companies to raise capital in U.S. financial markets."

"I'm curious, Adam," the senator said. "Was all of this discussed with the AG and the Director in the room?"

"No, this was after they left."

"It sounds like he was seeking your advice."

"Actually, it was more than that. He wants Puget Sound Security to become a U.S. intelligence contractor he can use for what he's calling his own 'special projects'."

Chapter Eighty

DRAKE AND LIZ flew out of Ronald Reagan Washington National Airport late Monday afternoon on United Airlines Flight 3447 to attend Michael Bridge's memorial service in Lincoln, Nebraska.

Drake had returned to the FBI's Field Office after brunch with his in-laws to meet SIAC Kate Perkins and answer a few questions, before rushing to the airport with Liz.

President Ballard was keeping a lid on the investigation of Secretary Berryman's role in the SkySage affair, for the time being, and had cleared his departure with the FBI. The president had asked him to deliver a hand-written letter to Congressman Bridge and his family, and his return to the capital could wait until after the memorial service.

Relaxing for the first time in a week during the five-hour flight to Nebraska, Drake and Liz had time to talk about the future.

Liz wasn't sure what kind of wedding she wanted and needed time to think about it.

Drake didn't have a vision yet about where he wanted to live but promised to give Liz's realtor the opportunity to show him everything.

Liz agreed to let Drake surprise her for their honeymoon and then listed the places on her bucket list she wouldn't mind seeing. Australia's Great Barrier Reef was at the top of her list.

By the time they were on final approach to the airport in Lincoln, Nebraska, they'd talked about their immediate future and getting started on living their lives together.

The one thing they didn't discuss was the president's request and what that might involve for their working lives at PSS. Privatized intelligence in America was dominated by five large corporations and the intelligence-contracting industry was worth upwards of fifty billion dollars a year.

Most of the work is top secret and can be lethal. Getting contracts for the work is extremely political, he knew, and the top five well-connected contractors would not welcome a newcomer and competitor warmly. Even if the newcomer's sponsor is the president of the United States.

Puget Sound Security would have to change. Drake wasn't sure how, exactly, but if they wanted to seize the opportunity to do what they had essentially been doing anyway and compete at the highest level of outsourced spying and intelligence gathering, they would do it.

As he followed Liz off the plane, he reminded himself why he was in Nebraska. Michael Bridge had been killed in the opening moves of a deadly game, the game he was thinking of getting into. A game that involved an adversary running a massive espionage operation and a long game that was dedicated to destroying America.

He had no idea how the president planned on using his new intelligence contractor or what his "special projects" might be. As a former Tier 1 operator, he knew he would never be able to refuse his president and Commander in Chief, if he was asked to serve.

The same would be true for his former partner and best friend. If the president wanted PSS to become a new intelligence contractor, the company's CEO would do whatever was necessary to accomplish that.

He was beginning a new season in his life with Liz and possibly a new iteration of PSS. The days ahead would be exciting and challenging, and they would require his best effort to make the most of each one of them. Liz deserved nothing less and so did his country.

By Associated Press:

A Hong Kong investor has been charged with espionage.

Federal prosecutors filed a sealed criminal complaint Monday charging Peter Cheng, 57, a Chinese national with fifteen counts of espionage. Cheng is the manager of HK Capital, LLC, a Hong Kong private equity firm. He was arrested this weekend at the Hay-Adams Hotel attending a dinner for Chinese businessmen being hosted by U.S. Secretary of the Treasurer, Walter Berryman.

Pursuant to an executive order signed by President Ballard, also on Monday, the United States will seek the death penalty in this and all future cases of espionage that compromise its national security.

BY THE WASHINGTON POST:

White House announces a summit meeting to be convened to secure freedom of navigation in the South China Sea

The four member nations of the Quadralateral Security Dialogue, Australia, Japan, India and the United States will meet in Washington D.C., to discuss President Ballard's proposal for a duty of its members to defend one another and help guarantee the freedom to navigate the seas.

The president also announced that regular Freedom of Navigation South China Sea patrols by the USS Nimitz Carrier Strike force and the USS Ronald Reagan will increase immediately.

"It's time that China's misguided belligerence is confronted and met with the unified resistance from the liberal democracies of the world. The Chinese Communist Party's goal to achieve world domination will not be allowed."

BY THE WASHINGTON EXAMINER:

The Secretary of the Treasury Department resigns.

The White House announced today that President Ballard had requested and received the resignation of Secretary of the Treasury Walter Berryman. Secretary Berryman is currently under investigation by the FBI to determine if he used his public office for private gain.

An unnamed source familiar with the investigation reports that Secretary Berryman introduced his son to contacts in China that allowed his son to receive financing for his son's private equity firm startup in the U.S.

The anonymous source also confirmed that Walter Berryman was being investigated for illegal foreign campaign contributions he received from China, when he ran for the governorship of California, and more recently to his PAC he formed to support a future run for the presidency of the United States.

Next in the Adam Drake series

China wants revenge for the Opium Wars of the past. The CCP will achieve it with an opium war of its own.

When Adam Drake hears a rumor of the plot on his honeymoon, he won't rest until he finds out if it's true. If it is, he vows to defeat it.

From a luxury resort in Australia, to a casino in Baja California, and an island off the coast of British Columbia, Drake chases after the billionaire head of a powerful and brutal Chinese triad to learn the truth.

Printed in Great Britain
by Amazon